THE ART TREASURES OF RUSSIA

ANCIENT GLASS

in the Hermitage collection

THE STATE HERMITAGE
ARS PUBLISHERS LTD

Written and compiled by
NINA KUNINA

Photography by
FERDINAND KUZIUMOV

*Consultations on glass
technology courtesy of*
FEODOR ENTELIS

ББК 85.103(3)
ISBN 5-900351-15-7

The author would like to thank the research assistants of the Ancient World Department, the State Hermitage Museum, headed by S.P.Boriskovskaya, for their kind attention and support in the course of my work on this book. I would like to especially thank those Hermitage research assistants who provided glass from the museum archives for publication, amongst them E.N.Khodza (curator of the Ancient World Department), Yu.P.Kalashnik, D.S.Gertsiger, Yu.I.Ilina, N.L.Grach, O.Yu.Sokolova, O.Ya.Neverov; N.B.Landa and A.A.Jerusalimskaya from the Oriental Department; and I.P.Zasetskaya from the Department of the Archaeology of Eastern Europe and Siberia. The author is also grateful to V.F.Zazovsky for financial assistance. Lastly, I am deeply indebted to the late Professor F.S.Entelis of the Mukhina State Academy of Art and Industry for consultations on glass technology and hold his memory forever sacred.

ARS Publishers Ltd would like to thank Lev Bayandurov, Managing Director of UNISTO, for help and support in publishing this book

In blessed memory of my teacher, Professor
V<small>ICTOR</small> G<small>AIDUKEVICH</small>

THE STATE HERMITAGE MUSEUM in St Petersburg is home to one of the world's leading collections of ancient glass. It possesses glasswork embracing an extensive period running from the days of the 18th dynasty of the New Kingdom of Ancient Egypt (15th century BC) to the sunset of the Roman Empire (5th century AD).

More than three thousand various vessels comprise the heart of the Hermitage collection. This is in addition to the enormous quantity of glass beads and pendants held in the museum archives. Miniature gems – copies of carved stones and original works – make up a special section of the collection. These include around two hundred seals and some seventy cameos mounted in signet rings. Amongst the cameos are phalerae – medallions with relief decorations that served as military decorations for the ancient Romans and were worn on their coats of armour.

The Hermitage's collection of ancient glass has been gradually built up over a long period of time. It draws its roots from both private collections bought between the late eighteenth and early twentieth centuries and glass found by archaeologists during excavations of ancient Greek towns in the Crimea and the Bug basin. Individual purchases and gifts continue to add to the museum's archives to this day.

The earliest established date of acquisition of ancient glass by the Hermitage is 1787, when Catherine the Great bought the extensive collection of gems belonging to Louis Philippe, Duc d'Orléans. The Duke's collection included two glass cameos (one of them cat.72). In 1792, when in Dresden, Catherine purchased the collection of J.B.Casanova, director of the Saxon Academy of Arts. This included forty glass cameos and phalerae (cat. 73–77).

In 1834 the Hermitage received the enormous collection of the Roman antiquarian S.Pizzati, which numbered some one and a half thousand objects – painted vases, bronzes, terracottas, including some thirty glass wares (amongst them sepulchral urns) from the days of the Roman Empire. The collection of Count G.Laval and Countess A.Laval, enriching the Hermitage with fine examples of antique sculpture and applied art, was bought from their daughters, Countess Borkh and Countess Kossakovskaya, in 1851. It included some fine examples of mosaic glass.

In 1884 the museum bought the collection of Count P.Saburov, Russian ambassador to Greece from 1870 to 1879. This collection of more than two hundred Tanagra terracotta statuettes included several ancient glass vessels. The A.Bazilevsky collection in Paris included various objects of applied art, some of them from medieval Western Europe. Acquired in 1855 by the Hermitage, it offered six examples of early Christian sandwich gold-glass vessels (cat. 434).

An important contributor to the collection of ancient applied art in the Hermitage was the J.Lemmé collection, acquired in 1893. It contained several hundred objects, amongst them more than 150 glass vessels found in southern Russia and mostly deriving from the necropoleis of ancient Greek cities.

More than sixty works by third and fourth century Syrian masters, including exquisitely decorated beakers, jars, flasks and unguentaria, were bought in 1898 from the Parisian antiquarian M.Sivadjan (cat. 403 – 407, 413).

The acquisition in 1900 of the A.Novikov collection proved most beneficial. The owner of an estate in the Crimean village of Eltegen (now Eltigen), lying to the south of Kertch, Novikov carried out excavations of the Nymphaion necropolis, one of the towns of the Bosporan kingdom on his land. He also bought up antiquities found during the course of excavation work at Kertch. Importantly, he lists the place of discovery – "Kertch" or "Eltegen" – in the inventory of his collection. The Novikov collection contains more than two hundred pieces. They are made from various materials, including around 150 glass vessels, mostly dating from the time of the Roman Empire. Amongst them is an exquisite blue-glass jug (cat. 250).

BOTTOM OF VESSEL
WITH FAMILY PORTRAIT
Rome. 4th century AD. Cat. 434

CAMEO WITH REPRESENTATION
OF HEAD OF ATHENS
Italy (?). 1st century AD. Cat. 72

SEAL WITH PORTRAIT
OF GAIUS CAESAR
*Italy. Late 1st century BC –
1st century AD. Cat. 71*

DOUBLE TUBE
Syria. 4th century AD. Cat. 413

JUG
Eastern Mediterranean. 1st century AD. Cat. 250

FLASK
Syria. 3rd – 4th centuries AD. Cat. 403

JUG
Master Frontinus. Gaul. 3rd – 4th centuries AD. Cat. 172

From the 1860s to the start of the twentieth century, the Hermitage acquired antiquities found in southern Russia from a number of private individuals. These came mostly from Kertch and from the village of Parutino (now Nikolaev region, Ukraine). The Odessian antique dealers L.Gokhman (Gaukhman) and G.Kallo were amongst those active in collecting the treasures uncovered in Parutino. The Kallo collection was acquired by the Hermitage in 1900, along with a wonderful glass pyxis with a painted colour design (cat. 181).

In 1909 Grigory IV, Patriarch of Antioche, presented the Hermitage with 52 glass items, most of them coming from the Syro-Palestinian region.

Amongst individual purchases made in the following years, the acquisition in 1914 of the Hermitage's sole 4th century jug bearing the brand of the Gaul master, Frontinus (cat. 172), merits special attention.

Following the October Revolution and the nationalization of private collections, the Hermitage became the recipient of many of these. Thus the collections of the Shuvalovs, the Stroganovs, Gaman-Gamon, Botkin, N.Romanchenko and others found their way into the Hermitage.

The collection of Count Sergei Stroganov, founder and president of the Imperial Archaeological Commission, numbered some hundred glass vessels, including various works by ancient masters. Many are extremely rare, such as the pyxis with a representation of Eros on its lid, made on the island of Cyprus in the 1st century AD (cat. 182). The collection of Countess Shuvalova added some fifty vessels to the museum's collection.

In 1923 the Hermitage was presented with an interesting and diverse collection of works of applied art from the museum of the former Baron Stieglitz Central School of Technical Drawing. It included wonderful examples of mosaic glass.

From the State Academy of the History of Material Culture in Leningrad in 1931 came a large collection of antiquities. They had previously been the property of Count A.Bobrinsky, president of the Imperial Archaeological Commission and vice-president of the Academy of Arts. He had put his collection together in southern Russia, mostly in Kertch, and had collected some two hundred glass vessels, dating from the 6th century BC to the 4th century AD.

Around the same time, the Hermitage received from the Academy of Sciences of the USSR the collection of the former Russian Archaeological Institute in Constantinople, numbering more than eighty glass items.

The following years saw the museum continue to receive ancient glass from private collections. In 1949 and 1953 the Hermitage purchased glass vessels from the collection of the famous St Petersburg philologist I.Tolstoy. And in 1984 V.Tikhonova presented the Hermitage with the collection of her father, the chemist and restorer V.Kononov, offering more than seventy examples of mosaic glass (cat. 91, 92).

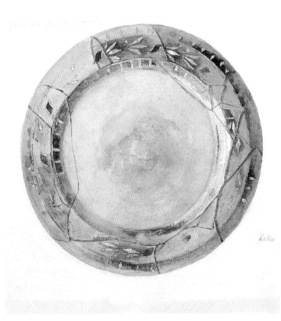

PYXIS
Alexandria (Egypt) or Syria. 1st century BC. Cat. 181

PYXIS LID

RESTORING THE PAINTED DESIGN ON THE LID OF A PYXIS
M.V. Farmakovsky. 1914
Pencil and water-colour

FRAGMENTS OF VESSELS
*Eastern Mediterranean, Egypt,
Italy, Syria (?). 1st century BC—
1st century AD. Cat. 91, 92*

The most substantial part of the Hermitage's "glass treasure-house", however, consists of ancient works unearthed during archaeological excavations in the south of Russia. These constitute approximately one third of the museum's collection. Well documented, they represent valuable material for studying not only glass and the history of ancient glass-making, but also the history and culture of the ancient towns lying along the Black Sea. It has been possible to submit glass wares found in interments, together with coins and other burial objects, to quite exact dating. By grouping them according to place of discovery, one can identify the local peculiarities of these and other glass vessels. Hypotheses can also be drawn as to their place of manufacture, even when glass-firing kilns have not been found in that region.

Excavation of ancient Greek towns lying along the north and north-west regions adjoining the Black Sea and their necropoleis has been going on since the 1830s. In the last century excavation work was carried out in the north-east and south-west Crimea, on the Taman peninsula and along the

PANTIKAPAION (KERTCH)   mouth of the Dnieper and Bug rivers.

The towns of the Bosporan kingdom stood along both shores of the Gulf of Kertch (the Bosporos Kimmerios of ancient times), and on the Kertch and Taman peninsulas. The capital, Pantikapaion, stood on the site of what is the present-day town of Kertch. The ancient Greek city of Chersonesos was situated in the south-west of the Crimea, on the outskirts of the modern day town of Sebastopol, whilst Olbia stood in the region of the Dnieper and Bug estuaries, near the village of Parutino.

Excavations at Chersonesos, Olbia and the Bosporan towns have yielded the Hermitage entire burial complexes, containing prized collections of works of Greek art and craftsmanship.

The Pantikapaion necropolis has provided the museum with more than six hundred glass vessels. Amongst them are a mosaic glass bowl (cat. 93), a painted amphora (cat. 178), an amphora bearing the brand of the master Ennion (cat. 109), an elegant krateriskos (cat. 183) and many other fine works. Excavation of the Pantikapaion necropolis has additionally embellished the Hermitage collection with unique examples of ancient glass-work dating from the 4th century BC, like the masterly executed gold-bound

THE SHORE OF THE STRAIT OF
KERTCH NEAR NYMPHAION

MEDALLION WITH SPINNER
*Eastern Mediterranean. Second half
of the 4th century BC. Cat. 67*

TRACING OF THE PICTURE
ON THE MEDALLION

TRACING OF THE REPRESENTATION OF
A SPINNER ON AN ATTIC VASE
4th century AD. Metropolitan Museum

DETAIL OF THE DESIGN ON
AN ATTIC VASE
FROM PANTIKAPAION
4th century BC. State Hermitage

glass gem (cat. 68) and cast "medallions" with drawings (cat. 65–67). From the Olbia burial ground came a wonderful painted bowl with a representation of an antelope (cat. 180) and an enormous modiolus (cat. 186). The Chersonesos necropolis has given the collection a beautiful vessel in the shape of a fish, made from multi-coloured glass (cat. 200), a figurative flask in the form of the head of the young Dionysus (cat. 153) and an elegant oenochoe of clear free-blown glass (cat. 249).

Besides the aforementioned works of ancient art, excavations carried out in the nineteenth and early twentieth centuries have yielded hundreds of utilitarian glass objects. Numerous and well documented, these represent a valuable source of history.

Throughout the Soviet period, the Hermitage conducted (and conducts to this day) excavations on three ancient sites. Work has gone on at Chersonesos (5th century BC – 14th century AD) since 1938, at the Bosporan town of Nymphaion (6th century BC – 4th century AD) since 1939, and at the Greek settlement on the island of Berezan (dating from the 7th century BC, the oldest along the northern Black Sea coast) since 1962.

EXCAVATING AT NYMPHAION
Northern Black Sea coast

Many glass vessels were discovered in the 1970s, in the graves of the Nymphaion necropolis (1st–4th centuries AD). Excavation work was carried out here by the Nymphaion Archaeological Expedition, headed by N.Grach. As was typical of Bosporan burial sites, a considerable number of items came from the eastern Mediterranean. One of the late 1st century vaults, however, revealed a jug brought from the western Roman Empire, probably Cologne, with a brand on its bottom (cat. 168). The jug, blown in open form, was found in the Nymphaion necropolis in 1974. Of special interest amongst the finds on the territory of the actual town of Nymphaion itself is the miniature glass sculptured female head (height 3.5 cm), found in 1983 (cat. 78). Its facial features (low forehead, widely-set eyes, small mouth with thin lips, small chin) are reminiscent of Lybia, wife of the Emperor Augustus. A rare example of an ancient sculpture made from high quality glass, it is the only glass sculptural portrait of Lybia. Unique not only for the regions adjoining the Black Sea, it joins the series of very few miniature glass sculptures dating from Roman times, another of which is the head of Augustus Caesar currently in Cologne. Research carried out by Soviet archaeologists in the lands to the north of the Black Sea in the post-war period has led to interesting revelations in the history of local ancient glass-work. In 1956, M.Smishko was excavating a 3rd–4th century settlement near the village of Komarovo (Chernovitsk region, Ukraine). Here he discovered fragments of pots used for founding glass, two fragments of a clay mould employed in the manufacture of semi-spherical ribbed cups, refuse from production (splinters, fragments and drops of glass, glass "foam"), instruments (a trulla for pouring out molten glass, iron pincers, knives, spoons, an oven fork and hammer) and fragments of hollow iron pipes 1 cm in diameter[1].

T.Vysotskaya, excavating 1959 to 1961 on the site of the ancient settlement of Alma-Kermen (central Crimea), uncovered the ruins of a glass workshop. She found the remains of two kilns (one circular kiln for founding glass and one rectangular one for fritting), melted raw glass, reject items, fragments of glass vessels and mollusc shells. This was the site for the production of vessels with applied ornamental designs made from coloured threads. They are dated the second half of the 2nd and early 3rd centuries AD. Vysotskaya believes that the glass masters were Romans, and links the existence of the workshop to the stationing here of the 11th Claudius Legion[2].

G.Belov, head of the Hermitage's Chersonesos Archaeological Expedition, unearthed a large fourth century glass-work complex in Chersonesos in 1963 and 1965. Here he found the remains of a kiln, an enormous accumulation of fragments and refuse from production. This workshop

[1] *Смишко М.Ю.* Поселення III—IV ст. н. е. із слідами скляного виробництва біля с. Комарів, Чернівецької области // Матеріали і дослідження з археології Прикарпаття і Волині. Київ, 1964. Випуск 5. С. 67—80; *Щапова Ю.Л.* Мастерская по производству стекла у с. Комарово (III—IV вв.)// Советская археология. 1973. № 3. С. 230—242.

[2] *Висотська Т.М.* Про виробництво скла в пізньоантичному Криму // Археологія. Київ, 1964. Т. XVI. С. 7—20

PORTRAIT OF LYBIA (?)
Eastern Mediterranean
After 42 year AD. Cat. 78

PORTRAIT OF AUGUSTUS CAESAR
Second half of the 1st century AD
Römisch-Germanisches Museum,
Cologne

PLASTER MOULD OF
THE HEAD OF LYBIA (?)

PORTRAIT OF LYBIA
Marble. 1st century AD
Ruhr University, Bohum

N.GRACH
*Head of the State Hermitage's
Nymphaion Archaeological
Expedition, 1966-1990*

G.BELOV
*Head of the State Hermitage's
Chersonesos Archaeological
Expedition, 1947-1978*

F.ENTELIS
*Expert on glass technology.
Professor of the Mukhina State
Academy of Art and Industry,
St Petersburg*

produced window glass and crockery. Material from earlier excavations gave Belov reason to believe that Chersonesos possessed several workshops for the manufacturing of glass wares[3].

Instruments used by ancient glass masters were discovered in 1964 in the Bosporan town of Tanais, on premises destroyed by a fire in the 240s. Excavation work was carried out there by the Lower Don Expedition, Institute of Archaeology of the Academy of Sciences, headed by D.Shelov. Ye.Alexeyeva and T.Arsenieva believe that this was the site of a workshop that made vessels (particularly bowls with grinded ornamental designs) and beads[4]. Large formless pieces of poured glass and remains of unworked glass – "a reliable witness to production"[5] – were found amongst 3rd century material in Fanagoria, on the Taman Peninsula. In 1971 and 1972 slag and dross thrown into a rubbish hole were also come upon[6].

PLAN OF EXCAVATION
OF A GLASS-FOUNDING KILN
(2ND-3RD CENTURIES)
AT ALMA-KERMEN, CRIMEA
*Т.Н.Высотская. О производстве
стекла в позднеантичном Крыму.
// Археология. Т. XVI. Киев. 1964.
С. 10, рис. 4*

PLAN OF EXCAVATION
OF A GLASS-FOUNDING KILN
IN COLOGNE
*O.Doppelfeld. Römisches und
Fränkisches Glas in Köln.
S. 15, Abb. b*

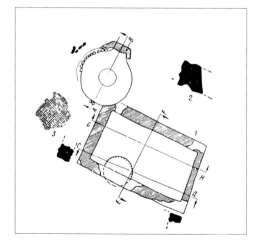
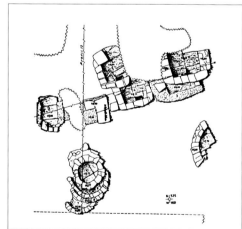

---

[3] *Белов Г.Д.* Стеклоделие в Херсонесе // Советская археология. 1965. № 3. С. 237—239; Стеклоделательная мастерская в Херсонесе // Краткие сообщения Института археологии. 1969. Вып. 116. С. 80—84

[4] *Алексеева Е.М. Арсеньева Т.М.* Стеклоделие Танаиса // Советская археология. 1966. № 2. С. 176—188

[5] *Щапова Ю.Л.* Очерки истории древнего стеклоделия. М. 1983. С. 162—163

[6] *Долгоруков В.С.* Исследования береговой части Фанагории в 1971—1972 гг. // Краткие сообщения Института археологии. 1975. Вып. 143. С. 55, 56

JUG
*Syria. Second half of 3rd century —
early 4th century AD*
Cat. 393

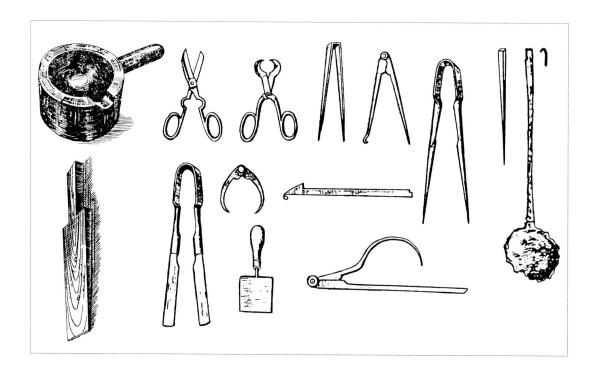

INSTRUMENTS USED BY ANCIENT GLASS
MASTERS (according to
A.S.Ostroverkhov, M.A.Bezborodov
and Yu.L.Schapova).
*А.С.Островерхов. Технология
античного стеклоделия.
Киев. 1993. С. 78, рис. 12*

In 1973 excavation of the Yagorlyk settlement yielded the remains of a glass workshop dating back to the 4th century BC, the oldest in the Black Sea area. It was the site for the manufacture of beads by pressing, winding softened glass thread onto a metal rod and many other techniques[7].

A 6th century workshop was uncovered on the site of an ancient settlement in Ilich (Taman Peninsula). This workshop manufactured glass for windows, icon-lamps, dinner services and beads[8].

The Armenian archaeologist Jores Khachatrian cites the existence of glass production in ancient Armenia on the evidence of finds made during excavations at Artashat and other sites in the 1970s. A collapsible plaster four-valved mould in the shape of a pine cone for blowing a glass vessel was found at Artashat. There is reason to believe that Armenian glassmakers were already making beads, clasps and stones with engraved designs in the 1st millenium BC. Khachatrian refers to several 2nd and 1st century BC Hellenic vessels and a series of vessels blown in the 1st—4th centuries AD, which he believes to be the work of Armenian masters[9].

[7] *Островерхов А.С.* Ягорлыцкое поселение // Археологические открытия 1973 года. М. 1974. С. 323; *Безбородов М.А., Островерхов А.С.* Стеклоделательная мастерская в Северном Причерноморье в VI в. до н. э. // Стекло и керамика. 1978. № 2. С. 32, 33; *Островерхов А.С.* Древнейшее античное производство стеклянных бус в Северном Причерноморье. Советская археология. 1981. № 4. С. 214—228

[8] *Николаева Э.Я.* Стеклоделие на Боспоре // Краткие сообщения Института археологии. 1991. Вып. 204. С. 50—55.

[9] *Хачатрян Ж.Д.* Стеклоделие в древней Армении (II—I века до нашей эры) // Историко-филологический журнал. Ереван. 1975. № 1 (68). С. 256—258; *Хачатрян Ж.* Армения и Сирия — центры стеклоделия (производственные общности) // Вестник общественных наук. Ереван. 1983, № 7 (487). С. 60—65.

On the basis of all these finds, confirmed by analysis of the typology and stylistics of a series of glass objects originating from northern Black Sea region excavations, one can trace the development of local glass production in ancient times.

Vital contributions to the study of ancient and medieval glass in both its historico-archaeological and chemical-technical aspects have been made by the archaeologists N.Sorokina, N.Ugrelidze, M.Saginashvili, T.Vysotskaya, Ye.Alexeyeva, T.Arsenieva, J.Khachatrian, A.Ostroverkhov, M.Smishko, E.Nikolaeva, as well as the Hermitage research assistants A.Voschinina, L.Galanina, I.Zasetskaya, Z.Lvova and the chemical technologists M.Bezborodov, F.Entelis, Yu.Schapova and V.Galibin. Their work, as well as occasionally their good offices, were of enormous assistance in the course of work on this book.

Over the centuries, mankind has opened up for himself the enormous technological and decorative possibilities of glass. Glass is born in the fire of the kiln. In its heated state it can be formed, modelled, rolled, pressed, cut and blown. The fire lends it its shine. When cooled, glass can be

TEMPLE WALL(7th century BC)
Nymphaion (environs of Kertch)

polished, ground, punched, engraved and perforated. It can be coloured in various lasting hues and tints and its surface can be painted and gilded. It possesses a rare quality — complete transparency. Its curves, ribs and edges play in the light, while it gathers colour in runs and protuberances. With its delicate, ultra-light walls, glass products at times seem not so much objects as metaphors for objects. Chemically stable, glass has long been put to various uses.

Glass-making first began in the countries of the ancient East — Mesopotamia and Egypt — probably as far back as the third millenium before the birth of Christ. Sand, lime and soda (or plant ashes and, later, wood ashes) were mixed in order to acquire the molten material necessary for glassware. This would then be heated in kilns, in pots and crucibles.

There are many ancient glass workshops known to us (more than ten of them still with the remains of kilns) in Egypt, Mesopotamia, Asia Minor, the Syrian coast, across Europe and along the Black Sea. The most ancient workshop (in Egypt) dates back to the second millenium before Christ, and the youngest to the time of the Roman Empire and the Middle Ages.

The process of glass founding was a long one and passed through several stages, at a temperature of around 1000 degrees centigrade.

In the third and second millenia BC the technique of founding colourless clear glass was still unknown. The result was viscous, paste-like and unclarified. Glassmakers therefore then painted it various colours. They employed copper oxide and protoxide as colouring agents which, depending on the conditions of firing, resulted in colours of red, green and light blue. Cobalt oxide turned glass dark blue, manganous oxide turned it purple-violet and lead oxide turned it yellow. Adding tin turned glass a milky-white.

Later, during the 1st millenium BC, masters learned how to found clear glass. Nevertheless, it still displayed a slight tone for a long time, depending on the composition of the raw material, which could not be purified of the superfluous admixtures. Like it or not, the iron inherent in the sand coloured the glass in light, almost indiscernable greenish, greeny-yellow and greeny-blue tones.

Beads, pendants, stamps and mosaic plaquettes used for decorating furniture were made from glass in the 2nd millenium BC in Mesopotamia, Egypt and the Aegean world. The oldest known technique employed in the manufacture of such glass wares was pressing in form.

Beads were made by twisting the glass mass on a metal rod. A somewhat more involved form of this technique, the "core technique", was used to manufacture hollow vessels. These first appeared in the middle of the 2nd millenium BC in Mesopotamia, and then in Egypt in the form of small thick-walled vases — krateriskoi and flasks for incense. The clay pig — the core — was put on a metallic rod and lent the form of the future vessel. Plaits of hot glass were then wound round the core which, uniting, formed the body of the vessel. The glass was generally either opaque (dulled) or semi-clear. Oriental aesthetics, however, demanded bright ornamentation, hence the vessel would be decorated in multi-coloured and often multi-tiered ornamental designs.

Multi-coloured glass threads were wound round the body rotated on the rod. In order to achieve a zigzag ornamental design, the threads were "combed" by special instruments (tooth combs) before being smoothed out and rolled out on a stone slab. During this process, the ornamental design of the coloured thread would join to the body of the vessel, forming a common smooth surface. The rod with the clay core was extracted from the cooled object. Then, heating the vessel, the rim was formed and the foot and handles (which were often semi-clear) affixed.

The favoured choice of colour for the glass was a lapis lazuli navy blue, though bright blues, red-browns, turquoises, milky-whites and dark shades running to black are also to be found. The threads for the ornamental design were either made from glass of another colour or of several colours — usually yellow, blue-turquoise or white.

A plain decoration in the shape of one or more coloured girdles (circular, spiral, undulating) might be employed alongside the multi-tiered pattern (zigzag, scalloped, plumose). Monochrome unornamented vessels are also occasionally encountered.

ARYBALLOS, OENOCHOE AND
AMPHORISKOS
Eastern Mediterranean.
Late 6th century —
early 5th century BC. Cat. 23, 19, 31

The oldest example of ancient glass in the Hermitage is the krateriskos, made by the core technique, which dates from the 14th century BC (cat. 1). This primitive means of producing vessels existed 1500 years before the birth of Christ.

During the 9th century BC, the main centres for glass-work were the Syrian coast and Mesopotamia. In the 7th and 6th centuries BC, glass workshops appeared on the islands of Rhodes and Cyprus and, it is thought, on the Greek mainland. The oldest workshop uncovered by archaeologists along the north Black Sea coast also dates from the 6th century BC. The heyday of the core technique was, however, the period embracing the 6th, 5th and 4th centuries BC. Bright multi-coloured flasks, filled with fragrant oils, were transported by sea merchants across the entire ancient world, even as far afield as the Pontus Euxinus (Black Sea). Inasmuch as these wares were spread throughout the Greek population, glassmakers lent them forms typical of Greek vessels made from other materials (ceramics, metal). Typical examples of glass flasks formed on cores were the alabastron, amphoriskos, aryballos and oenochoe (cat. 2–38). The Greek custom of accompanying the dead into the next world with an assortment of ritual objects, including flasks with incense, has provided archaeologists with a wealth of objects. As a rule, these thick-walled vessels have survived well.

Glass beads, produced in abundance in the ancient world, were also made by the core technique. A cylindrical sandy-clay core was placed on a wire pivot, covered in a layer of heated unitone or monochrome glass and extracted after cooling. If the rod passed right through, then the result was

RECONSTRUCTING A KILN
IN A WORKSHOP, TEL-EL-AMARNA
(according to W.Flinders Petrie
and Yu.L.Schapova).
*Ю.Л.Щапова. Очерки истории
древнего стеклоделия.
М. 1983. С. 76, рис. 14*

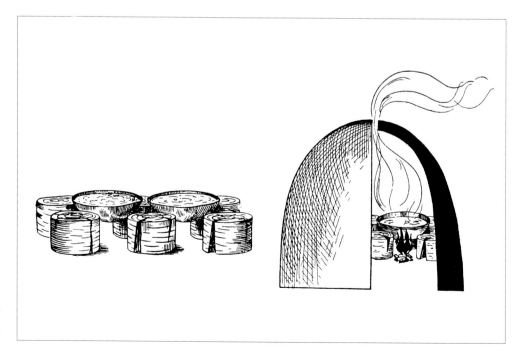

*"I heard from the glassworkers at Alexandria that there was in Egypt
a kind of vitreous earth without which many-coloured and costly designs
could not be executed."*

Strabo, Geog. XVI, 2.25 cap. 758

RECONSTRUCTING THE PROCESS
OF MANUFACTURING GLASS
BY THE CORE TECHNIQUE
(according to D.F. Grose).
*D.F. Grose. Early Ancient Glass.
New York. 1989. Fig. 4*

a transpierced bead. Besides these, there were also pendants without orifices, to which an ear would be attached. Amulet pendants (height 3– 5 cm) in the shape of the heads of demons, birds and (usually bearded) men (cat. 39–44) were made from the 7th to the 3rd centuries BC throughout the Mediterranean, particularly on the Syro-Phoenician coast and in Carthage. These amulets alternated with beads. When manufacturing pendants in the shape of male heads, the core was generally covered in dull turquoise glass. The face, coiffure and beard would be modelled from dull glass of various colours and applied to the body, so that the colour of the body could only be seen from the reverse side. A studied decorative modelling and colour scheme, sculptural expressiveness of the form and expression of the image were typical features of these exquisite miniatures. Large cylindrical beads, decorated with modelled representations of human faces on both sides (cat. 45), were also made from glass. Their purpose is not entirely clear. These beads had a thick channel running through them, so it is possible that they were used as finger-rings. Glass beads and pendants were put on one string with beads made from coloured stone.

A means of creating attractive bowls from decolourized glass by casting in mould was come upon, first in Assyria in the 9th and 8th centuries BC, then spreading across the whole Middle East, especially to Persia. The resulting bowls were thick-walled. After cooling, their surface was subjected to cold mechanical working – polishing, sometimes carving, with the help of which the relief ornamental design, attained in the mould, was finished off. The individual elements of the decoration were completed by carving alone. The form and decoration of these bowls imitated vessels made from precious metals, usually silver. There is an example of such a bowl, dating from the 4th century BC, in the Hermitage collection (cat. 47).

The casting method was employed in Egypt from the 4th to 2nd centuries BC to make exquisite bowls with open-work plant geometric ornamental designs, made from gold foil between two layers of colourless glass. The complex technology, rich material, triumphant beauty of the ornamentation and mastery of execution hint at the unique nature of such wares, all the more so when few such vessels are to be found in museum collections. The Hermitage possesses one of the finest bowls from this series, found in a burial mound in the northern Caucasus (cat. 48).

The casting technique was long utilized in the production of ancient glass. The eastern Mediterranean and Italy were sites for the production of smooth-walled ribbed bowls made from coloured glass, simple in form yet with austere proportions, the latest of which date back to the 1st century AD (cat. 50–56)

BOWL
Persia. Late 5th century –
first half of 4th century BC
H. 5.4. Cat. 47

RECONSTRUCTING THE PROCESS
OF MANUFACTURING GLASS
BY THE PRESSING TECHNIQUE
(according to D.F.Grose).
D.F.Grose. Early Ancient Glass.
New York. 1989. P. 245, fig. 118

GOLD-BOUND GLASS BOWL
Alexandria, Egypt
Second half of 3rd century —
early 2nd century BC
Cat. 48

Two-handled cups, skyphoi and kantharoi (cat. 57–62) were manufactured by means of casting, carving and polishing in the 1st century BC. They were cast in moulds together with their handles and feet. On the vessel's cooling, the orifices in the handles, the details of the feet and the decorations were finished off by chisel.

The clear outlines of the glass cups reproduce the chased forms of the silver utensils of that time. Such vessels were, as a rule, made from colourless glass. Besides colourless ones, the Hermitage also possesses a rare example made from blue glass (cat. 62).

KANTHAROS
*Eastern Mediterranean. First half
of 1st century AD. Cat. 62*

KANTHAROS
Silver. Italy. 1st century AD
Louvre

DETAIL OF THE PAINTWORK
ON A CRYPT
Kertch. 4th century AD

One more ancient means of decorating wares, extremely complicated and time-consuming, yet highly effective, was the glass mosaic technique. Mosaic tiles had decorated furniture in Ancient Egypt as far back as the 2nd millenum BC, yet as far as vessels are concerned, the heyday of this decorative technique was the 1st century BC and 1st century AD. Basically, bundles were gathered from rods of various-coloured glass, giving a set pattern in cross-section (meander, diamond, rosette).

The rods were then founded, resulting in a solid half-finished product, which was subsequently heated and stretched out. During the stretching process the pattern decreased in size many times over (to the necessary dimensions), whilst still retaining the original mutual arrangement of its elements. The resulting long rod was cut into "slices" – plaquettes displaying the required pattern. The various means of cutting the rods up into "slices" (diagonal cutting, for example), along with other manipulations (the heated rod could be rolled up prior to cutting and so on), opened up a wealth of possibilities for variations on the ornamental design. The slices were stacked in form. The gaps between them were filled with crushed glass, which consequently formed the basic colour of the product. During heating the glass would fill up the form. It was then separated from the vessel by pressing and polished on cooling. The same virtuoso technique was employed in the production of beads (cat. 103–108). Mosaic glass was made in Egypt, Syria and Rome. The Hermitage possesses a fine bowl with a spiral imitation agate ornamental design (cat. 93), in addition to whole mosaic vessels and a good few other fragments (cat. 86–94).

Imitation of the structure and natural patterns of coloured stones (agate, jasper), from almost complete imitation to deliberate stylization, is a typical feature of ancient glass-work. This same technique was also used during the creation of free compositions from wide stripes of coloured glass with gold foil held between layers of colourless glass. The foil cracks when heated, forming a shining, living texture. Researchers have still to fully understand the technology of this manufacturing technique. Its wonderful decorative effect is unsurpassed even by modern masters. Small flasks (of which there were two types), alabastra and pyxides, combining stripes of blue, green, purple and white glass with a gold stripe, were manufactured in Alexandria, Egypt and, probably, in Rome in the 1st century BC and the early 1st century AD. Several examples of these small masterpieces can be found in the collection of the Hermitage (cat. 95–98).

The mid–1st century BC brought about a revolution in glass-making on the Syrian coast with the invention of the glass-blowing pipe. This meant that glass, which had previously been pressed and cast, could now be blown. A lump of molten glass from the kiln was gathered on the end of a long iron pipe and rolled out onto a stone tile. Air was then blown into the

"...between Ace and Tyre is a sandy beach, which produces the sand in making glass. Now the sand, it is said, is not fused here but it is carried to Sidon and there melted and cast. Some say that the Sidonians, among others, have the glass-sand that is adopted to fusing though others say that any sand anywhere can be fused."

Strabo, Geog. XVI, 2.25 cap. 758

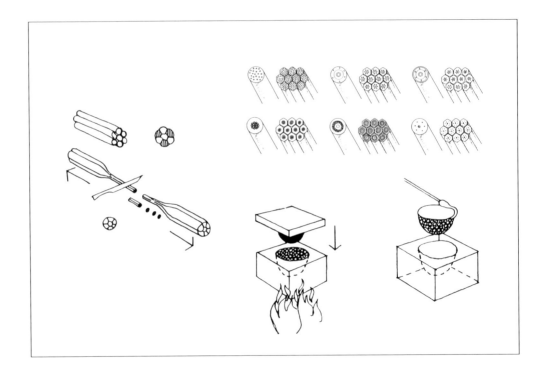

RECONSTRUCTING THE PROCESS
OF MANUFACTURING GLASS
BY THE MOSAIC TECHNIQUE
(according to D.F. Grose)
*D.F. Grose. Early Ancient Glass.
New York. 1989. P. 32, fig. 6
A. von Saldern. Glas von der
Antike bis zum Jugendstil. Mainz
am Rhein. 1982. P. 20, 21*

BOWL
*Eastern Mediterranean or Italy.
Late 1st century BC —
early 1st century AD. Cat. 93*

FLASKS AND PYXIS
Alexandria (Egypt) or Italy
First half of 1st century. Cat. 95—97

resulting half-finished product. A portion of glass, necessary for the future ware, was gathered on it and blown into a bubble. The finished product was then formed with the help of manipulations of the pipe and other instruments (rotation, stretching, clamps). Since the neck of the vessel was attached to the pipe, they had to be separated in order to form the brim. And so an iron rod (pontil) was attached to the bottom of the object and, holding the vessel on it, they would knock off its neck from the pipe and thus form the brim. After this the pontil was broken off, often leaving a pontil-mark on the bottom.

The free-blowing technique greatly simplified and accelerated the process of glass production, thus aiding the spread of glass-making throughout the entire ancient world. In the first three centuries AD large quantities of glass began to be blown not only in Rome and throughout the Roman Empire, but also far beyond its frontiers – from Mesopotamia to Spain, from Egypt to Britain and from Cyprus to the far shores of the Black Sea. Glass workshops were established in Gaul and Germany, with the leading centre situated in Cologne (Colonia Agrippina). Its goods were noted for their originality of form and decoration (cat. 168).

As before, the most prized masters of glass came from Syria, particularly those working in the town of Sidon. It is believed that Sidon was home to the second techique of blowing glass – in mould. This technique used a

*"Now the Italian river Volturnus also furnishes a white sand which is found
for six miles along the seashore, from Cumae to Liternum. This sand is very
soft, and is ground in mortars or between mill-stones. It is then mixed with
three parts of nitrum, by weight or measure, brought to a state of fusion,
and transferred to another furnace in which a mass called hammonitrum
is formed. This is fused for a second time and vitrum purum is obtained,
a mass of colourless glass. Similar methods are now en vogue in the Gauls
and Spains for converting sand into glass."*

Pliny, Nat. Hist. 36.194

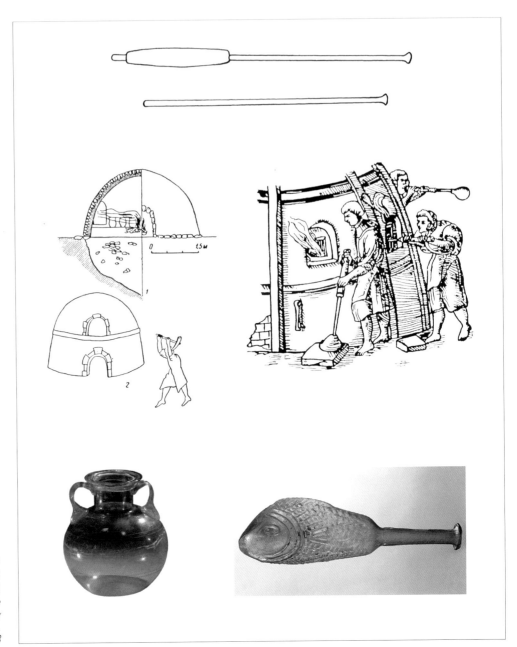

RECONSTRUCTING GLASS-BLOWING
PIPES AND A CIRCULAR KILN
(according to Agricola)
*Т.Н.Высотская. О производстве
стекла в позднеантичном Крыму
// Археология. Т. XVI. Киев. 1964.
С. 9, рис. 3*

OENOCHOAE AND JUG
Syria. Second half of 1st century AD
Cat. 123–125

negative detachable matrix, made from clay or stone, to produce objects bearing relief decorations and inscriptions (names of masters, toasts, wishes), as well as sculptured figurative vessels in the shape of heads of deities and humans, fruit, fish and shells (cat. 145–159).

The advantage of this technique was that the same matrix could be used over and over again. Whole series of identical vessels could be created from glass of different colours, varying the details – the rim, foot and handles – by hand. Employing multi-section forms, the masters sometimes combined various parts of different matrices, standard in size but with different ornamental motifs. This greatly increased the diversity of combinations of the individual elements of the ornamentation.

Blowing in mould first sprung up in Syria and rapidly spread across Italy, Gaul and the other regions of the ancient world. Masters freely moved across these regions, founding new branches of their enterprises. Several of their names are known to us. Amongst them pride of place belongs to that of Ennion (cat. 109), the 1st century AD master from Sidon who opened a branch of his workshop in Italy.

The Hermitage collection well reflects the diversity of wares created in closed detachable negative matrices (cat. 109–159). For a serial production of vessels of simple configuration, a means of blowing in an open undetachable mould was employed. The bubble of glass was blown into a hollow four-sided (or multi-sided) matrix and the body of the vessel thus acquired its form. The neck, brim and handle could then be completed by hand (cat. 162–172).

JUG
*Eastern Mediterranean
or Bosporan Kingdom
2nd century AD. Cat. 264*

Despite the technical superiorities of blowing in mould, the method that held sway in ancient glass-making was nevertheless the technique of free blowing. This may have been because it allowed masters unlimited possibilities for varying the forms and ornamentation of their vessels. Ancient glass-blowers thus created hundreds of different-shaped bowls and beakers, jugs and dishes, bottles and unguentaria. The diapason of their output ranged from flasks for incense to sepulchral urns.

The transparency of the glass had an important role to play in thin-walled blown products. But this had to be understood. Following the invention of blowing, in the 1st century AD, masters for a time still preferred to adhere to tradition and to paint their vessels in bright colours. In Alexandria and Rome they were decorated with enamel paints, completely covering the surface (cat. 178, 180). In Italy a popular technique was to adorn an item with bright specks of glass of varying colours. A hot bubble of glass, held onto a pipe, was then rolled in crumbs of coloured glass. On melting, they would turn into brightly-coloured spots, covering the vessel's exterior. Thus the popular imitation of coloured stone (jasper) became a less time-consuming process than it was when attempted by the mosaic technique. Amphoriskoi, sometimes modioli tankards, and small flasks thus tended to display brightly spotted surfaces (cat. 184, 185, 187–190, 193, 194).

With time, masters of glass came to fully comprehend the unique quality of their material – its transparency. They began to create the large part

RIBBED BOWLS
Northern Italy. Second –third quarters of 1st century AD
Cat. 206–208

"And at Rome, also, it is said that many discoveries are made both for producing
the colours and for the facility of manufacture, as, for example, in the case
of glassware, where one can buy a glass beaker or drinking-cup for a copper."

Strabo, Geog. XVI, 2.25 cap. 758

JUGS
Cyprus. Second half of 1st century AD
Cat. 242, 243

VASE-UNGUENTARIUM
Syria. 4th –5th centuries AD. Cat. 414

FLASKS
Syria. 3rd –4th centuries AD. Cat. 404, 405

FLASKS
Syria. 4th century AD. Cat. 409, 410

FLASKS
Syria. 4th century AD. Cat. 411, 412

of their work using colourless or specially painted glass, adorning vessels with engraved girdles, ground hollows and coloured glass threads.

The development of the forms and ornamentation of ancient glass reflects the general tendencies of the development of ancient artistic craftwork. The strict architect-onic forms, combined with the utilitarian purpose of the vessels, gave way in the late 3rd and 4th centuries AD to increasingly whimsical forms. Decoration began to take centre stage in glass production. This is best of all reflected in the works of the Syrian glass-blowers (cat. 404–414).

The art of ancient glass-making has gathered much experience throughout its long history. Masters have learned to make extremely high-quality glass and have developed many different means of producing and decorating of glass.

The experience of the ancient glass-blowers came to Venice from Syria and Byzantium. When the Venetians conquered Constantinople, alongside valuables and works of art they also seized the masters of glass, along with the secrets and skills of their trade. They invented the celebrated *latticinio* glass of Venice by developing the ancient "millefiori" (a thousand flowers) technique. This won them the reputation as the leading masters of glasswork in Europe and marked the beginning of the history of the art of glass in the modern era.

The main recipes for making glass and the technical devices of the ancient masters have withstood the test of time and are used to this day. Ancient glass is thus an inexhaustible treasure-trove, both for the masters of glass and for wide sections of the public.

Nina Kunina

illustrations

ANCIENT GLASS 1
core-formed glass

1. KRATERISKOS
*Egypt. Late 15th century —
first half of 14th century BC*
H. 9.2. Cat. 1

2. ALABASTRA
Eastern Mediterranean
5th century — early 4th century BC
H. 9.3; 10.9. Cat. 11—13

3. ALABASTRON
Eastern Mediterranean or Italy
Last quarter of 4th century BC
H. 24.1. Cat. 16

4. ALABASTRON
Eastern Mediterranean
Late 6th century — early 5th century BC
H. 12. Cat. 2

5. ALABASTRON
Eastern Mediterranean
Last quarter of 4th century BC
H. 14.9. Cat. 14

6. ALABASTRON
Eastern Mediterranean or Italy
Late 4th century — early 3rd century BC
H. 17.5. Cat. 17

7. ALABASTRON
Eastern Mediterranean
2nd century — 1st century BC
H. 13.2. Cat. 18

8. ALABASTRON
Eastern Mediterranean
First half of 5th century BC
H. 10. Cat. 4

9. ALABASTRA
Eastern Mediterranean
Early 5th century BC
H. 8.5; 11.8. Cat. 5, 6

10. ALABASTRA
Eastern Mediterranean
5th century BC
H. 9.6; 10.3. Cat. 9, 10

11. ALABASTRON
Eastern Mediterranean. Late 6th century –
first half of 5th century BC
H. 14.4. Cat. 3

12. OENOCHOE
Eastern Mediterranean (Rhodes ?)
Mid—5th century BC
H. 11.8. Cat. 21

13. ARYBALLOS, AMPHORISKOS
Eastern Mediterranean
Second half of 6th century —
first half of 5th century BC
H. 5.1; 7.6. Cat. 22, 32

14. ARYBALLOS, AMPHORISKOS
Eastern Mediterranean
5th century BC
H. 6.5; 7.5. Cat. 25, 30

15. AMPHORISKOE
Eastern Mediterranean
5th century BC
H. 6.6; 6.7. Cat. 33–35

16. ARYBALLOS, AMPHORISKOE
Eastern Mediterranean
Second half of 6th century — 5th century BC
H. 6; 9.1; 8.7. Cat. 24, 28, 29

17. OENOCHOE, ARYBALLOS, AMPHORISKOS
Eastern Mediterranean
5th century BC
H. 7.6; 5.5; 7.2. Cat. 20, 26, 36

18. AMPHORISKOS
Eastern Mediterranean
Second half of 6th century BC
H. 11. Cat. 27

19. AMPHORISKOS
Eastern Mediterranean
Early 1st century AD
H. 13.8. Cat. 37

20, 21. BEAD WITH DOUBLE-SIDED
REPRESENTATION OF HUMAN FACES
Eastern Mediterranean (Carthage ?)
4th — 3rd centuries BC
H. 2.8. Frontal view. Rear view. Cat. 45

22. PENDANTS IN SHAPE OF HEADS
OF DEMON AND COCKEREL
Eastern Mediterranean
Late 6th — early 5th centuries BC;
4th century BC
H. 3.1; 3.3. Cat. 39, 40

23. PENDANT IN SHAPE
OF BEARDED MALE HEAD
*Eastern Mediterranean
4th — 3rd centuries BC*
H. 5.8. Cat. 41

24. PENDANTS IN SHAPE
OF BEARDED MALE HEAD
*Eastern Mediterranean
4th — 3rd centuries BC*
H. 3.2; 3.1; 5. Cat. 42—44

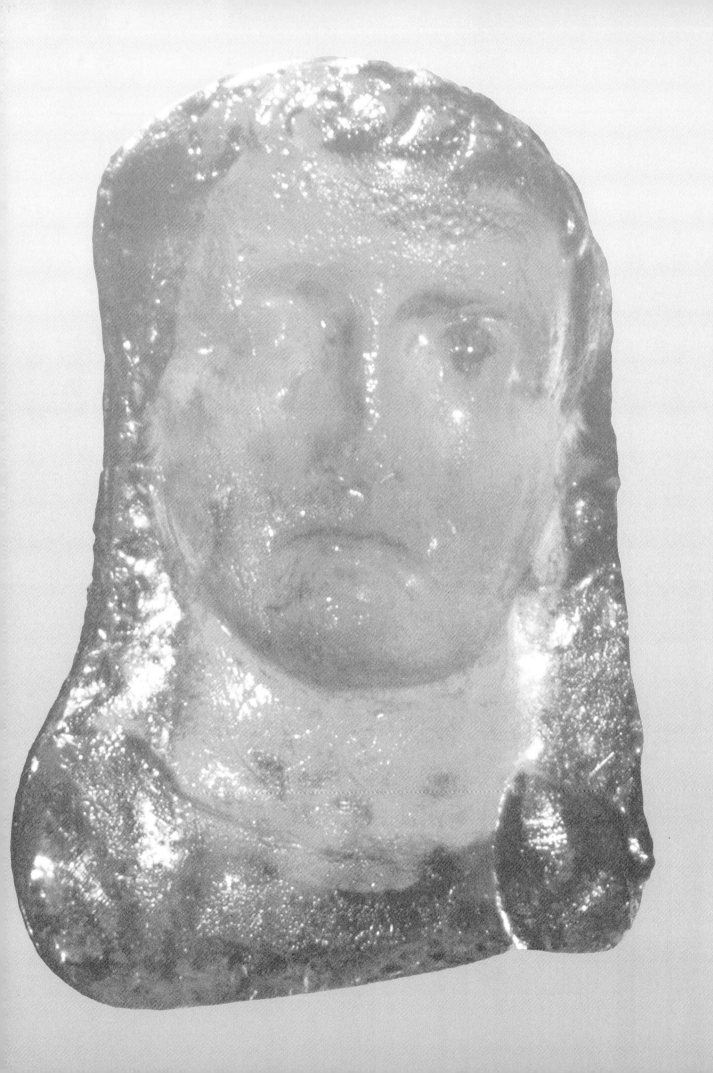

ANCIENT GLASS 2
cast and pressed glass

25. BOWL
Alexandria,Egypt
Second half of 3rd century —
early 2nd century BC
H. 8.5. Cat. 48

26. Bowl
*Syria. Late 1st century BC —
early 1st century AD*
H. 5.2. Cat. 52

27. Bowl
*Persia. Late 5th century —
first half of 4th century BC*
H. 5.4. Cat. 47

28. BOWL
Eastern Mediterranean
1st century AD
H. 5.9. Cat. 53

29. BOWL
Syria. Late 1st century BC —
early 1st century AD
H. 5.5. Cat. 51

30. RIBBED BOWLS
Eastern Mediterranean
1st century AD
H. 4.5; 5.5. Cat. 56, 55

31. RIBBED BOWLS
Eastern Mediterranean
1st century AD
H. 4.8. Cat. 54

34. KANTHAROS
Eastern Mediterranean
First half of 1st century AD
H. 9.8. Cat. 61

32, 33. PLATE
Eastern Mediterranean or Italy
40s—70s AD
D. 18.1. Cat. 63

35. KANTHAROS
Eastern Mediterranean
First half of 1st century AD
H. 9.3. Cat. 60

36. KANTHAROS
Eastern Mediterranean
Mid—2nd century BC
H. 9.6. Cat. 59

37. SKYPHOS
Eastern Mediterranean
Late 2nd century —
early 1st century BC
H. 8.2. Cat. 57

38. MEDALLION
WITH BUST OF WOMAN
Eastern Mediterranean
Second half of 4th century BC
Cat. 66

39. MEDALLION WITH SPINNER.
TRACING
Eastern Mediterranean
Second half of 4th century BC
Cat. 67

40. MEDALLION
WITH HEAD OF YOUTH
Eastern Mediterranean
Second half of 4th century BC
Cat. 65

41. CAMEO WITH REPRESENTATION
OF HEAD OF ATHENS
Italy (?). 1st century AD
Cat. 72

42. SEAL WITH PORTRAIT
OF GAIUS CAESAR
Italy. Late 1st century BC — 1st century AD
Cat. 71

43. PORTRAIT OF LUBIA (?)
Eastern Mediterranean
After 42 AD
H. 3.5. Cat. 78

44. SIGNET-RING
WITH PORTRAIT OF BERENICE
Alexandria (?),Egypt
3rd century BC
Cat. 69

45. FINGER-RING WITH PORTRAIT
OF MITHRADATES VI EUPATOR
Northern Black Sea coast (?)
Late 2nd century —
early 1st century BC
Cat. 70

46, 47. GEM. VIEW FROM THE BOTH SIDES
Eastern Mediterranean (?)
Second quarter — mid 4th century BC
Cat. 68

48. PHALERA WITH REPRESENTATION
OF DIONYSUS (MÆNADES ?)
Roman Empire
1st century AD
Cat. 74

49. PHALERA WITH REPRESENTATION
OF DIONYSUS (MÆNADES ?)
Roman Empire
1st century AD
Cat. 75

50. PHALERA WITH PORTRAIT
OF DRUSUS THE YOUNGER
Roman Empire
Early 1st century AD
Cat. 73

ANCIENT GLASS 3
mosaic glass

51. FLASK
Eastern Mediterranean
First half of 1st century AD
H. 10. Cat. 99

52, 53. ALABASTRON
*Eastern Mediterranean
or Alexandria
1st century BC*
H. 16.3. Cat. 94

54. SMALL BOWL
*Eastern Mediterranean
(Syria ?)
First half of 1st century AD*
H. 4. Cat. 86

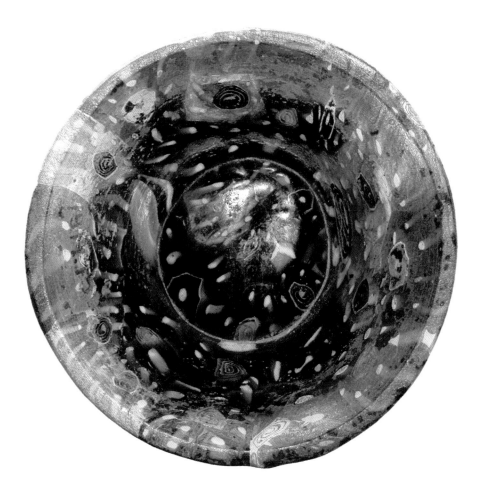

57. SMALL BOWL
Eastern Mediterranean or Italy
1st century AD
H. 5.7. Cat. 88

55. FOOT OF BOWL
Eastern Mediterranean
or Italy
First half of 1st century AD
Cat. 90

56. SMALL BOWL
Eastern Mediterranean (Syria ?)
First half of 1st century AD
H. 4. Cat. 87

58. FLASK
Eastern Mediterranean or Italy
First half of 1st century AD
H. 11.5. Cat. 102

59. FLASK
Eastern Mediterranean or Italy
First half of 1st century AD
H. 8.6. Cat. 101

60. BOWL
Eastern Mediterranean or Italy
Late 1st century BC —
early 1st century AD
H. 5. Cat. 93

61. FRAGMENT OF BOWL
Eastern Mediterranean
or Italy
1st century AD
H. 5.6. Cat. 89

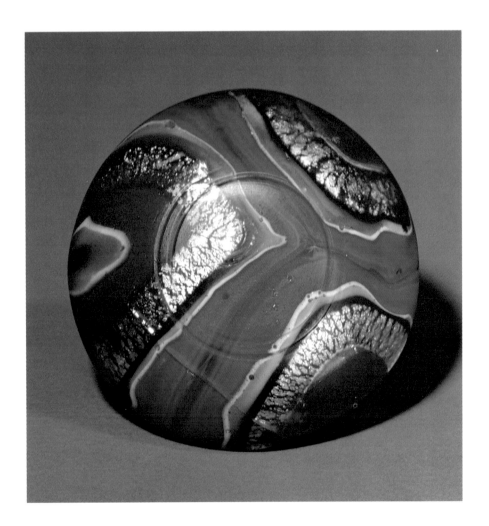

63. FLASK
Eastern Mediterranean
First half of 1st century AD
H. 8.5. Cat. 100

64. BOTTOM OF FLASK
Alexandria, Egypt
First half of 1st century AD
Cat. 98

65. FLASKS AND PYXIS
Alexandria (Egypt) or Italy
First half of 1st century AD
H. 6; 7.4; 4.3. Cat. 95—97

66. BEADS, PLAQUE, BEAD
Alexandria, Egypt
Late 1st century BC — 3rd century AD
Cat. 103—108

67. BEAD
*Mediterranean
or Alexandria (Egypt)
1st–3rd centuries AD*
Cat. 108

ANCIENT GLASS 4

mould-blown glass

68. **AMPHORA**. MASTER ENNION
Syria,Sidon
Early 1st century AD
H. 17.7. Cat. 109

69. AMPHORA. DETAIL
Master Ennion's stamp
Cat. 109

70. OENOCHOE. ENNION'S WORKSHOP (?)
Syria, Sidon
First half of 1st century AD
H. 18.   Cat. 112

71. OENOCHOE. ENNION'S WORKSHOP (?)
Syria, Sidon
First half of 1st century AD
H. 17.9. Cat. 110

72. OENOCHOE. ENNION'S WORKSHOP (?)
Syria, Sidon
First half of 1st century AD
H. 18.1. Cat. 111

75. BEAKER
*Eastern Mediterranean
or Italy*
First half of 1st century AD
H. 7.2. Cat. 116

73. BEAKER INSCRIBED
"WIN A VICTORY"
Syria. 1st century AD
H. 6.6. Cat. 113

74. BEAKER INSCRIBED
"BE HEALTHY AND HAPPY"
Syria. 1st century AD
H. 7.4. Cat. 115

76. BEAKER WITH REPRESENTATION OF JUPITER,
BACCHUS, SILVANUS AND NEPTUNE
Syria. Second half of 1st century AD
H. 12.5. Cat. 117

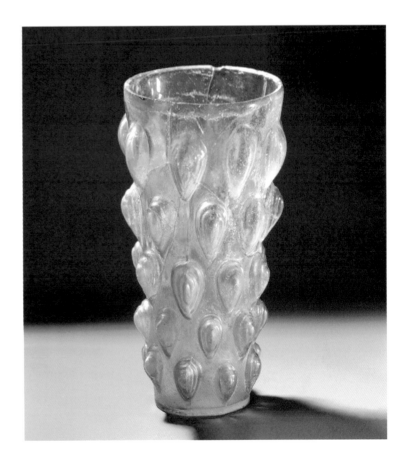

77. BEAKER
*Eastern Mediterranean
or Northern Italy
Second half of 1st century AD*
H. 14.2. Cat. 118

78. BEAKER
*Syria. Late 1st century —
first half of 2nd century AD*
H. 9. Cat. 119

79. FLASK
Syria
Second half of 1st century AD
H. 17.1. Cat. 126

80. OENOCHOAE, JUG
Syria
Second half of 1st century AD
H. 11.3, 12.2; 11.3. Cat. 123, 125, 124

81. GRAPE FLASKS
Eastern Mediterranean (Syria ?)
2nd century AD
H. 9.9; 12.5; 12. Cat. 149–151

82, 83. FISH BOTTLE
Eastern Mediterranean (?)
2nd – 3rd centuries AD
L. 25. Cat. 152

84. FLASKS AND AMPHORISKOS
*Syria (Sidon ?). Second half of 1st century —
early 2nd century AD*
H. 7.2; 7.1; 6.7. Cat. 139—141

85. SMALL JUG
Syria
1st century AD
H. 10.2. Cat. 130

86, 87. DOUBLE-HEAD FLASK
*Syria. Late 2nd century —
early 3rd century AD*
H. 7.5. Cat. 155

88. DOUBLE-HEAD JUG
AND DOUBLE-HEAD FLASKS
*Syria. Late 2nd century —
early 3rd century AD*
H. 7.1; 8.3; 7.5. Cat. 157, 156, 158

→
89. DIONYSUS HEAD FLASK
*Eastern Mediterranean (Syria ?)
Second half (?) of 2nd century AD*
H. 12.1. Cat. 153

→
90. BOY'S HEAD FLASK
*Eastern Mediterranean (Syria ?)
3rd century — early 4th century AD*
H. 16.6. Cat. 159

91. DATE FLASKS
Syria
Mid-1st century — mid-2nd century AD
H. 8; 6.3; 7.1. Cat. 146—148

92. SHELL FLASK
Eastern Mediterranean (Syria ?)
1st century AD
H. 11.5. Cat. 145

93. BOWLS
Syria
Second quarter — mid-1st century AD
H. 4.5. Cat. 121, 122

94. AMPHORISKOS
Syria (Sidon ?)
First half of 1st century AD
H. 8.9. Cat. 129

95. BOWL
Eastern Mediterranean
(Syria ?)
First half of 1st century AD
H. 4.4. Cat. 120

96, 97. RECTANGULAR JUG
Eastern Mediterranean
Second half of 1st century AD
H. 17.6. Cat. 165

98. PATERA
Northern Italy (?)
First half of 1st century AD
H. 6.2. Cat. 160

→
99. SMALL RECTANGULAR JUG
WITH TWO COMPARTMENTS
Rhineland or Gaul
1st – 2nd centuries AD
H. 11.5. Cat. 169

→
100. RECTANGULAR JUG
Rhineland (Cologne ?)
Third quarter of 1st century AD
H. 11.7. Cat. 166

101. CYLINDRICAL JUG. MASTER FRONTINUS
Gaul. 3rd — 4th centuries AD
H. 17.8. Cat. 172

102. FLASK
Bosporos' (?)
4th century AD
H. 28.8. Cat. 174

103. JUG WITH LION'S MASK
South-eastern Mediterranean (Egypt ?)
4th century AD
H. 30. Cat. 175

104. FLASK
Bosporos' (?)
4th century AD
H. 18. Cat. 173

105. JUG
Syria
4th century AD
H. 18.1. Cat. 176

106. FLASK
Syria
4th century AD
H. 19.5. Cat. 177

ANCIENT GLASS 5
free-blown glass

107. AMPHORA
Northern Italy
First half of 1st century AD
H. 30. Cat. 178

108. AMPHORA
Detail of painted design
Cat. 178

109. AMPHORA
*Eastern Mediterranean
or Egypt
Second half of 1st century AD*
H. 28.5. Cat. 179

110 — 112. BOWL
Northern Italy
Second quarter of 1st century AD
H. 7. Cat. 180

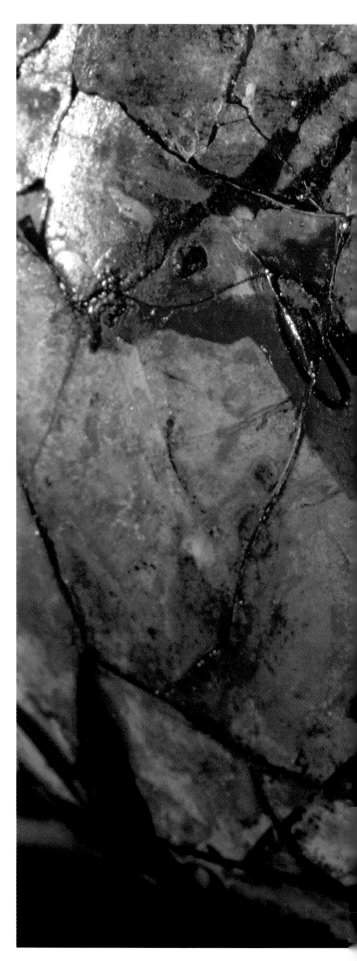

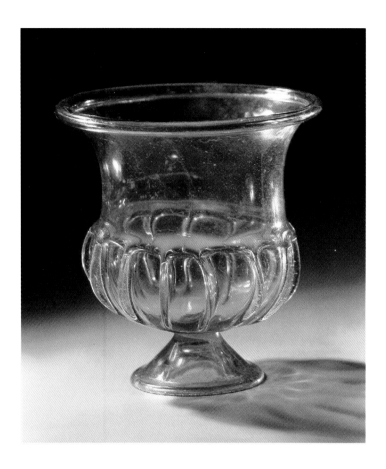

115. MODIOLUS
Northern Italy
Early 1st century AD
H. 12.1. Cat. 185

113. KRATERISKOS
Northern Italy
First half of 1st century AD
H. 15. Cat. 183

114. MODIOLUS
Western territory of the
Roman Empire or Italy
1st century AD
H. 20.4. Cat. 186

116. KRATERISKOS
Northern Italy
1st century AD
H. 14.6. Cat. 184

117. AMPHORISKOE
Northern Italy
1st century AD
H. 12.7; 12.6; 11.9. Cat. 187—189

118. AMPHORISKOE
Northern Italy,
Eastern Mediterranean
1st century AD
H. 11.2; 10; 11.8. Cat. 190—192

119. FLASK
Eastern Mediterranean
First half of 1st century AD
H. 11.5. Cat. 198

120. SMALL FLASKS
Northern Italy
First half of 1st century AD
H. 7.8; 7.4. Cat. 193, 194

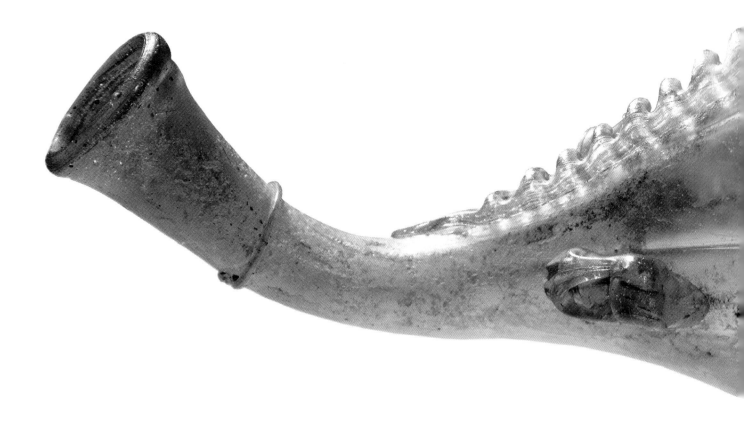

121, 122. FISH VESSEL
Eastern Mediterranean (Syria ?)
2nd – 4th centuries AD
L. 23.5. Cat. 201

123, 124. FISH VESSEL
Eastern Mediterranean. 2nd century AD
L. 17.3. Cat. 200

125. RIBBED BOWL
Northern Italy
Second – third quarters of 1st century AD
H. 7. Cat. 205

126. RIBBED BOWL
Northern Italy
First half of 1st century AD
H. 7. Cat. 204

127. RIBBED BOWLS
Northern Italy
First half — third quarter
of 1st century AD
H. 5; 4.6; 6.1. Cat. 209—211

128. DISH
Eastern Mediterranean
1st century AD
H. 2.8. Cat. 203

129. FLASK
Eastern Mediterranean
1st century AD
H. 11.1. Cat. 199

130. FLASK
Eastern Mediterranean
1st century AD
H. 17.1. Cat. 212

131. FLASK
Eastern Mediterranean
Second half of 1st century AD
H. 12.9. Cat. 216

132. FLASK
Eastern Mediterranean (Cyprus ?)
Second half of 1st century AD
H. 18.4. Cat. 215

→
133. FLASK
Syria
First half of 2nd century AD
H. 19. Cat. 219

→
134. FLASK
Eastern Mediterranean
Second half of 4th century AD
H. 16.2. Cat. 226

137. FLASK
*Eastern Mediterranean (Syria ?)
2nd – 4th centuries AD*
H. 14.5. Cat. 227

→

138. UNGUENTARIUM
*Eastern Mediterranean
Late 1st century AD*
H. 21.3. Cat. 221

→

139. ARYBALLOS
*Eastern Mediterranean
Second half of 1st century –
early 2nd century AD*
H. 11.5. Cat. 228

135. SMALL JUG
*Eastern Mediterranean
1st century AD*
H. 12.7. Cat. 246

136. AMPHORA
*Eastern Mediterranean
Second half of 1st century AD*
H. 12.7. Cat. 229

140. JUG
Eastern Mediterranean
Second half of 2nd century AD
H. 26. Cat. 241

141. JUG
Eastern Mediterranean
Second half of 1st century —
first half of 2nd century AD
H. 22. Cat. 233

142. JUG
Eastern Mediterranean
Second half of 1st century AD
H. 14.4. Cat. 232

143. SMALL JUG
Eastern Mediterranean or Bosporan Kingdom
Late 1st century — early 2nd century AD
H. 12.7. Cat. 255

144. BEAKER AND JUG
Eastern Mediterranean
Mid — second half of 1st century AD
H. 9.4; 19.5. Cat. 300, 240

145. SMALL JUGS
Cyprus
Second half of 1st century AD
H. 8.5; 14; 13.5. Cat. 242–244

146. SMALL JUG
Eastern Mediterranean
Second half of 1st century —
early 2nd century AD
H. 12.5. Cat. 248

147. JUG
Eastern Mediterranean. 1st century AD
H. 19. Cat. 250

148. OENOCHOE
Roman Empire. 1st century AD
H. 18.4. Cat. 249

151. JUG
Bosporan Kingdom (?)
Late 1st century —
early 2nd century AD
H. 20.1. Cat. 262

149. JUG
Bosporan Kingdom
Late 1st century —
early 2nd century AD
H. 22.6. Cat. 261

150. OENOCHOE
Eastern Mediterranean
1st century AD
H. 12.2. Cat. 271

152. JUG
Bosporan Kingdom
Late 3rd century — early 4th century AD
H. 18. Cat. 280

153. SMALL JUGS
Eastern Mediterranean
2nd century AD
H. 10.6; 10.3. Cat. 276, 277

154. SMALL JUGS
Bosporan Kingdom. 3rd century AD
H. 12.4; 10.5. Cat. 278, 279

155. SMALL JUG
Eastern Mediterranean. 2nd century AD
H. 14.2. Cat. 275

156. SKYPHOS
Italy or Syria. 1st century AD
H. 5. Cat. 282

157. BOWL
Eastern Mediterranean or Italy
1st century AD
H. 4.8. Cat. 284

160. BEAKER
Eastern Mediterranean
2nd – 3rd centuries AD (?)
H. 8.4. Cat. 325

158. BOWL
Eastern Mediterranean. 1st century AD
H. 6.5. Cat. 285

159. BOWL
Eastern Mediterranean. 1st century AD
H. 6.4. Cat. 286

161. BEAKER (PYXIS ?)
Eastern Mediterranean (Cyprus ?)
First half of 1st century AD
H. 7.3. Cat. 292

162. BEAKER (PYXIS ?)
Eastern Mediterranean
(Cyprus ?)
First half of 1st century AD
H. 6. Cat. 291

163. BOWL
Eastern Mediterranean
Late 1st century –
early 2nd century AD
H. 5.6. Cat. 290

→
164. BEAKER
Eastern Mediterranean
Mid – third quarter
of 1st century AD
H. 13.1. Cat. 297

→
165. KANTHAROS
Gaul or Rhineland
2nd century AD
H. 10. Cat. 331

166. JARS
Eastern Mediterranean. 1st century AD
H. 5.8; 5.2; 6.5. Cat. 312–314

167. JAR
Eastern Mediterranean. 1st century AD
H. 6. Cat. 315

168. BEAKER
Northern Italy (?). 1st century AD
H. 7.5. Cat. 302

169. BEAKER
Syro-Palestinian region
Second — third quarter of 1st century AD
H. 11.7. Cat. 295

170. BEAKERS
Cyprus, Eastern Mediterranean
Second half of 1st century AD
H. 6.5; 8.8; 8.1. Cat. 305–307

→
171. AMPHORA AND BEAKER
Syria or Northern Italy,
Eastern Mediterranean (Cyprus ?)
Mid – third quarter of 1st century AD
H. 20.6; 14.8. Cat. 337, 310
→
172. AMPHORA
Syria or Northen Italy
Mid – second half of 1st century AD
H. 25. Cat. 336

173. JUG, BOWL AND BEAKER
Eastern Mediterranean,
Syro-Palestinian region
Mid — third quarter of 1st century AD
H. 14.2; 6.4; 11.4. Cat. 230, 287, 296

174. INK-WELLS OR PYXIDES
Eastern Mediterranean
1st century AD
H. 3.5; 5.8. Cat. 382, 383

175. AMPHORISKOS AND SMALL JUGS
Eastern Mediterranean. 1st century AD
H. 7.5; 9.3; 7.5. Cat. 343—345

176. AMPHORISKOE
Eastern Mediterranean. 1st century AD
H. 6.9; 7. Cat. 341, 342

177. AMPHORISKOS
Eastern Mediterranean or Northern Italy
Second — third quarter of 1st century AD
H. 12.4. Cat. 338

178. UNGUENTARIA
Egypt
Mid – third quarter of 1st century AD
H. 11.5; 14.7. Cat. 361, 362

179. SMALL FLASKS
Eastern Mediterranean
First half of 1st century AD
H. 5.9; 5.7; 5.5. Cat. 352, 351, 350

180. GUTTUS
Eastern Mediterranean (?)
Second half of 1st century AD
H. 10. Cat. 378

181. GUTTUS
Eastern Mediterranean (?)
Second half of 1st century AD
H. 12.1. Cat. 377

182. ASKOS
Eastern Mediterranean
1st century AD
H. 20.8. Cat. 376

→
183, 184. BOWL
Rhineland (Cologne ?)
3rd century —
early 4th century AD
H. 7.7. Cat. 333

187. URN
Rhineland or Gaul
1st – 3rd centuries AD
H. 26.1. Cat. 387

185. GUTTUS
Eastern Mediterranean
1st century AD
H. 7.7. Cat. 381

186. URN WITH LID
Rhineland or Gaul
1st – 2nd centuries AD
H. 20.2. Cat. 386

188. JUG
Syria
Late 3rd century —
early 4th century AD
H. 25.2. Cat. 396

189. JUG
Syria (?)
Second half of 3rd century —
early 4th century AD
H. 21.3. Cat. 390

→
190. AMPHORA
Rhineland (Cologne ?)
4th century AD
H. 33.5. Cat. 400

→
191. JUG
Syria. Mid — 5th century AD
H. 27.8. Cat. 399

192. FLASK
Syria
3rd – 4th centuries AD
H. 23.4. Cat. 403

193. JUG
Syria
4th century AD
H. 34.3. Cat. 398

←
194. JUG
Eastern Mediterranean. 3rd – 4th centuries AD
H. 19.8. Cat. 392

←
195. OENOCHOE
*Eastern Mediterranean
(Syro-Palestinian region ?)
3rd century – first half of 4th century AD*
H. 16.6. Cat. 388

196. JUG
*Eastern Mediterranean (Syria ?)
Second half of 3rd century AD*
H. 19.3. Cat. 391

198. JUG
Syria
Late 3rd century – early 4th century AD
H. 30.3. Cat. 394

199. DOUBLE TUBE
Syria. 4th century AD
H. 11.1. Cat. 413

201. FLASKS
Syria. 4th century AD
H. 11; 13. Cat. 410, 409

→
202. AMPHORA
Syria. 4th century AD
H. 22.1. Cat. 401

→
203. FLASKS
Syria
3rd – 4th centuries AD
H. 19; 21.5. Cat. 404, 405

200. JUG (WITH TWO SECTIONS)
Eastern Mediterranean (Syria ?)
3rd – 4th centuries AD
H. 20.3. Cat. 397

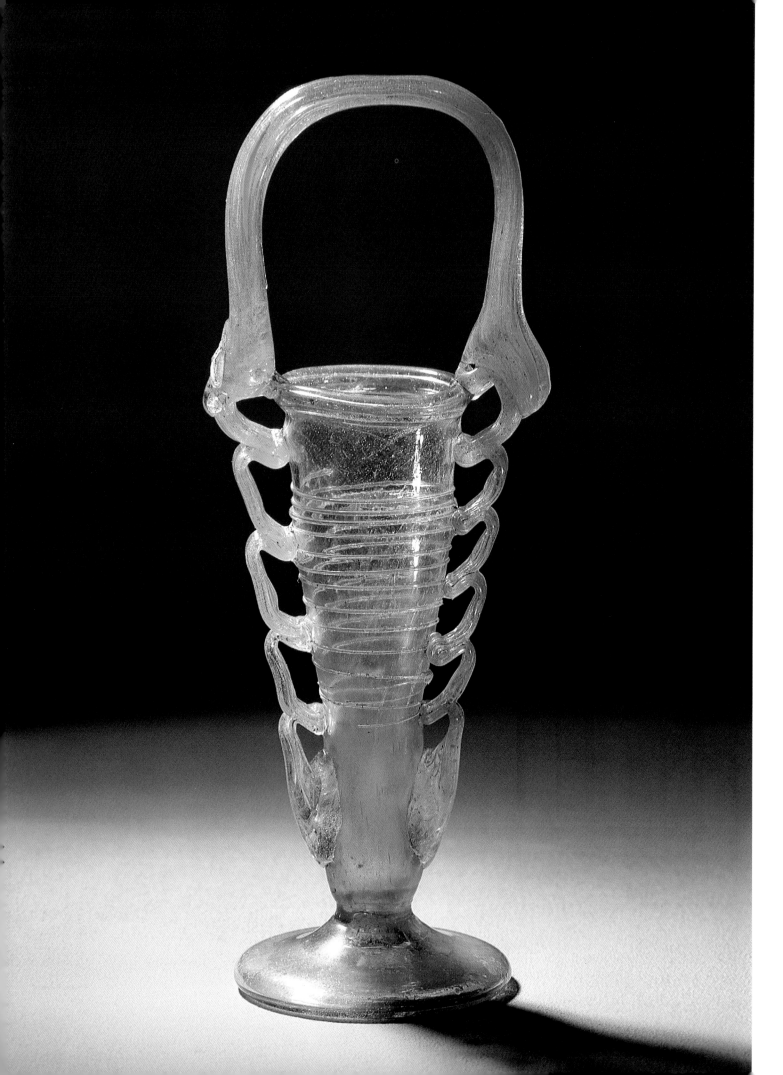

←
204. VASE-UNGUENTARIUM
Syria. 4th – 5th centuries AD
H. 12.9. Cat. 414

←
205. FLASKS
Syria. 4th century AD
H. 11.6; 12.7. Cat. 411, 412

206. JAR
Syria. 4th century AD
H. 10.2. Cat. 407

207. JAR
Syria. 4th century AD
H. 10. Cat. 408

208. JAR
Syria
4th century AD
H. 8.6. Cat. 406

209. SMALL JUG
Eastern Mediterranean
4th – 5th centuries AD
H. 12.4. Cat. 417

210. JAR
Eastern Mediterranean (Syria ?)
Late 4th century —
early 5th century AD
H. 13.3. Cat. 415

211. JAR
Eastern Mediterranean (Syria ?)
Late 4th century —
early 5th century AD
H. 12.5. Cat. 416

214. BEAKER
Syria. 4th century AD
H. 11.1. Cat. 418

212, 213. SMALL PLATE
Eastern Mediterranean or Egypt
3rd – 4th centuries AD
D. 11.6. Cat. 428

215. LAMPADA
Egypt or Syria
4th century AD
H. 20.3. Cat. 425

216. LAMPADA
Egypt or Syria. 4th century AD
H. 13.9. Cat. 424

217. BEAKERS
Eastern Mediterranean,
Black Sea coast (?)
4th century — early 5th century AD
H. 7.1; 10. Cat. 422, 423

218. Dish
Egypt or Syria. 4th century AD
D. 24,2. Cat. 431

219. Bottom of Vessel
with Family Portrait
Rome. 4th century AD
D. 8.1. Cat. 434

catalogue

EXPLANATORY GUIDE TO CATALOGUE
LIST OF ABBREVIATIONS

H — Height
D — Diameter
G — Greatest
L — Length
W — Width
All dimensions are in centimetres

* — Unique exponent
□ — Illustrated in colour in album

A C
Imperial Archaeological
Commission

MAE
Peter the Great Museum of
Anthropology and Ethnography
of the Academy of Sciences

RAIC
Russian Archaeological Institute
in Constantinople

RAS
Russian Archaeological Society

SAM
State Anthropoligical Museum

SAHMC
State Academy of the History of
Material Culture

SH
State Hermitage

SHM
State Historical Museum

AA
Archäologischer Anzeiger

ABC
S.Reinach. Antiquités du Bosphore
Cimmerien (1854)Paris,1892

Abdul-Hak
S.Abdul-Hak. Contribution d'une
découverte archéologique récente
á L'etude de la Verreric syrienne à
L'époque romaine
// JGS, 1965, vol. VII, p. 26—34

AM
Mitteilungen des Deutschen
Archäologischen Instituts.
Athenische Abteilung

Antik Kunst
Antik kunsti dansk privateje.
Udstillingi Ny Carlsberg Glyptotek

16 maj — 31 august 1974.
Kobenhavn, 1974

Auth
S.H.Auth. Ancient Glass at the
Newark Museum from the
Eugene Schaefer Collection of
Antiquities. Newark, New Jersey,
1976

Basserman-Jordan
E.Basserman-Jordan. Die antiken
Gläser des Herrn Oskar Zettler
zu München. München, 1918

Benko
A.Benko. Üvegcorpus. Règeszeti
Füzetek. Ser. II-11 szam. Magyar
Nemzeti muzeum-Torteneti
muzeum. Budapest, 1962

Berger
L.Berger. Römische Gläser aus
Vindonissa. Basel, 1960

Bosporan Kingdom
N.Z.Kunina. Bosporan Kingdom
// The State Hermitage. Master
pieces from Museum's Collections.
London, 1994, p. 292—331,
cat. no. 286—291, 318

Bucovala 1968
M.Bucovala. Vase antice de sticla
la Tomis. Bucuresti, 1968

Bucovala 1984
M.Bucovala. Roman Glass Vessels
Discovered in Dobrudja // JGS,
1984, vol. 26, p. 59—63

Čadik
J.Čadik. Graeco-Roman and
Egyptian Glass. A Guide to the
Exhibition at the National Museum
in Prague. Prague, 1970

Calvi 1965
M.C.Calvi. La coppa vitrea di
Aristeas nella collezione Strada
// JGS, 1965, vol. VII, p. 9—16

Calvi 1968
M.C.Calvi. I vetri romani del
Museo di Aquileia. Aquileia, 1968

Cat. Damas
Abū-l-Faraj Al-Ush, A.Joundi,

B.Zouhdi. Catalogue du Musée
National de Damas. Damas, 1969

Clara Rhodos
Clara Rhodos. Studi e materiali
publicati a cura dell Istituto
storico-archeologico di Rodi.
Rodi

CR
Compte-rendu de la Comission
Impériale Archéologique.
St. Petersbourg

Doppelfeld
O.Doppelfeld. Römisches und
Fränkisches Glas in Köln. Köln,
1966

Dusenbery 1967
E.B.Dusenbery. Ancient Glass from
the Cemeteries of Samothrace
// JGS, 1967, vol. IX, p. 34—49

Dusenbery 1971
E.B.Dusenbery. Ancient Glass in
the Collections of Wheaton
College // JGS, 1971, vol. XIII,
p. 9—33

Edgar
C.C.Edgar. Catalogue général des
antiquités égyptiennes du Musée
du Caire. Graeco-Egyptian Glass.
Le Caire, 1905

Filarska
B.Filarska. Szkla starozythe.
Muzeum Narodowe w Warszawie,
Katalog. Warszawa, 1952

Fitzwilliam Mus.
Glass at the Fitzwilliam Museum.
Cambridge, 1978
(London, New York, Melburne)

Fogolari e Scarfi
G.Fogolari, B.M. Scarfi. Abria
antica. Venezia; Milano, 1970

Fortuna 1965
M.T. Fortuna. I vetri soffiati della
necropoli di Akko // JGS, 1965,
vol. VII, p. 17—25

Fortuna 1969
M.T.Fortuna Canivet. I vetri romani

di Cornus conservati al Museo
di Cornus Gagliari
// JGS, 1969, vol. XI, p. 19—26

Fossing
P.Fossing. Glass Vessels before
Glass-Blowing. Copenhagen, 1940

Fremersdorf 1938
Fr.Fremersdorf. Römische Gläser
mit buntgefleckter Oberfläche
// Festschrift für August Oxé.
Darmstadt, 1938, S. 116—121

Fremersdorf III
Fr.Fremersdorf. Die Denkmäler des
römischen Köln. Bd. III. Römisches
Buntglas in Köln. Köln, 1958

Fremersdorf IV
Fr.Fremersdorf. Die Denkmäler
des römischen Köln. Bd. IV.
Das naturfarbene sogenannte
blaugrüne Glas in Köln. Köln, 1958

Fremersdorf VII
Fr.Fremersdorf. Die Denkmäler des
römischen Köln. Bd. VII.
Die römischen Gläser mit
aufgelegten Nuppen. Köln, 1962

Fremersdorf VIII
Fr.Fremersdorf. Die Denkmäler des
römischen Köln. Bd. VIII.
Die römischen Gläser mit Schliff,
Bemalung und Goldauflagen
aus Köln. Köln, 1967

Fremersdorf IX
Fr.Fremersdorf. Die Denkmäler des
römischen Köln. Bd. IX.
Die farblosen Gläser der Frühzeit
in Köln 2. und 3. Jahrhundert.
Bonn, 1984

Froehner 1879
W.Froehner. La verrerie antique.
Description de la collection
J.Charvet. Le Pecq, 1879

Froehner 1903
W.Froehner. Collection Julien
Greau. Verrerie antique. Paris,
1903

Glass
N.Z. Kunina. Glass // The State
Hermitage. Masterpieces from

Museum's Collections. London,
1994, p. 250—259,
cat. no. 225—241

Glass of the Caesars
D.B.Harden, H.Hellenvemper,
K.Painter, D.Whitehouse. Glass of
the Caesars. Exhibition Catalogue.
Milan 1987

Grose 1982
D.F.Grose. The Hellenistic and
Early Roman Glass from
Morgantina (Serra Orlando),
Sicily // JGS, 1982, vol. 24,
p. 20—29

Grose 1984
D.F.Grose. Glass Forming Methods
in Classical Antiquity: Some
Considerations // JGS, 1984,
vol. 26, p. 25—34

Grose 1989
D.F.Grose. The Toledo Museum of
Art. Early Ancient Glass. Core-
formed, Rod-formed and Cast
Vessels and Objects from the Late
Bronze Age to the Early Roman
Empire, 1600 B.C. to A.D.50.
New York, 1989

Haevernick 1970
T.E.Haevernick. Die Verbreitung
der "zarten Rippenschalen"
// JRGZM, 14. Jahrgang, 1967,
1970, S. 153—166

Haevernick 1977
T.E.Haevernick. Gesichtsperlen.
Madrider Mitteilungen,18. 1977,
S. 152—231, Taf. 37—44

Haevernick 1978
T.E.Haevernick. Modioli
// Glastechnische Berichte, 51.
Jahrgang 1978, Nr. 12,
S. 328—330

Harden 1935
D.B.Harden. Romano-Syrian
Glasses with Mould-blown
Inscriptions // JGS,1935,vol. 25,
p. 163—183, pl. XXIII—XXVIII

Harden 1936
D.B.Harden. Roman Glass from
Karanis. Ann Arbor, 1936

Harden 1940
D.B. Harden. Roman Mould-blown Glasses // The Connoisseur, 1940, September, vol. 106, no. 469, p. 102—105

Harden 1944—1945
D.B.Harden. Two Tombgroups of the First Century A.D. from Yahmour, Syria, and a Supplement to the List of Romano-Syrian Glasses with Mould-blown Inscriptions // Syria,1944—1945, vol. XXIV, p. 81—95

Harden 1968
D.B.Harden. The Canosa Group of Hellenistic Glasses in the British Museum // JGS, 1968, vol. X, p. 21—47

Hayes
J.W.Hayes. Roman and Pre-Roman Glass in the Royal Ontario Museum. A Catalogue. Toronto, 1975

Hayward
J.Hayward. Roman Mould-blown Glass at Yale University //JGS, 1962, vol. IV, p. 49—60

Isings
C.Isings. Roman Glass from Dated Finds. Groningen; Djakarta, 1957

Israeli
Y.Israeli. Sidonian Mould-blown Glass Vessels in the Museum Haaretz // JGS, 1964, vol. VI, p. 34—41

JDI
Jahrbuch des Deutschen Archäologischen Instituts, Berlin

JGS
Journal of Glass Studies, Corning, New York

JRGZM
Jahrbuch des Römisch-Germanischen Zentral Museums Mainz. Mainz

JRS
Journal of Roman Studies. London

Kern 1954
J.H.C.Kern. A Pair of Mould-blown Glass Amphorisks, Ist Century A.D. // Oudheidkundige Mededelingen uit het Rijksmuseum van Oudheden te Leiden, Nieuwe reeks, 1954, XXXV, p. 38, 39

Kern 1956
J.H.C.Kern. Zwei buntgefleckte Glaskelche des I. Jhts n.Chr. in Leiden // Archeologia Classica, 1956, vol. VIII, fasc. I, p. 56—63, tav. XXII, 1—3

Kern 1963
J.H.C.Kern. Römische Modioli des I.Jahrhunderte n.Chr. // Mnemosyne, S: IV, vol. XVI⁴, Leiden, 1963, p. 400—405

Kisa I
A.Kisa. Das Glas im Altertume. Erster Teil. Leipzig,1908

Kisa II
A.Kisa. Das Glas im Altertume. Zweiter Teil. Leipzig,1908

Kisa III
A.Kisa. Das Glas im Altertume. Dritter Teil. Leipzig,1908

La Baume
P. La Baume. Glas der antiken Welt. Bd. 1. Römisch-Germanisches Museums Köln. Köln, 1973

Liepmann
U.Liepmann. Glas der Antike. Kestner-Museum Hannover. Hannover, 1982

Marconi
P.Marconi. Vetri romani nel museo di Zara // Bolletino d'Arte, 1932, vol. XXVI,Serie III, p. 33—41

Masterpieces
D.B.Harden, K.S.Painter, R.H.Pinder-Wilson, Hugh Tait. Masterpieces of Glass. London, 1968

Matheson
S.B.Matheson. Ancient Glass in the Yale University Art Gallery. Yale, 1980

Morin-Jean
Morin-Jean. La verrerie en Gaule sous l'Empire. Romain. Paris, 1913

Myres
J.L.Myres. The Metropolitan Museum of Art. Handbook of the Cesnola Collection of Antiquities from Cyprus. New York, 1914

Neuburg
F. Neuburg. Ancient Glass. London, 1962

Nolte und Haevernick
B. Nolte, T.E. Haevernick. Ägyptische und griechische frühe Glasgefässe // Wissenschaftliche Zeitschriftder Universität Rostock, 16. Jahrgang 1967. Gesellschafts und sprachwissenschaftliche Reihe. Rostock, 1967, Heft 7/8, S. 491—493, 611, Taf. 58—65

Oliver 1967
A.Oliver, Jr. Late Hellenistic Glass in the Metropolitan Museum // JGS, 1967, vol. IX, p. 13—33

Oliver 1969
A.Oliver, Jr. A Gold-Glass Fragment in the Metropolitan Museum of Art. // JGS, 1969, vol. XI, p. 9—16

Oliver 1970
A.Oliver, Jr. Persian Export Glass // JGS, 1970, vol. XII, p. 9—16

Petru 1969
S.Petru. Antično steklo iz Dolenjskih grobov. Antike Gläser aus Dolenjsko (Unterkrain) // Razprave, VI, Ljubljana, 1969, S. 163—177

Petru 1972
S.Petru. Emonske nekropole. Ljubljana, 1972

Pfeffer und Haevernick
W. von Pfeffer und T.E. Haevernick. "Zarte Rippenschalen" // Saalburg Jahrbuch, 1958, XVII, S. 76—88

RM
Mitteilungen des Deutschen Archäologischen Instituts, Römische Abteilung

Saldern 1959
A. von Saldern. Glass Finds at Gordion // JGS, 1959, vol. I, p. 23—50

Saldern 1964
A. von Saldern. Ancient Glass in Split // JGS, 1964, vol. VI, p. 42—46

Saldern 1966
A. von Saldern. Ancient Glass // Boston Museum Bulletin, 1966, vol. LXIV, no. 335, p. 4—17

Saldern 1975
A. von Saldern. Two Achaemenid Glass Bowls and a Hoard of Hellenic Glass Vessels // JGS, 1975, vol. XVII, p. 38—46

Sammlung Cohn
A. von Saldern. Glas von der Antike bis zum Jugendstil. Sammlung Cohn. Los Angeles, Cal; Mainz am Rhein, 1980

Sammlung Hentrich
A. von Saldern. Glassammlung Hentrich. Antike und Islam. Kataloge des Kunstmuseums Düsseldorf. Düsseldorf, 1974

Sammlung von Kirchner-Schwarz
Sammlung von antiken Gläsern, Terrakotten, Marmorskulpturen und Bronzen aus dem Besitze von Fr.D. Kirchner-Schwarz, Beirut. Auktion in München in der Galerie Helbing am 22 und 23. Juni 1914. München, 1914

Sammlung Löffler
Peter La Baume, Jan Willem Salomonson. Römische Kleinkunst. Sammlung Karl Löffler. Wissenschaftliche Kataloge des Römisch-Germanischen Museums Köln. Bd. 3. Köln. (sans date)

Sammlung Niessen
Beschreibung römischer Altertümer, gesammelt von Carl Anton Niessen. Bd. 1, 2. Köln, 1911

Sammlung Oppenländer
Axel von Saldern, Birgit Nolte, Peter La Baume, Thea Elisabeth Haevernick. Gläser der Antike. Sammlung Erwin Oppenländer. Hamburg, 1974

Sammlung Wolf
E.M.Stern, B. Schlick-Nolte. Frühes Glas der alten Welt 1600 v.Chr. — 50 n.Chr. Sammlung Ernesto Wolf. Stuttgart, 1994

Seefried
M.Seefried. Glass Core Pendants found in the Mediterranean Area // JGS, 1979, vol. 21, p. 17—26

Silvestrini
D.Silvestrini. La coppa vitrea greco-alessandrina di Locarno // Bolletino d'Arte, 1937, vol. XXXI, Serie III, p. 430—443

Simonett
Ch.Simonett. Tessiner Gräberfelder. Basel, 1941

Smith Collection
Glass from the Ancient World. The Ray Winfield Smith Collection. The Corning Museum of Glass. Corning, New York, 1957

Sokolow
Gleb Sokolow. Antike Schwarzmeerküste. Denkmäler der Architektur, Bildhauerei, Malerei und angewandte Kunst. Leipzig, 1976

Spartz
E.Spartz. Antike Gläser. Vollständiger Katalog. Staatliche Kunstsammlungen Kassel. Kassel, 1967

Toll
N.P.Toll. Excavations at Dura-Europos. Ninth Season 1935—1936, Part II (Necropolis). New-Haven, 1946

Vanderhoeven
M.Vanderhoeven. Verres Romains (Ier — IIIme siècle) des Musées Curtius et du Verre à Liège. Liège, 1961

Vessberg 1952
O. Vessberg. Roman Glass in Cyprus. Opuscula Archaeologica. Lund, 1952. VII, p. 109—165, pl. I—XXIV

Vessberg 1963
O.Vessberg. Notes on the Chronology of the Roman Glass in Cyprus // Studies Presented to David Moore Robinson. SaintLouis,Missouri,1963

Vetri romani
Vetri romani del cantone Ticino. Locarno, 1988

Voščinina
A.I.Voščinina. Frühantike Glasgefässe in der Ermitage (Gruppe der Salbgefässe in der Sandkern-Technik)
// Wissenschaftliche Zeitschrift der Universität Rostock, 16. Jahrgang 1967. Gesellschafts und sprachwissenschaftliche Reihe. Rostock, 1967, Heft 7/8, S. 555—560

Weinberg 1959
G.D.Weinberg. Glass Manufacture in Ancient Crete // JGS, 1959, vol. I, p. 11—22

Weinberg 1963
G.D.Weinberg. A Parallel to the Highdown Hill Glass // JGS, 1963, vol. V, p. 25—28

Weinberg 1970
G.D.Weinberg. Hellenistic Glass from Tel Anafa in Upper Galilee // JGS, 1970, vol. XII, p. 17—27

Weinberg 1973
G.D.Weinberg. Notes on Glass from Upper Galilee // JGS, 1973, vol. XV, p. 35—51

Zouhdi
B.Zouhdi. Les verres conservés au departement des antiquités syriennes des époques grecque, romaine et byzantine du Musée National de Damas // Bulletin des Journées Internationales du Verre, 1964, vol. 3, p. 41—54

АДЖ
М.Ростовцев. Античная декоративная живопись на юге России. Атлас. СПб., 1913; текст, СПб., 1914

Алексеева 1971
Е.М.Алексеева. Миниатюрная мозаика в стеклянных украшениях I в. до н. э. — II в. н. э. // СА. 1971, № 4, с. 178—185

Алексеева 1982 (1)
Е.М. Алексеева. Античные бусы Северного Причерноморья // САИ, М., 1982, вып. Г 1—12, 1982

Алексеева 1982 (2)
Е.М.Алексеева. Юго-восточная часть некрополя Горгиппии // Горгиппия II. Материалы Анапской археологической экспедиции. Краснодар, 1982, с. 5—116

АСГЭ
Археологический сборник Государственного Эрмитажа

Бларамберг
М.Бларамберг. Археологические розыскания в Керчи. ЗООИД, Т. II, отделения 2-е и 3-е, 1850, с. 815—820

Богданова
Н.А. Богданова. Могильник первых веков нашей эры у с. Заветное // Труды ГИМ. Археологические исследования

на юге Восточной Европы. 1989, вып. 70, с. 17—70

ВДИ
Вестник древней истории

ГМИНВ
State Museum of the Art of the Peoples of the Orient, Moscow

Гущина, Засецкая
И.И. Гущина, И.П. Засецкая. Погребения зубовско-воздвиженского типа из раскопок Н.И. Веселовского в Прикубанье // Труды ГИМ. Археологические иследования на юге Восточной Европы. 1989, вып. 70, с. 71—141

ДБК
Древности Босфора Киммерийского. СПб., 1854

Засецкая 1993
И.П. Засецкая. Материалы боспорского некрополя второй половины IV — первой половины V в. // Материалы по археологии, истории и этнографии Таврии. Вып. III. Симферополь, 1993, с. 23—105, табл. 1—64

ЗООИД
Записки Одесского Общества истории и древностей. Одесса

ИАК
Известия Императорской Археологической Комиссии. СПб. (1899—1913); Пг. (1914—1916)

Извлечение
Извлечение из всеподданейшего отчета об археологических разысканиях в 1853 году. СПб., 1855

Искусство Византии
Искусство Византии в собраниях СССР. Каталог выставки. Т. 1. М., 1977

Качалов
Н. Качалов. Стекло. М., 1959, с. 40—96

Кобылина
М.М. Кобылина. Раскопки некрополя Тиритаки в 1934 году // МИА. Археологические памятники Боспора и Херсонеса. 1941, № 4, с. 75—84

Кропоткин
В.В. Кропоткин. Римские импортные изделия в Восточной Европе (II в. до н. э. — V в н. э.) // САИ. Вып. Д 1—27. М., 1970

КСИА
Краткие сообщения Института археологии Академии наук СССР. М

Кунина 1964
Н. Кунина. Две стеклянные патеры из некрополя Пантикапея // СГЭ, 1964, вып. XXV, с. 37—39

Кунина 1968
Н.З. Кунина. Стеклянные стаканы с греческими надписями в собрании Эрмитажа // Античная история и культура Средиземноморья и Причерноморья. Л., 1968, с. 220—226

Кунина 1970
Н.З. Кунина. Группа полихромных стеклянных сосудов из некрополя Пантикапея // СА, 1970, № 3, с. 224—228

Кунина 1973
Н.З. Кунина. Сирийские выдутые в форме стеклянные сосуды из некрополя Пантикапея // Памятники античного прикладного искусства. Л., 1973, с. 101—150

Кунина 1974
Н. Кунина. Новые поступления стеклянных сосудов в Отдел античного мира // СГЭ, 1974, вып. XXXVIII, с. 83—84

Кунина 1975
Н. Кунина. Новое поступление античного стекла из коллекции Гаршиных // СГЭ, 1975, вып. XL, с. 102—104

Кунина 1981
Н.З. Кунина. Стеклянный сосуд гальского мастера из Ольвии // СГЭ, 1981, вып. XLVI, с. 44, 45

Кунина 1982
Н.З. Кунина. Два стеклянных кувшина из некрополя Нимфея // Художественные изделия античных мастеров. Л., 1982, с. 119—124

Кунина 1984
Н.З. Кунина. К вопросу о западном импорте стекла на Боспор (по материалам некрополя Пантикапея из собрания Отдела античного мира Эрмитажа) // ТГЭ, 1984, т. XXIV, с. 147—164

Кунина 1987
Н.З. Кунина. Античная стеклянная пиксида с расписной крышкой из собрания Эрмитажа // СГЭ, 1987, вып. LII, с. 36—38

Кунина 1995
Н.З. Кунина. Раннехристианская стеклянная чаша из Нимфея // СГЭ, 1995, вып. LVI, с. 46—48

Кунина 1997
Н.З. Кунина. О боспорском стеклоделии в I—III вв. н. э.

// Сборник научных трудов. Нижний Новгород. 1997, с. 39—82

Кунина, Сорокина
Н.З. Кунина, Н.П. Сорокина. Стеклянные бальзамарии Боспора // ТГЭ, 1972, т. XIII, с. 146—177

Максимова
М.И. Максимова. Античные резные камни Эрмитажа. Путеводитель по выставке. Л., 1926

МДАПВ
Матеріалі і дослідження з археології Прикарпаття і Волині

МИА
Материалы и исследования по археологии СССР

Неверов 1971
О.Я.Неверов. Античные камеи в собрании Государственного Эрмитажа. Ленинград. 1971

Неверов 1988
О.Я.Неверов. Античные камеи в собрании Эрмитажа. Каталог. Ленинград. 1988

Неверов 1994
О.Я.Неверов. Античные камеи. СПб., 1994

ОАК
Отчеты Императорской Археологической Комиссии. СПб

СА
Советская археология

Сагинашвили 1970
М.Н. Сагинашвили. Стеклянные сосуды Урбнисского могильника. Каталог. Тбилиси, 1970 (на рус. и груз. яз.)

Сагинашвили 1977
М.Н. Сагинашвили. Стеклянные сосуды из Тбилиси // КСИА. Античные памятники Колхиды и Иберии. 1977, вып. 151, с. 126—130

САИ
Свод археологических источников

СГЭ
Сообщения Государственного Эрмитажа

Скалон 1973
К. Скалон. О некоторых формах стеклянной посуды позднеантичного и раннесредневекового Боспора // СГЭ, 1973, вып. XXXVII, с. 50—52

Скалон 1974
К. Скалон. Стеклянные сосуды из боспорского некрополя

// СГЭ, 1974, вып. XXXVIII, с. 44—48

Смирнов
К.Ф. Смирнов. Северский курган. М., 1973

Соколов
Г. Соколов. Античное Причерноморье. Памятники архитектуры, живописи, скульптуры и прикладного искусства. Л., 1972

Сорокина 1957
Н.П. Сорокина. Тузлинский некрополь. М., 1957

Сорокина 1962
Н.П. Сорокина. Стекло из раскопок Пантикапея 1949—1959 гг. // МИА. Пантикапей, № 103, 1962, с. 210—236

Сорокина 1963
Н.П. Сорокина. Позднеантичное и раннесредневековое стекло с Таманского городища // Керамика и стекло древней Тмутаракани. М., 1963, с. 134—170

Сорокина 1965 (1)
Н.П. Сорокина. Сирийский стеклянный сосуд из собрания Одесского государственного археологического музея // Краткие сообщения о полевых археологических исследованиях Одесского Государственного археологического музея за 1963 г. Одесса, 1965, с. 185—189

Сорокина 1965 (2)
Н.П. Сорокина. Стеклянные сосуды из Танаиса // МИА. Древности Нижнего Дона. 1965, № 127, с. 202—248

Сорокина 1968
Н.П. Сорокина. Фигурный стеклянный сосуд из Кеп // СА, 1968, № 4, с. 181—189

Сорокина 1969
Н.П. Сорокина. К вопросу об экономических связях государств Северного Причерноморья в I в. н. э. // МИА. Древности Восточной Европы. 1969, с. 217—221

Сорокина 1971
Н.П. Сорокина. О стеклянных сосудах с каплями синего стекла из Причерноморья // СА, 1971, № 4, с. 85—100

Сорокина 1973
Н.П. Сорокина. Стеклянные сосуды из могильника Харакс // Кавказ и Восточная Европа

в древности. М., 1973, с. 183—189

Сорокина 1977
Н.П. Сорокина. Античные стеклянные сосуды из раскопок некрополя боспорского города Кепы на Таманском полуострове // Античный мир и археология. Саратов, 1977, вып. 3, с. 115—144

Сорокина 1978
Н.П. Сорокина. Античное стекло в собрании Одесского археологического музея // Археологические исследования Северо-западного Причерноморья. Киев, 1978, с. 267—274

Сорокина 1979
Н.П. Сорокина. Стеклянные сосуды IV—V вв. и хронология Цебельдинских могильников // КСИА, 1979, вып. 158, с. 57—67

Сорокина 1990
Н.П. Сорокина. Стеклянные капельники или гуттусы первых веков нашей эры из Северного Причерноморья // Труды ГИМ. Проблемы археологии Евразии. 1990, вып. 74, с. 71—78

Спасский
Г. Спасский. Боспор Киммерийский с его древностями и достопримечательностями. М., 1846

СПб
St Petersburg

Стекло древней Армении
Б.Н. Аракелян, Г.А. Тирацян, Ж.Д. Хачатрян. Стекло древней Армении (I—IV вв.) // Археологические памятники Армении. 3. Памятники древней эпохи. Ереван, 1969, Вып. I

ТГЭ
Труды Государственного Эрмитажа

Художественное ремесло
Государственный Эрмитаж. Художественное ремесло эпохи Римской империи (I в. до н. э. — IV в.). Каталог выставки. Л., 1980

Художественное стекло
Художественное стекло. Альбом по материалам выставки в Государственном Эрмитаже. Л., 1967

Шелковников
Б.А. Шелковников. Художественное стекло. Л., 1962

PART 1.
CORE-FORMED GLASS
Late 15th century BC — 1st century AD

1.

KRATERISKOS

Egypt. Late 15th century — first half of 14th century BC

H 9.2; D rim 4.1; base of leg 3.5; duct of leg 0.5
Received from S.Golitsyn collection
E 3719   ill.1

Fluted semi-spherical body; with shoulders, very wide, almost cylindrical neck, flanged rim; on high conic foot. Small, rounded handles. Dull dark-blue glass; arms of semi-clear blue glass. Yellow outlining along rim; continuous scallops ornamental design of white, turquoise (in centre) and yellow (bottom) threads on neck and in shape of white garlands between yellow undulating girdles along middle of body; yellow outlining of foot. Trace of core inside body, traces of polishing by buffing on foot.

Condition: Stuck together again from pieces; small losses along edge of foot.

Literature: Шелковников, ил. 1; Качалов, с. 58, ил. 13

Analogies: Fossing, p. 14, fig. 4; Nolte und Haevernick, Taf. 59, *1, 2*; Neuburg, Pl. I, c; Smith Collection, no. 5; Sammlung Oppenländer, Nr. 1; C.A.Keller. Problems in Dating Glass Industries of the Egyptian New Kingdom: Examples from Malkata and List // JGS, 1983, vol. 25, p. 22, fig. 4; compare: Nolte und Haevernick, Taf. 61, *2*; Recent Important Acquisitions // JGS, 1962, vol. IV, p. 139, no. 2; Auth, no. 1; Kisa I, S. 23, Abb. 11; Grose, p. 60, no. 7; Sammlung Wolf, S. 130, no. 5

2.

ALABASTRON

*Eastern Mediterranean
Late 6th century — early 5th century BC*

H 12; D rim 2.3; GD 3.3
Received in 1893 from J.Lemme' collection
E 474   ill.4

Fluted body widening downwards; without neck, with small rim; rounded bottom. Dull dark-blue glass; three-tiered

multi-row zigzag ornamental design of yellow and white threads; outlining along edge of rim and base of body.

Condition: Ears knocked off (one partly); surface iridescent, therefore yellow zigzags are hardly discernable from the white ones.

First ever publication

Analogies: SH, E 3167; Auth, no. 8; compare: Fossing, p. 67, fig. 39

3.

ALABASTRON

Eastern Mediterranean. Late 6th century — first half of 5th century BC

H 14.4; D: rim 3.6; GD 4.3
Received in 1893 from J.Lemme' collection
E 470   ill.11

Body widening downwards; with shoulders; high neck, wide irregular rim; rounded bottom. S-shaped ears. Semi-clear blue-green glass. Similar articles without ornamental design are rarely found.

Condition: Good.

First ever publication

Analogies: SH, E 1468 (form and colour); Fossing, p. 60, fig. 27; Grose, 1989, p. 133, no. 64 (col. ill., p. 95)

4.

ALABASTRON

Eastern Mediterranean. First half of 5th century BC

H 10; D: rim 3.3; GD body 3.2
Received in 1932 from LILI collection; found in 1906 in Pantikapaion necropolis (grave 5)
П.1906.6   ill.8

Body widening downwards; with shoulders, short neck, wide disc-shaped rim; rounded bottom. S-shaped ears. Dull white glass; outlining along edge of rim, ears and girdle beneath them from purple-violet threads.

Condition: Large part of one ear lost.

Literature: ИАК, 1909, вып. 30, с. 3; Voščinina, Taf. 117, *1* (right)

Analogies: Voščinina, Taf. 117, *1* (centre); Fossing, p. 61, fig. 28

5.

ALABASTRON

*Eastern Mediterranean
Early 5th century BC*

H 8.5; D rim 2.5; GD 2.6
Received in 1915; bought from inhabitant of Taman
E 2909   ill.9

Body widening downwards; wide neck, crudely made rim; rounded bottom. S-shaped ears. Semi-clear blue glass; dull white glass on neck; yellow outlining along edge of rim, continuous scallops (arches facing upwards: rarely found) ornamental design of white threads.

Condition: Surface, particularly neck, iridescent.

First ever publication

Analogies: Fossing, p. 65, fig.37; Sammlung Oppenländer, Nr. 183; Recent Important Acquisitions // JGS, 1964, vol. VI, p. 156—157, no. 3; Hayes, no. 4; Grose 1989, p. 142, no. 93 (col. ill, p. 98); Clara Rhodos, vol. III, sep. CXCVII, fig. 210; vol. IV, sep. XXVI, fig. 89; sep. CXIII, fig. 256

6.

ALABASTRON

*Eastern Mediterranean
Early 5th century BC*

H 11.8; D rim 3.7; GD 3.8
Received in 1928 from E.Shuvalova collection (bought in Italy ?)
E 1476   ill.9

Faintly fluted body widening downwards; with shoulders, short neck, wide rim; flat bottom. S-shaped ears. Dull dirty-white glass, semi-clear on rim and handles. Outlining along edge of rim and multi-row scallops ornamental design of dark-violet threads.

Condition: Surface iridescent in places and has lost its shine.

1   □   2   □   3*   □

4   □   5, 6   □   7   8*

9, 10   □   11—13   □   14   □

15   16*   □   17   □   18   □

Literature: Glass, p. 252, no. 227

Analogies: SH, E 120 (Voščinina, Taf. 122, 3);
ПАН.1688

7.
ALABASTRON

Eastern Mediterranean
5th century — early 4th century BC

H 10.5; D rim 3.5; GD body 3.4
Received in 1925 from Stieglitz Museum
collection, previously bought in Kertch from Ya.Buksil
E 1084

Body widening downwards; with shoulders, short neck, wide disc-shaped rim; rounded bottom. S-shaped ears. Dull white glass. Outlining along edge of rim; girdles, multi-row zigzag ornamental design of dark-purple threads.

Condition: Good.

First ever publication

Analogies: SH, E 1092, E 2050, П.1907.23 (Voščinina, Taf. 118, 2); Sammlung Oppenländer, Nr. 158; Fossing, p. 61, fig. 29; Clara Rhodos, vol. IV, sep. XXV, fig 85; sep. XXVI, fig. 89

8.
ALABASTRON

Eastern Mediterranean. Second half of 5th century BC

H 14.5; D rim 4.8; GD body 4.1
Received in 1851 from S.Pizzati collection; bought in Italy
E 123

Almost cylindrical body; with shoulders, high neck, wide disc-shaped rim; rounded bottom. Rounded ears. Dull black glass; spiral ornamental design of double and triple white threads.

Condition: Upper section of vessel glued back on; surface iridescent on one side.

Literature: Voščinina, Taf. 122, 2

Analogies: Compare form: Fossing, p. 68, fig. 42

9.
ALABASTRON

Eastern Mediterranean. 5th century BC

H 9.6; D rim 3; GD body 2.5
Received in 1893 from J.Lemme' collection
E 476   ill.10

Almost cylindrical body; with shoulders, very short neck, wide rim; rounded bottom. S-shaped ears. Semi-clear brown glass. Outlining along edge of rim and three-tiered ornamental design of triple girdles of dirty-white threads.

Condition: Surface iridescent in places.

First ever publication

Analogies: Fossing, p. 64, fig. 33; in shape,

compare: SH П.1905.44 (Voščinina, Taf. 117, 3, left); Grose, p. 137, no. 77 (col. ill., p. 97)

10.
ALABASTRON

Eastern Mediterranean. 5th century BC

H 10.3; D rim 3.1; GD body 2.9
Received in 1931 from SAHMC; previously in A.Bobrinsky collection
E 2058   ill.10

Cylindrical body; with short neck, wide rim; rounded bottom. S-shaped ears. Dull black glass. Outlining along edge of rim, continuous striped ornamental design of white threads.

Condition: One side of body and rim iridescent.

First ever publication

Analogies: Fossing, p. 67, fig. 40 (Southern Russia)

11.
ALABASTRON

Eastern Mediterranean. 5th century BC

H 9.3; D rim 3; GD 2.7
Received in 1931 from SAHMC; previously in A.Bobrinsky collection
E 2060   ill.2

Almost cylindrical body; with shoulders, short neck, wide rim; flat bottom. S-shaped ears; one without orifice. Dull dark-brown glass. Yellow and blue outlining along edge of rim; girdles and continuous multi-row zigzag ornamental design of turquoise-blue and yellow threads. Yellow spiral helix on turquoise background in centre of bottom.

Condition: Good.

First ever publication

Analogies: CH, П.1905.43 (Voščinina, Taf. 117, 3, right); Fossing, p. 67, fig. 41

12.
ALABASTRON

Eastern Mediterranean. 5th century BC

H 10.9; D rim 3.2; GD body 2.8
Received in 1931 from SAHMC; previously in A.Bobrinsky collection
E 2056   ill.2

Almost cylindrical body; with short neck, wide rim; rounded bottom. S-shaped ears. Dull red-brown glass; yellow glass on neck (top). Yellow outlining along edge of rim; girdles and multi-row zigzag ornamental design of yellow, bright-turquoise and light-green threads. Yellow and red-brown helixes with red-brown circle in centre of bottom.

Condition: Good.

Literature: Voščinina, Taf. 118, 1 (5)

Analogies: Numerous similar alabastra have been found in the necropoleis of Olbia, Pantikapaion and other northern Black Sea towns. See: Voščinina, S. 558, 559, Taf. 118; compare also: SH, ПАН.591 (from Kertch); Fossing, p. 67, fig. 41 (from Southern Russia), p. 68, fig. 42 (from Kertch); Sammlung Oppenländer, Nr. 184, 185; compare: Hayes, no. 7, 8; Auth, no. 264; compare with cat. 13

13.
ALABASTRON

Eastern Mediterranean
Late 5th century — early 4th century BC

H 10.9; D rim 2.8; GD body 2.8
Received in 1860; found before 1830 in Pantikapaion necropolis
ПАН.591   ill.2

Almost cylindrical body; with shoulders, short neck, wide rim; flat bottom. S-shaped ears. Dull red-brown glass. Yellow outlining along edge of rim; continuous multi-row zigzag ornamental design of yellow and blue threads.

Condition: Good.

First ever publication

Analogies: See cat. 12

14.
ALABASTRON

Eastern Mediterranean
Last quarter of 4th century BC

H 14,9; D rim 4,4; GD body 3,7
Received in 1905; found in 1902 in Pantikapaion necropolis (grave 83)
П.1902.44   ill.5

Faintly fluted body widening downwards; with shoulders, short neck, very wide disc-shaped rim; flat bottom. Rounded ears. Dull dark-blue glass. Yellow outlining along rim and shoulders; continuous multi-row zigzag ornamental design of yellow threads.

Condition: Good.

Literature: ИАК, 1904, вып. 9, с. 88

Analogies: Compare with cat. 15; Sammlung Wolf, S. 220, Nr. 51; compare ornamental design with Filarska, nr. 1, Tabl. 1, 1

15.
ALABASTRON

Eastern Mediterranean. Last quarter of 4th century BC

H 20.1; D rim 5.5; GD body 5
Received in 1891, bought in Kertch
E 314

Faintly fluted body widening downwards; with high neck, wide disc-shaped rim; flat bottom. Small ears, without orifices, set low down. Dull dark-blue glass. Yellow outlining along edge of rim and down body; multi-row zigzag ornamental design of yellow, yellow-green and white threads.

Condition: Part of rim lost; losses to upper part of body compensated by coloured paste; hole on bottom.

First ever publication

Analogies: Compare with cat. 14

16.
ALABASTRON

Eastern Mediterranean or Italy
Last quarter of 4th century BC

H 24.1; D rim 6.6; GD body 5.3
Received in 1862; found in 1862 in
Pantikapaion necropolis (grave 34)
П.1862.17   ill.3

Body widening downwards; almost shoulderless, high neck, very wide disc-shaped rim; flat bottom, Small, rounded, deeply set ears. Dull dark-blue glass. Yellow outlining along edge of rim; continuous multi-row feathery ornamental design of white and yellow threads.

Condition: Glued back together again from pieces; small piece near bottom lost, rim glued back on.

Literature: OAK for 1862, p. VIII; Художественное стекло, ил. 2; Voščinina, Taf. 118, *2*; М.А.Безбородов. Химия и технология древних и средневековых стекол. Минск, 1969, с. 125, ил. 29; Bosporan Kingdom, p. 304, no. 287

Analogies: Sammlung Oppenländer, Nr. 190; Sammlung Cohn, Nr. 19; Hayes, No. 5; Liepmann, Nr. 5; compare Grose 1989, p. 153, no. 125 (col. ill., p. 101)

17.
ALABASTRON

Eastern Mediterranean or Italy. Late 4th century — early 3rd century BC

H 17.5; D rim 4.6; GD body 4.2
Received in 1925 from Stieglitz Museum collection; bought in Rome
E 1085   ill.6

Faintly fluted (with five vertical indentations) body widening downwards; with high neck, wide crudely made rim; rounded bottom. Rounded, large ears. Dull dark-blue glass. Yellow outlining along edge of rim; multi-row scalloped (near shoulders) and feathery ornamental design of yellow, blue and white threads.

Condition: Good.

First ever publication

Analogies: Sammlung Cohn, Nr. 17; Sammlung Oppenländer, Nr. 190; Hayes, no. 25; Auth, no. 11; Fossing, p. 89, fig. 56; Liepmann, Nr. 5; Smith Collection, no. 19; Filarska, nr. 25, tabl. V, 3; SH, E 189; Sammlung Wolf, S. 216, Nr. 49, S. 218, Nr. 50; Grose, 1989, p. 152, no. 122 (col ill., p. 101)

18.
ALABASTRON

Eastern Mediterranean. 2nd—1st centuries BC

H 13.2; D rim 3; GD 3.7
Received in 1955 from MAE
E 3160   ill.7

Ovoid irregular body; with very high neck, thick crudely made small rim; sharp bottom. Handles without orifices. Dull dark-blue (almost black) glass. White outlining along edge of rim, neck and bottom; multi-row scallops ornamental design of white and yellow threads divided by verticals.

Condition: Good.

First ever publication

Analogies: Сагинашвили 1977, с. 129, ил. 2, *2* (compare ill. 2, *1* and 2, *3*); Fossing, p. 112, fig. 85; Hayes, no. 27, 30; Matheson, no. 33; compare: Voščinina, Taf. 124, *2*; Sammlung Oppenländer, Nr. 192; Liepmann, Nr. 7; Filarska, nr. 36, tabl. V, 4; Grose 1989, p. 168, no. 165, 167

19.
OENOCHOE

Eastern Mediterranean
Late 6th century — 5th century BC

H 7.4; rim: 2.6 x 2.4; D: body 4.6; foot 2
Received in 1900 from A.Novikov collection;
found in Kertch
E 703   ill. on p.27

Ovoid body; on small foot. Rounded handle. Dull blue glass; neck, handle and leg of semi-clear glass. Yellow outlining along edge of rim and foot; zigzag ornamental design of yellow and bright-blue threads between yellow girdles along middle of body; yellow run on neck.

Condition: Good.

Literature: Glass, p. 252, no. 226

Analogies: Sammlung Löffler, Nr. 1, Taf. 1, La Baume, Nr. B1, Taf. 2, *1*; Sammlung Oppenländer, Nr. 119; compare: Spartz, Nr. G 88, Taf. 2, *3*; Grose 1989, p. 150, no. 117; SH, ПАН.830

20.
OENOCHOE

Eastern Mediterranean or Egypt
5th century BC

H 7.6; rim: 2.9 x 2.4; D: body 4.4; foot 2.4
Received in 1930
E 1898   ill.17

Ovoid body; on small conic leg. Thick, rounded handle, curved above rim. Dull pale-turquoise glass, reminiscent of Egyptian faience. Outlining along edge of rim and foot, zigzag ornamen-

tal design between girdles (along middle of body) of dark-purple threads. Handle carelessly made.

Condition: Good.

First ever publication

Analogies: Compare: Sammlung Oppenländer, Nr. 155 (white glass); Fossing, p. 74; fig. 50

21.
OENOCHOE

Eastern Mediterranean (Rhodes ?)
Mid —5th century BC

H 11.8; rim: 3.7 x 3.2; D: body 6.1; foot 3.7
Received in 1928 from E.Shuvalova collection
(bought in Italy ?)
E 1479   ill.12

Spherical body; on wide conic foot. Wide, tapered handle, smoothly bent above rim. Dull dark-blue glass; rim and foot of semi-clear glass. Turquoise outlining along edge of rim; thin relief border of turquoise on neck; zigzag ornamental design between girdles of yellow and light-blue threads along middle of body; small yellow circle at lower end of handle.

Condition: Surface iridescent in places.

Literature: Художественное стекло, ил. 1; М.А.Безбородов. Химия и технология древних и средневековых стекол. Минск, 1969, с. 124, ил. 28

Analogies: Masterpieces, no. 12; Sammlung Oppenländer, Nr. 127 (compare: Nr. 119); Fossing, p. 76, fig. 52; Spartz, Nr. G88, Taf. 2, *3*; Matheson, no. 7, *9*; Grose, p. 149, no. 114 (col ill., p. 96); Sammlung Wolf, S. 212, Nr. 47

22.
ARYBALLOS

Eastern Mediterranean. Second half of 6th century — early 5th century BC

H 5.1; D: rim 2.5; body 4.6
Received in 1915 from AC; found in 1911 in
Pantikapaion necropolis (grave 17)
П.1911.14   ill.13

Fluted spherical body; with short neck, crudely made wide rim. Small ears. Dull red-brown glass. Yellow outlining along edge of rim; zigzag ornamental design of turquoise, yellow and light-green threads along middle of body; yellow and light-blue girdles along bottom of body.

Condition: Good.

Literature: ИАК, 1914, вып. 56, с. 8

Analogies: SH, П.1898.28 (blue with yellow ornamental design; from Pantikapaion necropolis); Auth, no. 270 (col. ill. on p. 23); compare: Sammlung Oppenländer, Nr. 149; Sammlung Hentrich, Nr. 9; Fossing, p. 124, fig. 99; Filarska, nr. 19, tabl. IV, 1

23.
ARYBALLOS

Eastern Mediterranean. 5th century BC

H 6.6; D: rim 3; body 5.6
Date and circumstances of acquisition unknown
E 48   ill. on p.27

Spherical body; with high neck, crudely made funnel-shaped rim. Figured ears. Semi-clear dark-blue glass. Light-blue outlining along edge of rim; zigzag ornamental design of yellow and light-blue threads between girdles (three yellow ones above and one yellow and one light-blue below) along middle of body.

Condition: Surface iridescent in places.

First ever publication

Analogies: Sammlung Wolf, S. 214, Nr. 48; see also analogies to cat. 24

24.
ARYBALLOS

Eastern Mediterranean. 5th century BC

H 6; D: rim 2.5; body 4.9
Received in 1917; bought in Kertch from Pekerev
E 2950   ill.16

Faintly fluted spherical body; with high neck, small rim. Figured ears. Dull dark-blue glass; semi-clear glass on rim. Yellow outlining along edge of rim; zigzag ornamental design of yellow and light-blue threads between yellow girdles.

Condition: Surface iridescent; colour of ornamental design altered.

First ever publication

Analogies: Similar aryballoe are commonly found throughout the ancient world; see cat. 23, 25; Fossing, p. 73, fig 48; Nolte und Haevernick, Taf. 64, *3*; Sammlung Oppenländer, Nr. 143, 144; Neuburg, p. 39, pl. V, *a*; Spartz, Nr. G 97, Taf. 2, *4*; Hayes, no. 14—16; Masterpieces, no. 14; Matheson, no. 10, 11

25.
ARYBALLOS

Eastern Mediterranean. 5th century BC

H 6.5; D: rim 2.8; body 5.3
Received in 1888; bought from A.Bludova
E 295   ill.14

Spherical body; with high neck, wide funnel-shaped rim. Figured ears. Dull dark-blue (almost black) glass. Light-blue outlining along edge of rim; zigzag ornamental design of yellow and greeny-blue threads between girdles along middle of body.

Condition: Surface destroyed in places.

First ever publication

Analogies: Sammlung Wolf, S. 214, Nr. 48; see also analogies to cat. 24

26.
ARYBALLOS

Eastern Mediterranean. 5th century BC

H 5.5; D: rim 2.6; body 4.3
Received in 1931 from SAHMC; previously in A.Bobrinsky collection
E 2066   ill.17

Spherical body; with short neck, thick crudely made rim. Figured ears. Dull dark-blue (almost black) glass. White outlining along edge of rim; zigzag ornamental design of greeny-yellow and light-blue threads between girdles (along middle of body).

Condition: Silvery film of iridization on one of the handles and beneath it.

First ever publication

Analogies: Compare with Hayes, no. 14; compare dimensions and proportions with Fossing, p. 73, fig. 49

27.
AMPHORISKOS

Eastern Mediterranean
Second half of 6th century BC

H 11; D: rim 3.6; body 6.8; foot 1.3
Received in 1904 from AC; found in 1903 in Pantikapaion necropolis (grave 104)
П.1903.82   ill.18

Fluted ovoid body; with conic base; with high cone-shaped neck, wide funnel-shaped rim, flat foot. Thick, vertical handles, with rounded curve under rim. Dull white glass. Outlining along edge of rim and foot, two-tier ornamental design of dark-brown threads.

Condition: Pieces of body and part of rim lost.

Literature: ИАК, 1905, вып. 17, с. 25, 26, ил. 21 (on p. 26)

Analogies: SH, E 134, E 3419, П.1907.79; ИАК, вып. 35; 1910, с. 15, ил. 1 (from Pantikapaion necropolis); Fossing, p. 69, fig. 43, Nolte und Haevernick, Taf. 64, *5*; Masterpieces, no. 13; Sammlung Oppenländer, Nr. 156, 157; Sammlung Cohn, Nr. 1; Matheson, no. 21, 22; Auth, no. 19; Liepmann, Nr. 1; Filarska, nr. 12, tabl. II, *6*; Grose 1989, p. 143, no. 94, 95 (col ill., p. 96)

28.
AMPHORISKOS

Eastern Mediterranean. Second half of 6th century — 5th century BC

H 9.1; D: rim 2.5; body 5.3; foot 1.7
Received in 1928 from E.Shuvalova collection (bought in Italy ?)
E 1478   ill.16

Cone-shaped body; with wide shoulders, high neck, funnel-shaped rim; on wide, flat foot. High, vertical handles with smooth curve at rim. Dull dark-blue glass; yellow glass at top of foot and edge of base; rim and handles of semi-clear glass. Yellow outlining along edge of rim and in rows along neck; zigzag ornamental design on centre of body between simple (top) and undulating girdles of yellow and greeny-blue threads.

Condition: Surface has lost its shine.

First ever publication

Analogies: Hayes, no. 9—12

29.
AMPHORISKOS

Eastern Mediterranean. 5th century BC

H 8.7; D: rim 2.4; body 4.5; foot 1.3
Received in 1928 from E.Shuvalova collection (bought in Italy ?)
E 1461   ill.16

Biconic body; with high neck, crudely made flanged rim, on flat foot. Vertical handles, with smooth curve at rim. Dull dark-blue glass. Yellow outlining along edge of rim; spiral ornamental design on neck and zigzag ornamental design of yellow and turquoise threads between yellow girdles on body.

Condition: Part of rim lost.

First ever publication

Analogies: Matheson, no. 17; compare: Hayes, no. 3; Grose 1989, p. 146, no. 105; SH, П.1852.59

30.
AMPHORISKOS

Eastern Mediterranean. First half of 5th century BC

H 7.5; D: rim 2.2; body 5.3; foot 1.1
Received in 1928 from E.Shuvalova collection (bought in Italy ?)
E 1480   ill.14

Almost spherical body; with short neck, small funnel-shaped rim and short conic boot. Small, sloping handles, with curve near rim. Semi-clear blue glass; handles of light-blue (one) and yellow (other) glass. Bright-blue outlining along edge of rim; zigzag ornamental design of greeny-blue and yellow threads between girdles along middle of body.

Condition: Good.

First ever publication

Analogies: Auth, no. 17 (col. ill., p. 23); Hayes, no. 9, 11; Matheson, no. 14; Sammlung Oppenländer, Nr. 146; R.B.Wartke, Glas im Altertum. Zur Frühgeschichte und Technologie antiken Gläses. Sonderausstellung des Vorderasiatischen Museums, Berlin, 1982, Taf. s. 19 (left); SH, E 1480 (yellow outlining along edge of rim)

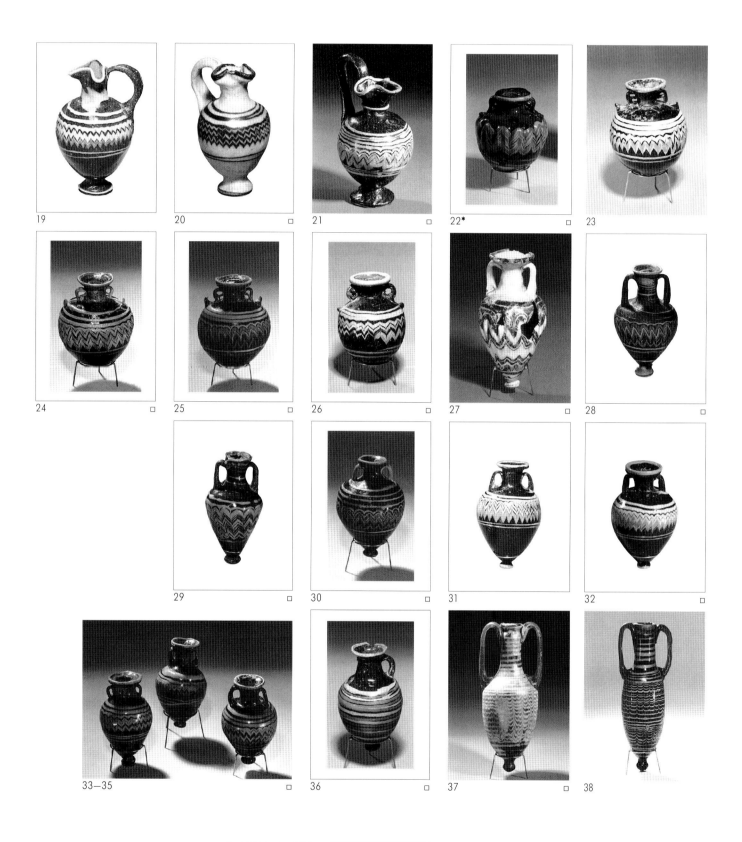

19

20

21

22*

23

24

25

26

27

28

29

30

31

32

33—35

36

37

38

39, 40

41—44

45a

456

31.
AMPHORISKOS

Eastern Mediterranean
First half of 5th century BC

H 8; D: rim 2.6; body 5; foot 1.1
Received in 1955 from MAE
E 3148

Ovoid body of harmonic proportions;
with high neck, small funnel-shaped rim;
with small flat bottom. Small handles,
with smooth curve near rim. Semi-clear
blue glass; dull yellow glass on lower
section of foot. Yellow outlining along
edge of rim; zigzag ornamental design
of light-blue and yellow threads between
doubled yellow girdles.

Condition: Good.

First ever publication

Analogies: Similar amphoriskoe were spread
throughout the ancient world. See Neuburg,
pl. 13, Nolte und Haevernick, Taf. 64, *2*;
Matheson, no. 13, 15; Fitzwilliam Mus, no. 23b;
Hayes, no. 10, 11; Masterpieces, no. 15;
La Baume, Nr. B4, Taf. 3, *1*; Sammlung Hentrich,
Nr. 7; Grose 1989, p. 144, no. 97

32.
AMPHORISKOS

Eastern Mediterranean
First half of 5th century BC

H 7.6; D: rim 2.8; body 4.8; foot 1
Received in 1908 from AC; found in 1907 in
Pantikapaion necropolis (grave 40)
П.1907.34   ill. 13

Ovoid body with conic base; with high
neck, wide funnel-shaped rim. Vertical
handles with smooth curve beneath rim.
Semi-clear dark-blue glass. Light-blue
outlining along edge of rim and yellow
outlining of foot; zigzag ornamental
design of bright-blue and lemon-yellow
threads between yellow girdles.

Condition: Good.

Literature: ИАК, 1910, вып. 35, с. 22
Analogies: See cat. 31

33.
AMPHORISKOS

Eastern Mediterranean. 5th century BC

H 6.6; D: rim 2.6; body 4; foot 1.1
Received in 1931 from SAHMC; previously in
A.Bobrinsky collection
E 2067   ill. 15

Ovoid body with conic base; with short
wide neck, wide rim, crudely made foot.
Small rounded handles. Dull black glass.
Yellow outlining along edge of rim; zigzag ornamental design of yellow and
light-blue threads (across middle of body)
between yellow girdles.

Condition: Surface iridescent in places.
First ever publication

Analogies: Sammlung Oppenländer, Nr. 142;
Auth, no. 273

34.
AMPHORISKOS

Eastern Mediterranean. 5th century BC

H 6.6; D: rim 2.2; body 4.1; foot 1
Received in 1955 from MAE
E 3147   ill.15

Ovoid body; with high neck, wide rim;
with small flat foot. Vertical handles. Dull
red-brown glass. Yellow outlining along
edge of rim; zigzag ornamental design of
yellow and grey-blue threads between
carelessly traced yellow girdles.

Condition: Glued together again from
pieces; one side and lower section of
vessel iridescent.

Literature: Glass, p. 253, no. 228
Analogies: Sammlung Oppenländer, Nr. 140;
Grose, p. 146, no. 104 (col ill., p. 98)

35.
AMPHORISKOS

Eastern Mediterranean. 5th century BC

H 6.7; D: rim 2.3; body 4.2; foot 1.1
Received in 1925 from Stieglitz Museum
collection; bought in Kertch from Ya.Buksil
E 1079   ill.15

Faintly fluted (in the form of vertical
indentations) oval body; with short neck,
wide rim, with massive foot. Rounded
handles. Dull red-brown (on upper section up to shoulders) and dark-blue
glass. Bright-blue outlining along edge
of rim; zigzag ornamental design of
yellow and bright-blue threads between
yellow (top) and yellow-green girdles.

Condition: Silvery-iridescent film of
iridization on ornamental design on one
side of vessel.

First ever publication

Analogies: Compare: Sammlung Oppenländer,
Nr. 140

36.
AMPHORISKOS

Eastern Mediterranean. 5th century BC

H 7.2; D: rim 2.5; body 4.6; foot 1.1
Received in 1931 from Academy of Sciences
E 2443   ill.17

Almost spherical body; with high cone-
shaped neck, small rim; with small biconic
foot. Rounded handles. Semi-clear blue
glass. Double outlining (yellow above
light-blue) along edge of rim; continuous
striped ornamental design of alternating
yellow and light-blue threads.

Condition: One handle lost.
First ever publication

Analogies: Grose 1989, p. 147, no. 109
(col ill., p. 99); compare with SH, П.1904.29

37.
AMPHORISKOS

Eastern Mediterranean
Early 1st century BC

H 13.8; D: rim 2.1; body 5.3
Received in 1909; found in 1905 in
Pantikapaion necropolis (grave 23,
together with cat. 353—355, 359)
П.1905.24   ill.19

Ovoid body; with high shoulders, very
high neck, small bolster-shaped rim, foot
in form of sphere. High vertical handles;
curving ovally above rim. Dull brown
glass; handles and foot of clear olive-
green glass. Continuous striped (on neck
and shoulders and near bottom) and
scallops (on body) ornamental design of
light-blue threads.

Condition: Surface iridescent, colour of
glass has altered (except for light-blue
threads on shoulders).

Literature: ИАК, 1909, вып. 30, с. 8, 9; Кунина,
Сорокина, с. 170, ил. 11, *18*

Analogies: Cat. 38; SH, E 57; E 319; E 469;
E 1465; 2233/37; Dusenberry, 1967, p. 38,
fig 5—8; Smith Collection, no. 22—24;
Masterpieces, no. 19; Sammlung Oppenländer,
Nr. 207; Neuburg, pl. 20; Sammlung Cohn,
Nr. 4; Hayes, no. 34—37; Auth, no. 26, 27,
279—287; Matheson, no. 26—31; Cat. Damas,
pl. VI; Fitzwilliam Mus. no. 28a, b, c; Fossing,
p. 121, fig. 94, 95; Grose 1989, p. 172,
no. 176, Гущина, Засецкая, с. 129,
табл. II, 25; с. 96, кат. 25

38.
AMPHORISKOS

Eastern Mediterranean. Early 1st century BC

H 14.3; D: rim 2; body 4.3
Received in 1912; found in 1910 in
Pantikapaion necropolis (grave 47(5),
together with cat. 122, 178)
П.1910.39

Spindle-shaped body; with high wide
neck; bolster-shaped rim; with foot
spherical. High vertical handles, curving
ovally above rim. Dull dark-blue glass;
handles and foot of clear blue glass.
Continuous striped/scallops ornamental
design of yellow and light-blue threads.

Condition: Cracks on body; one side of
vessel iridescent.

Literature: ИАК, 1913, вып. 47, с. 57 сл.,
с. 59, ил. 10; Сорокина 1965 (1), с. 186,
ил. 2, *2*; Кунина, Сорокина, с. 158, ил. 6, *4*;
Художественное стекло, с. 6 (without ill.)

Analogies: Grose 1989, p. 170, no. 170
(col. ill., p. 107); see also cat. 37

39.
PENDANT IN SHAPE OF HEAD OF DEMON

Eastern Mediterranean
Late 6th century — early 5th centuriy BC

H with loop 3.1; D duct 0.5
Received in 1900; found in 1898 in Pantikapaion necropolis (earth tomb at "Artemis excavations")
П.1898.27   ill.22

Pendant with loop. Dull dark-blue (face and ear) glass. Details of face modelled from coloured dull glass: eyes from blue and white glass; eyebrows, ears and beard from red-brown glass. Vertical duct from core inside.

Condition: Minor damage to surface.

Literature: Haevernick 1977, Nr. 315 (without ill.); Алексеева 1982 (1), табл. 47:21, с. 41, тип 462

Analogies: Haevernick 1977, Taf. 40, Nr. 329, 330, Taf. 43, Nr. 661; Seefried, p. 19, fig. 2 (Type A); Grose 1989, no. 37

40.
PENDANT IN SHAPE OF HEAD OF COCKEREL

Eastern Mediterranean. 4th century BC

H 3.3; D duct 0.4
Found in Kertch
ПАН.1844   ill.22

Dull dark-blue glass. Details modelled from coloured dull glass: eye from blue and white glass; outlining of eyes, comb and tuft from yellow glass. Zigzag ornamental design in imitation of plumage on body. Orifice for suspension drilled through head, possibly after loop was lost: chip can be seen on the back of the cockerel's head.

Condition: Chips on neck (front and back) and on head (back and below).

Literature: Алексеева 1982, табл. 47:34, с. 42, тип 472

Analogies: Compare: Seefried, p. 25, fig. 24 (top left — from excavations at Al Mina Sueidia, Syria); ibidem, p. 22, fig. 16 (Type E 4)

41.
PENDANT IN SHAPE OF BEARDED MALE HEAD

Eastern Mediterranean. 4th—3rd centuries BC

H with loop 5.8; D duct 1
Received in 1960; found in 1960 in Nymphaion
НФ.60.467   ill.23

Pendant with loop. Body of turquoise dull glass (colour seen from behind). All details modelled from coloured dull glass. Hair

from series of locks; beard divided into strands by flutes. White face and moustache; dark-blue and white eyes; dark-blue locks, eyebrows and beard; yellow lips and ear decorations in shape of spheres. Vertical duct from core inside.

Condition: Chip on loop; surface heavily iridescent, majority of locks have yellowed, difficult to determine colour of loop.

Literature: В.Скуднова. Раскопки Нимфея 1960 г. // СГЭ, 1964, вып. XXV, ил. на с. 62; Haevernick 1977, Nr. 496 (without ill) — place of discovery wrongly given as Pantikapaion; Алексеева 1982 (1), табл. 47:20, с. 41, тип 463

Analogies: SH, cat. 44; compare: Haevernick 1977, Nr. 516, 546; Алексеева 1982 (1), табл. 47:29; Seefried, p. 20, fig. 8 (Type C 2)

42.
PENDANT IN SHAPE OF BEARDED MALE HEAD

Eastern Mediterranean
Second half of 4th century BC

H with loop 3.2; D duct 0.5—0.8
Received in 1909; found in 1902 in Pantikapaion necropolis (grave 109)
П.1902.49   ill.24

Pendant with loop. Beard divided into strands by flutes. Body of dull blue glass. All details modelled from coloured dull glass. Yellow face, blue and white eyes, blue eyebrows and beard, white mouth and earrings. Blue head-dress edged with braid of blue and white stripes. Duct from core inside.

Condition: Part of braid from head-dress and lower section of beard lost; chip on back.

Literature: Алексеева 1982, табл. 47:13, с. 41, тип 462

Analogies: Haevernick, 1977, Taf. 43, Nr. 620; compare: ibidem, Taf. 42, Nr. 560; Алексеева 1982 (1), табл. 47:14; compare: Grose 1989, no. 42

43.
PENDANT IN SHAPE OF BEARDED MALE HEAD

Eastern Mediterranean. 4th—3rd centuries BC

H 3.1; D duct 0.5
Received in 1839; found in 1839 in Pantikapaion necropolis (kurgan VI, grave 3)
П.1839.40   ill.24

Pendant with loop. Body of dull turquoise glass. All details modelled from coloured dull glass. Hair from series of locks. White face and moustache, dark-blue and white eyes, dark-blue locks and eyebrows, turquoise beard, yellow lips. Duct from core inside.

Condition: Loop, part of hair, nose and most of beard lost; chips on back; surface damaged and has lost its shine.

First ever publication

Analogies: Compare: Siegfried, p. 20, fig. 8 (Type C 2); SH, П.1867/68.1025

44.
PENDANT IN SHAPE OF BEARDED MALE HEAD

Eastern Mediterranean. 3rd century BC

H with loop 5; D duct 0.8
Received in 1953; found in Chersonesos
X.1953.233   ill.24

Pendant with loop. Body of dull turquoise glass. All details modelled from coloured dull glass. Hair from series of locks. Beard divided into strands by flutes. White face; dark-blue and white eyes; dark-blue hair, eyebrows and beard; yellow lips and decorations in the shape of spheres on brow and ears.

Condition: Part of coiffure lost; cracks on nose, beard and back of pendant; surface has lost its shine.

Literature: Качалов, с. 86, ил. 45; Г.Д.Белов. Эллинистический дом в Херсонесе // ТГЭ, 1962, вып. VII, с. 175, ил. 386; Haevernick, 1977, S. 166, Abb. 5, Nr. 98

Analogies: See cat. 41

45.
BEAD (WITH DOUBLE-SIDED REPRESENTATION OF HUMAN FACES)

Eastern Mediterranean or Carthage
4th—3rd centuries BC

H 2.8; D: 2.4; duct 1.4
Received before 1854; found in Kertch
ПАН.664   ill.20, 21

Cylindrical form with wide duct running through it. Dull dark-blue glass. Modelled relief representations of human faces on both sides; white face with eyes of blue and white glass, dark-blue eyebrows and yellow mouth on one; yellow face, with eyes of blue and white glass, dark-blue eyebrows and white mouth on other. Row of white relief spheres on upper edge of bead, similar one on lower edge, two vertical rows of yellow relief spheres separating faces. Trail from core on inside of duct.

Condition: Surface heavily iridescent; brown spots and streaks on yellow face.

Literature: DBK, tabl. LXXII, 17, 18; Haevernick 1977, S. 203, Nr. 425 (incorrect inv. no. given); Alexeyeva 1982 (1), tabl. 47:4

Analogies: Haevernick 1977, S. 159, Abb. 3, Nr. 379, 380, 403; ibidem, Taf. 42, Nr. 416, 466; Alexeyeva 1982 (1), tab. 47:3 (from Olbia); Seefried, p. 22, fig. 19 (Type F1); Grose, 1989, no. 48; Sammlung Wolf, S. 192—193, Nr. 37

PART 2.
CAST & PRESSED GLASS
Late 15th century BC — 1st century AD

46.

PYXIS WITH LID

Crete or Greece. 3rd — 1st centuries BC

H 4.2; D: rim 9.9; base 13.1; thickness of rim 0.4; base 0.3
Lid: H 2.5; D 11.4; protuberance 7.8; thickness of border 0.4
Received in 1884 from P.Saburov collection
E 235

Cylindrical body with slightly concave walls; wide and flat bottom. Lid with protuberance in middle, wide flat border and inner flange (H 0.3) for fixing. Semiclear greenish glass (pyxis); almost colourless glass (lid); with spherical bubbles. Narrow polished groove along outside of rim; two grooves in shape of concentric circles on top of lid.

Manufacturing technique: Cast in mould, polished by buffing (concentric fissures and grooves are visible on the surface). Lid does not fit tightly onto pyxis due to their different diameters.

Condition: Minor chips; surface of pyxis iridescent.

Literature: Художественное стекло, с. 7 (without ill.); on technique see: Fr. Schuler. Ancient Glassmaking Techniques: The Molding Process // Archeology, 1959, vol. 12, no. 1, p. 47

Analogies: Weinberg 1959, p. 11—23; fig. 1—21; Liepmann, Nr. 9; Sammlung Wolf, S. 282, Nr. 78

47.

BOWL

Persia. Late 5th century — first half of 4th century BC

H 5.4; D rim 18.4; thickness of rim 0.3
Received in 1894 from Academy of Sciences
E 529   ill.27

Almost semi-spherical body; with slightly flanged rim. Clear greenish glass. Relief ornamental design in shape of twelve-petalled rosette from pointed lotus leaves alternating almond leaves outside on bottom and up to middle of walls. Smooth border separated from lower section by

relief girdle of two grooves; smooth, shining inner surface.

Manufacturing technique: Cast in mould, polished by firing inside; after cooling finished by chiselling outside, which explains certain irregularities in the execution of the ornamental design. Flat circle (D 1.4) in centre of rosette (on bottom) in very narrow relief (H < 0.1). Contours of leaves cut out in narrow grooves; almonds protrude 0.2—0.4 cm above surface. Height of relief increases towards rim. Contours of almonds accentuated by chiselling. Form and decoration hint at an attempt to imitate vessels made from precious metals, mostly silver.

Condition: Minor cavities and scratches on both sides; chip and cracks along rim; surface iridescent in many places.

Literature: Художественное стекло, ил. 3; Л.К.Галанина. Стеклянные сосуды из Курджипского кургана // АСГЭ, 1970, вып. 12, с. 44; Appendix, № 12; Oliver 1970, p. 13, fig. 8; М.Н.Сагинашвили, Ю.М.Гагошидзе. Алгетская фиала // "Мацна". Академия наук Грузинской ССР. Серия: Истории, археологии, этнографии и истории искусств. Тбилиси, 1973 (in Georgian), № 4, с. 96, табл. 10

Analogies: For the manufacturing of cast cups in the Near and Middle East 9th—2nd centuries BC see Saldern 1975, p. 38, note 1; Oliver 1970, p. 9—14; Л.К.Галанина, op. cit., с. 43, 44; М.Н.Сагинашвили, Ю.М.Гагошидзе, op. cit., с. 83—98; on form and decoration: ibidem ill on p. 96; Fossing, p. 84, fig. 54; Saldern 1975, p. 37, fig. 1, 2; p. 38, fig. 3, 4; Л.К.Галанина, op. cit., с. 38, ил. 3, 4—9; SH, Ку 1896 1/99 (bowl with omphalos, embedded rosette petals); prototypes in bronze and silver: Oliver, op. cit., p. 12, fig. 7; p. 13, fig. 9; compare: Recent Important Acquisitions // JGS, 1974, XVI, p. 125, No. 2

48.

GOLD BAND GLASS BOWL

Alexandria, Egypt. Second half of 3rd century — early 2nd century BC

H 8.5; D rim 15.5
Received in 1939 from Northern Ossetian Museum of Local Lore, History & Economics

(Ordzhonikidze); found in the 1930s in kurgan at Gosudarstvennaya, near the town of Mozdok
Кз.5323   ill.25

Cone-shaped body; with sandwich gold-glass walls; decoration of gold foil between walls, rounded bottom. Clear yellowish glass; continuous geometric plant ornamental design of double rosette on bottom and three-tier frieze on walls with double girdles between tiers. Upper frieze: garland of bundles of pointed leaves with berries and binding in shape of double short strokes; second frieze: ivy branch with leaves and flowers in zigzag frame of double diamonds serving as base for large rosette of alternating acanthus and trianglar leaves with vein in centre. Ornamental design of component diamonds between leaf tips.

Manufacturing technique: Cast in form; ornamental design in gold leaf traced on outer walls of inner cup, edges of cup alloyed by firing.

Condition: Good.

Literature: Н.В.Тревер. Памятники греко-бактрийского искусства. М.—Л., 1940, с. 158—162, ил. 12 on с. 159, табл. 50; В.Г.Луконин. Искусство древнего Ирана. М., 1977, ил. on с. 119; C.Picard. Sur une coupe de verre à dorures d'un kourgane du Caucase septentrional // Revue archéologique, XXV, 1946, p. 173—182, fig. 1 (p. 174); K.Parlaska. Das Verheltnis der megarischen Becher zum alexandrinische Kunsthandwerk // JDI. Band 70, 1955, S. 145, Abb. 9; A.Adriani. Un vetro dorato Alessandrino dal Caucaso // Bulletin de société d'Alexandrie, no. 42, Le Caire, 1967, p. 105—127, tav. I; Шелковников 1962, ил. 9; Художественное стекло, ил. 4; Saldern 1959, p. 47, no. 7 (without ill.); Harden 1968, p. 39 (without ill.); Качалов, с. 90, ил. 49

Analogies: Compare with cup from Corning Museum of Glass: Recent Important Acquisitions // JGS, 1972, vol XIV, p. 153, no. 3; for system of ornamentation and individual elements of ornamental design compare with cup from Geneva: Saldern, op. cit., p. 47, fig. 32; cup from Rothschild collection: A.Adriani, op. cit., tav. VI; fragment

46*

47 a

47 б

48* a

48 б

49

50

51

52

53

54

55, 56

of cup from Metropolitan Museum: Oliver 1969, p. 10, fig. 1—3

49.
FRAGMENT OF GOLD BAND GLASS BOWL
Alexandria, Egypt. 3rd century BC

W 4.7
Received in 1924 from SAHMC; found in 1903 in Olbia
On.1903.222

Fragment of rim with part of wall. Clear colourless, double-layered glass; with laying of ornamental design of gold foil between layers. Geometrical and floral ornamental design of three friezes with motifs of wave, shoots and acanthus leaves.

Literature: ИАК, 1906, вып. 13, с. 181, ил. 133; Harden 1968, p. 38, fig. 36; Художественное стекло, с. 7 (without ill.)

Analogies: For manufacturing technique see cat. 48; for ornamental design see Harden, op. cit., p. 24, fig. 1—4, p. 25, fig. 5—9, p. 38, fig. 34 (one cup from Canosa, see also Masterpieces, p. 33, no. 38)

50.
BOWL
Eastern Mediterranean (Syria ?)
Late 2nd century — early 1st century BC

H 9.9; D rim 17.1; thickness of rim 0.3
Received in 1884 from P.Saburov collection
E 236

Conic form, rounded bottom. Semi-clear greenish glass. Three polished grooves (one wide one between two narrow) on inside beneath rim, two in the shape of concentric circles on outside of bottom. Form: imitation of metallic examples of the late Hellenistic period.

Condition: Minor damage; "runs" of iridescence on surface

First ever publication

Analogies: Weinberg 1970, p. 20, fig. 1; Weinberg 1973, p. 40, fig. 3, *9;* Hayes, no. 39; Sammlung Oppenländer, Nr. 244; Recent Important Acquisitions // JGS, 1959, vol. I, p. 106, 107, no. 5; Matheson, no. 34; Dusenbery 1971, p. 10, fig. 2; Auth, no. 288; Recent Important Acquisitions // JGS, 1971, vol. XIII, p. 135, p. 134, 135, no. 2; Fitzwilliam Mus., no. 30 a,b,c; Sammlung Hentrich, Nr. 15

51.
BOWL
Syria. Late 1st century BC — early 1st century AD

H 5.5; D: rim 10.9; bottom 8
Received in 1926 from S.Stroganov collection
E 1256   ill.29

Form widening slightly upwards; with straight walls; flat bottom. Semi-clear honey-brown (of various intensities) glass. Two horizontal grooves (the lower one doubled) on inner surface.

Manufacturing technique: Outer wall 0.8 cm lower than rim, ground by buffing; rest of surface polished by firing.

Condition: Silvery-lilac film of iridescence on greater part of surface.

First ever publication

Analogies: Hayes, no. 42; Matheson, no. 36; Fitzwilliam Mus., no. 31; Weinberg 1970, profile 16; Weinberg 1973, Catalogue, p. 42, no. 9, p. 40, fig. 3, *9*

52.
BOWL
Syria. Late 1st century BC — early 1st century AD

H 5.2; D: rim 16.2; bottom 6.3
Received in 1884 from P.Saburov collection
E 233   ill.26

Semi-spherical body; slightly concave bottom. Semi-clear blue glass. Two horizontal relief grooves (the lower one doubled) on inner walls.

Manufacturing technique: Inner surface and narrow stripe outside (0.8 cm lower than rim) polished by buffing; outer surface polished by firing and has retained its shine.

Condition: Good.

First ever publication

Analogies: Matheson, no. 37; Weinberg 1970, p. 20, profiles 17, 18; Weinberg 1973, p. 40, fig. 3, *16*

53.
BOWL
Eastern Mediterranean. 1st century AD

H 5.9; D rim 12; thickness of walls at top 0.3
Received in 1926 from S.Stroganov collection
E 1209   ill.28

Semi-spherical body; with smooth rim and narrow external ribs converging at the bottom; flat bottom. Semi-clear brown glass.

Manufacturing technique: Inner surface and upper part of walls on outside ground by buffing (ground groove 0.8 cm lower than rim on inside; double on bottom); rest of surface polished by firing.

Condition: Surface iridescent on both sides.

Literature: Художественное ремесло, кат. 298 (without ill.)

Analogies: Sammlung Oppenländer, Nr. 249, 250; Weinberg 1973, p. 41, no. 29; Hayes, no. 46; Auth, no. 40; Grose 1982, p. 27, fig. 8

54.
RIBBED BOWL
Eastern Mediterranean. 1st century AD

H 4.8; D rim 14.8
Received in 1931 from SAHMC; previously in A.Bobrinsky collection
E 2191   ill.31

Semi-spherical body; with smooth edge and thick external ribs converging at the bottom. Clear honey-yellow glass.

Manufacturing technique: Upper ends of ribs sliced off; traces of polishing by buffing outside on smooth walls and inner surface in the form of narrow ground girdle above rim and doubled concentric circles on bottom (lengths 8.4 and 1.3); rest of surface ground by firing.

Condition: Good.

First ever publication

Analogies: Isings, Form 3a; Matheson, no. 44; La Baume, Nr. C 2, Taf. 7, *2;* Sammlung Oppenländer, Nr. 249 (in colour), 254; Sammlung Hentrich, Nr. 29—31; Auth, no. 41

55.
RIBBED BOWL
Eastern Mediterranean. 1st century AD

H 5.5; D rim 13.8; thickness of walls at top 0.3
Received in 1931 from library of Academy of Sciences; previously in RAIC collection
E 2438   ill.30

Semi-spherical body; with high walls narrowing downwards and twelve external relief ribs. Clear aquamarine glass.

Manufacturing technique: Upper ends of ribs sliced off; inner surface and upper section of walls polished by buffing (circle of two engraved furrows inside cup); rest of surface polished by firing.

Condition: Surface iridescent.

First ever publication

Analogies: See cat. 54; Simonett, S. 145, Abb. 124, *21,* Taf. 12, *8 (3);* Fremersdorf IV, Taf. 7, top; compare: Berger, Taf. 18, *33 (24);* Benko tabl. XXVI, 3 (8e/5); L. Krakovska. Roman Glass Vessels from Slovakia // JGS, 1981, vol. 23, p. 13, fig. 3; Сорокина 1962, с. 216, ил. 3, 4; Гущина, Засецкая, с. 136, табл. IX, 73

56.
RIBBED BOWL
Eastern Mediterranean
Second half of 1st century AD

H 4.5; D rim 11.4; thickness of walls at top 0.2
Received in 1906; found in 1905 in Pantikapaion necropolis (grave 120 /12)
П.1905.108   ill.30

Semi-spherical body; with smooth rim and eleven external relief ribs converging at the bottom. Clear light-aquamarine glass.

Manufacturing technique: Upper ends of ribs sliced off; traces of polishing by buffing in the form of engraved grooved girdles can be found on upper section of inside walls (half-way down) and on smooth section outside; rest of surface polished by firing.

Condition: Surface iridescent, top layer lost.

57 □

58 □

59 □

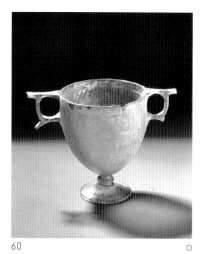

60 □

61 □

62* □

63*a □

63 б □

64

Literature: ИАК, 1909, вып. 30, с. 36, 37; Кунина, Сорокина, с. 155, ил. 5, *11*

Analogies: SH, E 670; cat. 55; Fortuna 1969, p. 24, fig. 21; Isings, Form 3a; Hayes, no. 52; Bucovala 1968, N. 28; Fremersdorf IV, Taf. 7, (bottom); compare: Sammlung Oppenländer, Nr. 254, 258; La Baume, Nr. C 2, Taf. 7, *2, 3*; Weinberg 1973, p. 41, no. 39, 40, 42; Fogolari e Scarfi, tav. 58, *2*; Сорокина 1962, с. 216, ил. 3, *3*

57.
SKYPHOS

Eastern Mediterranean
Late 2nd century — early 1st century BC

H 8.2; D: rim 10.2; pad-base 6.3; L upper plate of handles 4.2; thickness of walls at top 0.3
Found in 1845 in kurgan II near Titorovskaya, Krasnodar region
T.1845/46.2   ill.37

Spherical body; on massive foot widening downwards slightly. Figured handles, with horizontal upper and curved lower plates. Clear yellowish glass, with multitude of small bubbles. Ground groove beneath inside rim.

Manufacturing technique: Carved lines (one horizontal one between two vertical) under handles: traces of marking during manufacture; surface on both sides polished by buffing. Form of vessel in imitation of metallic examples.

Condition: Dents on walls on one side.

Literature: М.И.Ростовцев. Скифия и Боспор. Л., 1925; с. 558; Смирнов, с. 21, ил. 10, *3*; Oliver 1967, p. 31, no. 17

Analogies: Смирнов, с. 21, ил. 10, табл. I, II; Oliver 1967, p. 32; fig. 24, 25; Saldern 1966, p. 8, no. 335, fig. 4; Froehner 1879, pl XIII, 77; Сокровища курганов Адыгеи // Материалы Кавказской археологической экспедиции ГМИНВ 1981—1983 гг. Каталог выставки М., 1985, кат. 440, с. 44, ил. XXI

58.
SKYPHOS

Eastern Mediterranean. First half of 1st century AD

H 9.3; D: rim 12.6; foot 9.6; L upper plate of handles 4.5; thickness of walls 0.4—0.7
Received in 1904; found in 1899 at Zubovsky, Krasnodar region (kurgan II)
2234/52

Wide body; with walls narrowing slightly upwards and abrupt bend toward low pad-base. Figured handles, with horizontal upper and curved lower plates; semicircular notches at ends of upper plates. Clear glass, with light yellow-green tint.

Manufacturing technique: Two concentric circles — internal relief one (D 1.6) and external one in form of ground groove (at a distance of 1.1

from pad-base) — on inside on bottom. Surface on both sides ground by buffing.

Condition: Glued back together again from pieces; losses; chips along rim in places.

Literature: ИАК, 1901, вып. 1, с. 101, ил. 24; Смирнов, с. 21, ил. 10, *л*; Кропоткин, с. 245, ил. 74, *9*, (№ 869); Гущина, Засецкая, с. 121, кат. 146; с. 140, табл. XIII, 146

Analogies: Смирнов, с. 21, ил. 10, *к*; Neuburg, pl. 85; Fogolari e Scarfi, Tav. 57, *1*; Гущина, Засецкая, с. 131, табл. IV, 33

59.
KANTHAROS

Eastern Mediterranean. Mid—2nd century BC

H 9.6; D: rim 9.4; foot 4.1; L upper plate of handle 4.2; thickness of upper walls 0.4
Received in 1906; found in 1900
at Akhtanizovskaya, Krasnodar region
Axt. 35

Ovoid body; on thick, cone-shaped, gently ground foot. Figured handles, with horizontal upper and slightly curved lower plates. Semi-clear almost colourless glass, with yellow tint where glass is thicker.

Manufacturing technique: Traces of marks left during manufacture under handles; surface on both sides ground by buffing.

Condition: Part of upper plate on one of handles lost.

Literature: OAK for 1902, с. 107, ил. 208; ИАК, 1909, вып. 29, с. 36, ил. 34; Смирнов, с. 21, ил. 10 н; Кропоткин, с. 245, ил. 74, *1* (№ 862); Oliver 1967, p. 31, no. 23

Analogies: Masterpieces, no. 37

60.
KANTHAROS

Eastern Mediterranean. First half of 1st century AD

H 9.3; D: rim 7.3; foot 4.5; L upper plate of handles 3.1
Received in 1927; found in 1914 in the northern Caucasus near Maikop (kurgan II, Bare Mountain)
2248/31   ill.35

Ovoid body; on profiled foot, with wide cone-shaped base. Elegant narrow handles with horizontal upper and curved lower plates. Semi-clear colourless glass. Ground girdle under inside of rim.

Manufacturing technique: Surface ground on outside (inside ?) by buffing.

Condition: Pieces of rim, lower protuberance of one of handles and part of upper protuberance of other handle lost; surface iridescent in places.

Literature: OAK for 1913—1915, с. 158; Смирнов, с. 21, ил. 10 о; Кропоткин, с. 245, ил. 74, *6* (№ 892); Oliver 1967, p. 31, no. 24; Гущина, Засецкая, с. 114, кат. 112, с. 137, табл. X, 112

Analogies: See cat 61, 62; Recent Important Acquisitions // JGS, 1971, vol. XIII, p. 135, no. 3 (Corning Museum of Glass, no. 70.1.29 — from blue glass)

61.
KANTHAROS

Eastern Mediterranean. First half of 1st century AD

H 9.8; D: rim 8.5; foot 4.9; L upper plate of handles 3.2
Received in 1916; found in 1902 in the northern Caucasus near Armavir (kurgan I; grave 5)
2240/5   ill.34

Ovoid body; on elegant leg boot profiled cone-shaped base. Figured handles, with horizontal upper and curved lower plates; relief scroll-shaped helixes and shoots near places where handles join the edge. Clear colourless glass.

Condition: Foot glued together from pieces; corner of upper plate of one of handles broken off; scratches on body.

Literature: OAK for 1902, с. 87, ил. 194; Смирнов, с. 21, ил. 10 п; Кропоткин, с. 245, ил. 74, *5* (№ 861); Качалов, с. 82, ил. 41; Гущина, Засецкая, с. 105. кат. 73, с. 136, табл. IX, 73

Analogies: See cat. 60, 62

62.
KANTHAROS

Eastern Mediterranean. First half of 1st century AD

H 10; D: rim 8.3; foot 4.4; L upper plate of handles 3.1
Received in 1900 from G.Kallo collection; found in Southern Russia
E 807   ill. on p.32

Ovoid body with elegant profiled foot. Figured handles with horizontal upper and curved lower plates. Clear blue glass. Figured notches on handles and transitions to rim. Profile of foot in imitation of metal kantharoi.

Condition: Glued back together again from pieces; losses; surface heavily iridescent.

Literature: K.Gorbunova and I.Saverkina. Greek and Roman Antiquities in the Hermitage. Leningrad, 1975, no. 110

Analogies: See cat. 60, 61

63.
PLATE

Eastern Mediterranean or Italy
40s—70s AD

H 2.9; D: rim 18.1; pad-base 9.7
Received in 1872; found in 1872 in Pantikapaion necropolis (grave 3, together with cat. 163, 213, 298)
П.1872.98   ill.32, 33

Clearly profiled rim and walls, low pad-base. Carmine glass. Relief circumference (D 1.7) with dot in the middle in centre of the inner side.

Manufacturing technique: Surface of vessel ground and polished by buffing. Successful imitation of plate made from coloured stone (described as jasper in an old State Hermitage inventory book).

Condition: Glued back together again from pieces; losses and chips; bottom covered in whitish spots of iridescence.

Literature: OAK for 1872, c. XXII

Analogies: Compare: Berger, Taf. 3, *30* (Taf. 17, *2*) — in shape, from dull greyish-white glass; fragment of dull red-glass vessel see ibidem, Taf. 3, 40; dull red-glass cups see: Sammlung Oppenländer, Nr. 287; SmithCollection, Nr. 179 a, b, c; see also Masterpieces p. 43, no. 48 — made from clear glass

64.
PLATE

Eastern Mediterranean. First half of 1st century AD

H: 2.4; pad-base 0.5; D: rim 18.7; pad-base 8.5; thickness of pad-base 0.3—0.4
Received in 1879; found in 1879 in Pantikapaion necropolis (grave 38)
П.1879.25

Flanged rim, roundly curved walls, short circular pad-base; flat bottom. Clear greenish glass.

Manufacturing technique: Rim ground, pad-base sliced off and ground. Traces of buffing on both sides of plate.

Condition: Surface heavily iridescent and in many places, particularly on the inside, corroded by cavities.

Literature: OAK for 1878, 1879, c. LVIII—LIX; N.Garschin von Engelhardt. Eine Kertscher Kamee mit dem Bildnis Drusus Jüngeren // JDI, 1926, Band XLI, S. 245, Abb. 6; Islings, p. 21, Form 5

Analogies: Isings, Form 5; compare: Smith Collection, no. 377

65.
MEDALLION WITH HEAD OF YOUTH

Eastern Mediterranean. Second half of 4th century BC

Dimensions of flat side: 1.9 x 1.5
Received in 1873; found in 1873 in Pantikapaion necropolis (together with cat. 66)
П.1873.163   ill.40

Ovoid form; with one flat and one protuberant side; lopped off at edge. Clear, greenish glass. Linear representation in black paint of head of youth, with oval face, straight nose, full lips, rounded chin and wavy hair slightly raised over his forehead across white prime coating on flat side. Three-quarters turn of the head, slightly bent to the right. Wide-open eyes together with sharp turn of the head create the impression of an intense glance. Thick neck with folds ends in arched (upwards) line. The absence of information regarding the circumstances of the discovery make it difficult to determine the object's purpose (inset for a wooden or bone casket ?).

Condition: Surface slightly iridescent, mostly on protuberant side.

First ever publication

66.
MEDALLION WITH BUST OF WOMAN

Eastern Mediterranean
Second half of 4th century BC

D 3.2
Received in 1878; found in 1878 in Pantikapaion necropolis (child's grave 14, together with cat. 67)
П.1878.35   ill.38

Round form; with flat and slightly protuberant sides. Clear greenish glass. Linear representation of bust of woman, with head slightly turned to the right, oval face and thick wavy hair over her forehead, across thin light prime coating on flat side. Wide-open eyes, eyelids underlined by distinct double lines. Large straight nose; wavy line of lips, dimple on chin; stout neck. Large earrings with pyramidal pendants in her ears. A necklace was depicted about her neck, of which two arched lines and a trace of a third one have survived. The upper section of her clothes can be seen: the horizontal folds of the tunic and the folds of the cloak gathered on her right shoulder.

Condition: Surface heavily iridescent and corroded by cavities; top layer on protuberant side almost lost; top layer on flat side lost near rim; pieces of drawing on woman's neck, bust and left shoulder lost.

Literature: OAK for 1878, c. XXXVI; OAK for 1880, c. 98, 99; табл. IV, 21

67.
MEDALLION WITH SPINNER

Eastern Mediterranean
Second half of 4th century BC

D 3.3
Received in 1878; found in 1878 in Pantikapaion necropolis (child's grave 14; together with cat. 66)
П.1878.34   ill.39

Round form; with one flat and one slightly protuberant side. Clear greenish glass. Linear representation in black paint of a woman sitting in a chair (with high curved back and curved legs) across thin light prime coating on flat side. The woman's head is *en face*, the torso in three quarters, the legs in profile. There is a distaff in the woman's raised left hand, a thread stretches down in a diagonal direction towards the spindle (under the seat between the legs of the chair). The medallion may represent Aphrodite, worshipped as the goddess of fate. This subject is common to monuments of antique art.

Condition: Surface iridescent; parts of upper coat along with priming along edges on flat side lost; part of coiffure, upper section of face, end of one leg of chair, part of space under chair have vanished. Top layer of glass on protuberant side almost totally lost.

Literature: OAK for 1878, c. XXXVI; OAK for 1880, c. 98, 99; табл. IV, 20; regarding representations of the spinning Aphrodite as the goddess of fate: Elmer G.Suhr. The Spinning Aphrodite. New York, 1969, p. 93—150, fig. 4—8, 23—25, 28—33, 35—39

Analogies: For the subject on red-figure vases see Suhr E.G., op. cit. p. 101, fig. 23

68.
GOLD BAND GEM

Eastern Mediterranean
Second quarter —mid 4th century BC

Dimensions of inset (without mounting): 1.5 x 1.6
Received in 1859; found in 1858 in Pantikapaion necropolis (stone tomb 2, Pavlovsky kurgan)
ПАВ.4   ill.46, 47

Ovoid form; in form of inset, with one flat and one slightly protuberant side, with golden frame and hoop. Blue glass, with applied figures stamped from gold foil, coated with clear glass. Representation of two Barbarians dancing in short tunics and pointed hats and earth stylied as horizontal patterned stripe on protruding side; representation of swimming dragon surrounded by dolphins and fish on flat side. Setting in form of rim with spiral ornamental design and ribbed wire piping. Inset is connected to ends of hoop by gold pins, allowing the inset and hoop to rotate. Form of hoop and design of gem testify that the object, similar to a ring, was worn as a pendant (on the wrist, chest or waist).

Condition: Heavily worn frames indicate that the gem was used for a long time and might have been a family heirloom.

Literature: OAK for 1859, c. 11 and 122, табл. III, 4, 5; АДЖ, c. 107; A.Furtwängler. Die Antiken Gemmen. Leipzig und Berlin, 1900, S. 135; М.И.Артамонов. Сокровища скифских курганов в собрании Государственного Эрмитажа. Прага, 1966, табл. 274, 275; J.Boardman. Greek Gems and Finger Rings. London, 1970, p. 233, pl. 822; S.G.Miller. Two Groups of Thessalian Gold. Berkeley, 1979, p. 20, pl. 11 e-f; Л.К.Галанина. Курджипский курган. Л., 1980, с. 42, 43, ил. 17, 18; R.Higgins. Greek and Roman Jewellery. 2nd edn. London, 1980, pl. 31 b; D.Musti et al. L'oro dei Greci. Novarra, 1992, no. 127; D.Williams and J.Ogden. Greek Gold. Jewellery of the Classical World. London, 1994, p. 171, no. 108; Д.Уильямс, Д.Огден. Греческое золото. Ювелирное искусство классической эпохи. V—IV века до н. э. СПб., 1995, с. 171, № 108

Analogies: See gems with gold relief representations on glass, covered with clear glass or rock crystal: with hoop; with representations on two sides from Homolion, Northern Greece (B.Deppert-Lippitz. Griechischer Goldschmuck. Mainz, 1985, S. 193, Taf. 16; S.G.Miller. op. cit. p. 20, pl. 11c); finger-ring with representations on both sides (one has survived) from a London auction (Sotheby's, July 10th 1992, lot 318); finger-ring in the Louvre (S.G.Miller, op. cit. pl. 11, d); finger-ring in SH, 2495/70 — found in Kurdzhipsky kurgan in the Kuban region (Л.К.Галанина, op. cit., с. 89, № 34, с. 42, 43); finger-ring wholly of glass (including hoop) in the Metropolitan Museum (D.Williams and J.Ogden, op. cit., p. 221, No. 159); finger-ring wholly of glass (including hoop) in the British Museum (D.Williams and J.Ogden, op. cit., p. 221, No.160); Д.Уильямс, Д.Огден, op. cit., с. 221, N 160)

69.
SIGNET-RING WITH PORTRAIT OF BERENICE

Egypt (Alexandria ?). 3rd century BC

Ring: 2.3 x 2.2; disc 2.2 x 1.8; W hoop in middle section 0.4
Received in 1929; previously in A.Nelidov collection, bought in Constantinopole
Ж 608   ill.44

Oval flat inset and glass hoop form a single whole. Semi-clear greenish glass. Sunken carved profile portrait of head of the Queen of Egypt (Berenice I or Berenice II), head turned to the left, on inset. Manufacturing technique: Casting, possibly finished by carving.

Condition: Good.

Literature: L.Pollak. Klassisch-antike Goldschmidearbeiten im Besitz, A.J. von Nelidov. Leipzig, 1903, Nr. 424, S. 146; J.Boardman. Greek Gems and Finger Rings. London, 1970, p. 146, no. 460

Analogies: SH, Ж 607 — from the same sort of glass and of the same shape; with representation of female head, possibly Demetra (Pollak, op. cit., Nr. 423, S. 145); compare: A.Furtwängler. Die antiken Gemmen. Berlin, 1900. Bd. II, Taf. XXXII, 32 (on stone)

70.
FINGER-RING WITH PORTRAIT OF MITHRADATES VI EUPATOR

Northern Black Sea coast (?)
Late 2nd century — early 1st centuriy BC

Ring: 2.8 x 2.7; inset: 1.8 x 1.5; H 0.4
Received in 1893 from J.Lemme' collection; possibly found on Northern Black Sea coast
Ж 464   ill.45

Made from thin gold leaf with filling (sulphur ?) with protuberant oval glass inset fixed in socket with the help of a vertical rim. Clear purple-violet glass imitating the amethyst. Sunken carved profile portrait (in profile to the left) of Mithradates VI Eupator, King of Pontos and Bosporos with diadem in his hair. K.Gebauer believes it to be a portrait of Alexander the Great. The inset was recently attributed by O.Ya. Neverov as being a copy from an original gem of coloured stone, with a portrait of Mithradates VI, dating prior to 88 BC.

Condition: Part of gold leaf broken off under inset, grey mass filling the ring visible; surface of inset shabby.

Literature: Collection Lemme' a Odessa decrite par M.F. Odessa, 1884, pl. VIII, 8; K.Gebauer. Alexanderbildnis und Alexandertypus. AM, 63/64, 1938—1939, S. 82; Неверов. Золотой перстень с портретом эллинистического царя (к иконографии Митридата VI) // ВДИ, 1969, № 1, с. 172—175, ил. 1 (с. 172) и 2 (с. 173); Митридат — Дионис // СГЭ, 1973, вып. XXXVII, с. 43, ил. д, е

Analogies: H.B.Walters. Catalogue of the Engraved Gems. London, 1962, pl. XVI, no. 1228

71.
SEAL WITH PORTRAIT OF GAIUS CAESAR

Italy. Late 1st century BC—1st century AD

1.6 x 1.2
Received in 1909; found in 1905 in Pantikapaion necropolis (grave 26)
П.1905.135   ill.42

Oval flat inset. Clear, greenish glass. Sunken carved portrait of head (in profile to the right) of Gaius Caesar, grandson of Roman Emperor Caesar Augustus. The mounting is modern.

Condition: Good.

Literature: OAK for 1906, с. 63, ил. 73; ИАК, 1909, вып. 30, с. 10, ил. 8; Неверов. Итальянские геммы в некрополях северопонтийских городов // Из истории Северного Причерноморья в античную эпоху. Л., 1979, с. 108, № 10, табл. I, 10

Analogies: P.Fossing. Catalogue of the Antique Engraved Gems and Cameos. The Thorwaldsen Museum Copenhagen. Copenhagen, 1929, no. 1185

72.
CAMEO WITH REPRESENTATION OF HEAD OF ATHENS

Italy (?). 1st century AD

1.5 x 1.2
Received in 1787 from Duc d'Orleans collection (Paris); previously in P.Crozat collection (Paris)
Ж 79   ill.41

Oval inset. Dull tricolour glass in imitation of tricolour sardonyx. Embossed bust of Athens (in profile to the right) on dark-brown, almost black, background (thickness 1 mm). Brown helmet and aegis, white face, neck, shoulder, helmet and plumage.

Manufacturing technique: Cast in mould.
Condition: Good.

Literature: Description sommaire des pierres gravées du Cabinet de feu Mr. [Pierre] Crozat par Piesre-Jean Mariette. Paris, 1741, no. 886; [Belly]. Catalogue des pierres gravées du Cabinet de feu Son Altesse serenissime Monseigneur M. le Duc d'Orléans. Premier Prince du Sang. Paris, 1786, no. 904; Максимова, с. 100; Неверов 1988, с. 156, кат. 415 (ил.)

Analogies: Compare with Неверов 1988, с. 111, cat. 111 (from sardonyx)

73.
PHALERA WITH PORTRAIT OF DRUSUS THE YOUNGER

Roman Empire. Early 1st century AD

3 x 2.1
Received in 1792 from J.B.Casanova collection (Dresden)
Ж 272   ill.50

Fragment of phalera in frame. Clear blue glass. Golden 18th century frame. Relief portrait of the head of Drusus the Younger, son of the Roman Emperor Tiberius.

Condition: Good.

Literature: Максимова, Резные камни, с. 99; Неверов 1971, № 83; Неверов 1988, с. 151, 155, № 400; Неверов 1994, с. 120, № 48; Z. Kiss, L'iconographie des princes Julio-Claudiens, p. 106, fig. 368

Analogies: L.Curtius, Ikonographische Beiträge, VII, RM, 50, 1935, Taf. 29. A.Alfödi, Römische Porträt-medallions aus Glas, Urschweiz, XV, 1951, Taf. II—III

74.
DIONYSUS (MÆNADES ?) PHALERA

Roman Empire. 1st century AD

2.6 x 2.1
Received in 1792 from J.B.Casanova collection (Dresden)
Ж 222   ill.48

Circular disc in frame. Clear violet glass. Golden 18th century frame. Relief portrait

65*

66*

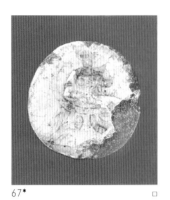

67*

68* a

68 б

69

70*

71

72

73

74

75

76

77

of the head of Dionysus (Mænades ?) on the frame.

Condition: Losses on the upper section.

Literature: Максимова, Резные камни, p. 100; Неверов 1988, p. 158, № 423

Analogies: SH, Ж 220, Ж 221, Ж 234 (Неверов 1988, кат. 424—427); E.Babelon. Catalogue des camées antiques et modernes de La Bibliothèque Nationale. Paris, 1897, No. 83; F.Fremersdorf, Glas-phalera aus Vechten // Bulletin van de Vereeniging tot Bevordering der Kennis van de Antike Beschaving, 1935, lg. X, S. 4, Abb. 7

75.
DIONYSUS (MÆNADES ?) PHALERA
Roman Empire. 1st century AD

2.4x2.2
Received in 1792 from J.B.Casanova collection (Dresden)
Ж 221   ill.49

Circular disc in frame. Clear colourless glass. Golden 18th century frame. Relief portrait of the head of Dionysus (Mænades ?) on the frame.

Condition: Good.

Literature: Максимова, Резные камни, с. 100; Неверов 1988, с. 158, № 424

Analogies: SH, Ж 220, Ж 222

76.
PHALERA
Roman Empire. 1st century AD

5 x 4.5
Received in 1792 from J.B.Casanova collection (Dresden)
Ж 237

Oval disc in frame. Clear greenish glass. Golden 18th century frame. Relief portrait of the head of Medusa on the frame.

Condition: Good.

Literature: Максимова, Резные камни, с. 100; Неверов 1988, с. 159, 160, № 428

Analogies: Verzeichniss Roemischer Altertuemer, gesammelt von Care Anton Niessen, Köln, 1896, Taf. XXVII, 4. SH Ж 6806 (Неверов 1988, кат. 429); E.Babelon. Catalogue des camées antiques et modernes de La Bibliothèque Nationale. Paris, 1897, No. 83; F.Fremersdorf, Glas-phalera aus Vechten // Bulletin van de Vereeniging tot Bevordering der Kennis van de Antike Beschaving, 1935, lg. X, S. 4, Abb. 8, 9

77.
PHALERA
Roman Empire. 1st century AD

D 4
Received in 1792 from J.B.Casanova collection (Dresden)
Ж 226

Circular disc in frame. Clear bluish glass. Golden 18th century frame. Relief bust of Alexander the Great in helmet, armour, a spear behind his left shoulder, on the frame.

Condition: Chips on the helmet, armour and behind.

Literature: K.Gebauer, Alexanderbildnis und Alexandertypus, Mitteilungen des Deutschen Archaeologischen Instituts. Athenische Abteilung, 63, 1938, Taf. 4, 17; Максимова, Резные камни, с. 100; Неверов 1988, с. 150, № 398; Неверов 1994, с. 122, № 49

Analogies: Le Musee, II, Geneve, 1875, pl. XI; M.Vollenweider. Les portraits romains, Geneve, 1960, t. 8, pl. IV

78.
PORTRAIT OF LYBIA (?)
Eastern Mediterranean. After 42 AD

H 3.5
Received in 1983; found in 1983 in Nymphaion
Нф.83.235   ill.43

Miniature sculptured portrait of female head; possibly fragment of lost statuette. Clear aquamarine glass. Head slightly bent to the right. Hair divided by parting in the middle, frames face in circular locks and gathered under diadem. Coiffure apparently ended in a knot, hanging down on neck, at place of break on back. Facial features (low forehead, widely-set eyes, small tightly-shut mouth with thin lips, small chin) and form of hairstyle are reminiscent of portraits of Lybia, wife of Augustus Caesar. A rare example of an antique sculpture from high-quality clear glass; the only glass sculptural portrait of Lybia.

Manufacturing technique: Cast in mould with aid of wax model, finished by chiselling.

Condition: Almost entire neck, part of right side of face (traces of broken off protuberance, purpose of which is unknown) and part of coiffure lost; one piece on back of neck glued on.

Literature: Tesori d'Eurasia, 2000 anni: Di Storia in 70 anni di Archeologia Sovietica. Venezia, Palazzo Ducale. 1s septembre 1987 febbrario 1988. Milano, 1987, p. 45, cat. 180; Bosporan Kingdom, p. 331, no. 318 on sculpture from glass see: Musée de Mariemont. [Catalogue des] Verres Antiques de la collection Ray Winfield Smith 8 mai —15 septembre 1954. Bruxelles, 1954, cat. 32 (pl. III), cat. 40 (pl. XI); Smith Collection, p. 113, 114, cat. no. 188—191, pl. IV, V, fig. 190, 191; Boston Museum Bulletin, 1966, vol. LXIV, no. 335, p. 11, 13, fig. 10; O.Doppelfeld. Das neue Augustus — Porträt aus Glas im Kölner Museum // Kölner Jahrbuch fur Vor-und-fruegeschichte. 8. Band. 1965/1966, S. 7—12,

Taf. 1—5; Recent Important Acquisitions // JGS, 1962, vol. IV, p. 140, no. 9; Filarska. nr. kat. 57, 58; on the iconography of Lybia see W.H.Gross. Julia Augusta. Untersuchungen zum grundlegung einer Livia-Ikonographie. Göttingen, 1962, Taf. 29

79.
ROD (?)
Eastern Mediterranean (Syria ?)
Second half of 1st century — first half of 2nd century AD

L 22.9
Received in 1866; found in 1866 in Pantikapaion necropolis (crypt 4, tomb 7)
П.1866.83

Spiral with ring at one end and small figure of bird at other. Clear colourless glass.

Condition: Glued together again from two pieces.

Literature: OAK for 1866, c. VI; CR pour l'année 1875. St Peterbourg, 1878, Atlas, Pl. II, 25

Analogies: SH, П.1900.21 (see Художественное ремесло, кат. 310, without ill.), cat. 80; Smith Collection, no. 298; Auth, no. 213; Fremersdorf IV, Taf. 134

80.
ROD (?)
Eastern Mediterranean (Syria ?)
Second half of 1st century — first half of 2nd century AD

L 23.6
Received in 1900 from A.Novikov collection; possibly found on Kertch peninsula.
E 736

Spiral, with ring at one end and small figure of bird at other. Clear light-blue glass.

Condition: Good.

Literature: Качалов, с. 87, ил. 46

Analogies: See cat. 79

81.
ROD (?)
Eastern Mediterranean
Second half of 1st century — first half of 2nd century AD

L 19.1
Received in 1906; found in 1903 in Pantikapaion necropolis (grave 83, inside urn with ashes)
П.1903.55

Spiral, with ring at one end and disc at the other. Made from three stripes: clear colourless glass; dull white glass (narrow stripe: thread); clear violet glass.

Manufacturing technique: Stripes laid in parallel and twisted into spiral.

78* a □ 78 б

  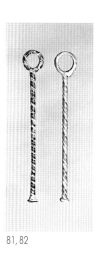  

79 80 81, 82 83 84* 85*

Condition: Glued back together again from two pieces; surface iridescent in places

Literature: ИАК, 1905, вып. 17, с. 21, ил. 16

Analogies: Cat. 82, 83; SH, П.1845.21;
Isings, Form 79; Vessberg, 1952, pl. X, 15—17;
Sammlung Oppenländer, Nr. 620;
Auth, no. 521; Fitzwilliam Mus., no. 96

82.
ROD (?)

Eastern Mediterranean
Second half of 1st century — first half of 2nd century AD

L 19
Received in 1866; found in 1866 in
Pantikapaion necropolis (grave 12, under kurgan)
П.1866.74

Spiral, with ring at one end and disc at other. Made from three stripes: clear amber glass; dull white glass; opaque light-blue glass.

Manufacturing technique: Stripes laid in parallel and twisted into spiral.

Condition: Good.

Literature: OAK for 1866, c. VIII

Analogies: See cat. 81

83.
ROD (?)

Eastern Mediterranean
Second half of 1st century — first half of 2nd century AD

L 21.7
Received in 1931 from A.Bobrinsky collection; bought in Kertch
E 2243

Spiral, with ring at one end and disc at other. Made from three stripes: clear dark-blue glass; dull white glass; bright-blue glass.

Manufacturing technique: Stripes laid in parallel and twisted into spiral.

Condition: Good.

Literature: Качалов, с. 87, ил. 46

Analogies: See cat. 81, 82

84.
"NEEDLE" (HAIR-PIN ?)

Eastern Mediterranean. First half of 1st century AD

L remnant 14.8; D rod 0.3—0.5
Received in 1877; found in 1877 in
Pantikapaion necropolis (grave 5)
П.1877.23

Long thin rod with one pointed end and the other forming a loop. Clear honey-yellow glass; inside of rod and helixes on loop made of white threads.

Condition: End of loop lost.

Literature: OAK for 1877, c. XI

Analogies: SH, П.1875.397 (from clear dark-blue glass with pointed loop and white threads); Vessberg 1952, pl. X, 18

85.
SPOON

Eastern Mediterranean
2nd — 3rd centuries AD

L remnant 19.1
Received in 1898; bought from M.Sivadjan; found in Syria
E 1304

Oval, with straight handle. Clear light-bluish glass.

Condition: End of handle lost.

First ever publication

Analogies: SH, E 1305; Vessberg 1952, pl. X, 19

86 □   87 □   88 □

89 □   90 a □   90 б □

91   92

   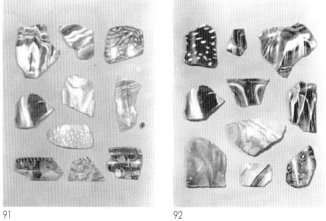   

93 a □   93 б □   94*

PART 3.
MOSAIC GLASS
Late 1st century BC — 3rd century AD

86.
SMALL BOWL

Eastern Mediterranean (Syria ?). First half of 1st century AD

H 4; D: rim 9.2; pad-base 4.1
Received in 1893 from J.Lemme' collection
E 497   ill.54

Rounded walls; with distinctly profiled protuberance outside rim, with crudely formed circular pad-base. Dark-violet, almost black, glass; insets in shape of irregular concentric circumferences with alternation of dimmed yellow (in centre), red and white glass and in shape of spirals of semi-clear, light-green glass with yellow core. Pad-base of violet glass.

Manufacturing technique: Cast in mould; pad-base made separately; sections from cut rods of coloured glass, passing through vessel walls, placed in background glass. Traces of polishing by buffing on inside, outside polished by firing; rim levelled off by lopping.

Condition: Cavities on surface in places, particularly on outside; whitish film of iridescence in places; top shining layer lost.

Literature: Художественное стекло, ил. 5

Analogies: Compare: cat. 87; Hayes, no. 59—63; Auth, no. 48; Sammlung Oppenländer, Nr. 314—321; Fitzwilliam Mus., no. 37; Liepmann, Nr. 11; Matheson, no. 49

87.
SMALL BOWL

Eastern Mediterranean (Syria ?)
First half of 1st century AD

H 4; D: rim 9.5; pad-base 4.1
Received in 1925 from Stieglitz Museum; bought in Kertch from Ya.Buksel
E 1095   ill.56

Rounded walls; with distinctly profiled rim protruding outwards, crudely formed circular pad-base. Dark, almost black (possibly dark-blue) glass, with insets in shape of flower with white pith surrounded by red, and "petals" in shape of yellow "strokes" and spirals.

Manufacturing technique: Cast in mould, pad-base made after casting; sections of slit glass rods of other colours, passing through whole bulk of vessel, placed in background glass. Traces of polishing by buffing inside, outside polished by firing, rim levelled off by lopping.

Condition: Glued back together again from pieces; whitish film of iridescence on outer surface.

Literature: Шелковников, ил. 6

Analogies: Compare: Sammlung Oppenländer, Nr. 314; Hayes, no. 63; Matheson, no. 49; Smith Collection, no. 137

88.
SMALL BOWL

Eastern Mediterranean or Italy
1st century AD

H 5.7; D rim 9.2
Received in 1852 from A. & G.Laval collection
E 196   ill.57

Semi-spherical form; with smooth rim and fourteen thick external ribs. Upper section of bowl on outside and the whole surface on inside both smooth. Clear honey-yellow glass with insets and veins of dulled white glass in imitation of jasper.

Manufacturing technique: Mosaic, made from separate sections of various colours; each section represents a stretched spiral. Ribs sliced off, surface polished on both sides.

Condition: Glued back together again from pieces; surface iridescent, with whitish film in places.

First ever publication

Analogies: Simonett, Taf. 9, *4*; Fremersdorf III, Taf. 3, *5*; Berger, Taf. 1, *17*; compare decoration: Matheson, no. 55; Smith Collection, no. 141; Sammlung Löffler, Nr. 42, Taf. 5, *2*

89.
FRAGMENT OF BOWL

Eastern Mediterranean or Italy
1st century AD

H 5.6; L fragment 8; estimated D rim 9.2
Received in 1852 from A. & G.Laval collection
E 201c   ill.61

Fragment of upper section of semi-spherical bowl, with smooth rim and external ribs. Glass made of dark-violet, light-green, clear colourless, semi-clear yellow and white (veins) sections; imitation of coloured stone.

First ever publication

Analogies: Compare: Smith Collection, no. 128; Matheson, no. 41; Hayes, no. 77, 78; Fremersdorf, III, Taf. 3, *4*

90.
FOOT OF BOWL

Eastern Mediterranean or Italy. First half of 1st century AD

H 2.5; D: bottom 3.1; foot 7.2
Received in 1924 from SAHMC
П.1914.19   ill.55

Cone-shaped form. Translucent cobalt-blue glass; with insets of coloured and clear glass.

Condition: Outer surface iridescent; original colours visible only on inside of walls.

First ever publication

Analogies: Berger, Taf. 2, 22; compare: Kisa II, S. 421, Abb. 204; compare pattern: Auth, no. 307

91.
FRAGMENTS OF VESSELS

Italy. Late 1st century BC — first half of 1st century AD (1—7); Alexandria or Italy. 1st century BC — 1st century AD (8); Eastern Mediterranean or Italy. 1st century BC — 1st century AD (9, 10)

L 3.1—4.9
Received in 1984 from V.Kononov collection (1, 2, 4—6, 8, 10); in 1852 from A. & G.Laval collection (3, 7); in 1912; discovered by accident in Kertch (9)
E 3267, E 3281, E 201d, E 3271, E 3286, E 3278, E 201e, E 3269, П.1909.143, E 3253a
(in order)   ill. on p.14

First ever publication

Analogies: Berger Taf. 2, *20*, Taf. 1, *8, 11*; Hayes, no. 70, 75; Sammlung Oppenländer,

Nr. 332; Sammlung Niessen, Taf. III, 9a, 9b, 11h; Taf. II, 9o, 9l, 9k; Сорокина 1962, c. 213, ил. 1

92.
FRAGMENTS OF VESSELS

Italy. 1st century BC — 1st century AD (1, 3, 4, 6); Alexandria or Italy. First half of 1st century AD (2, 5); Eastern Mediterranean or Italy. 1st century BC — 1st century AD (8); Alexandria. Second half of 1st century BC (9); Eastern Mediterranean, possibly Syria. First half of 1st century AD (10)

L 2.3—5.2
Received in 1984 from V.Kononov collection (1—9); in 1852 from A. & G.Laval collection (10)
E 3247a, E 3251b, E 3280, E 3271, E 3276, E 3262h, E 3259, E 3257c, E 3272, E 201g
(in order)   ill. on p.15

First ever publication

Analogies: Sammlung Niessen, Taf. II, 9a, 13b, 13d; Taf. III, 11h; Taf. 1, 12; Sammlung Oppenländer, Nr. 317, 332; Berger, Taf. 2, *20*; Hayes, no. 65; Fitzwilliam Mus., no. 34c

93.
BOWL

Eastern Mediterranean or Italy. Late 1st century BC — early 1st century AD

H 5; D rim 17.1
Received in 1852; found in 1852 in Kertch, possibly in Pantikapaion necropolis
П.1852.1   ill.60, 62

Semi-spherical form; with thick walls, smooth rim and external ribs. Semi-clear violet glass, with spiral dulled white insets, dim on the outside and more distinct on the inside, imitation of multi-layered agate.

Manufacturing technique: Mosaic; mould-pressed. Ribs sliced off; inner surface and outside rim polished by buffing; circumference of doubled grooves (D 7.5) with protuding dot in centre (D 0.8) on bottom; body with ribs polished by firing.

Condition: Small chips along rim; inner surface heavily iridescent, with whitish film.

Literature: ДБК, табл. LXXVIII, 5, 6; ABC, pl. LXXVIII, 5, 6; Шелковников, ил. 7; Художественное стекло, ил. 10; Художественное ремесло, кат. 299; Качалов, c. 90, ил. 50

Analogies: Marconi, pl. 37 (ill.); Sammlung Oppenländer, Nr. 328; Masterpieces, no. 51; Matheson, no. 40; Smith Collection, no. 127; Sammlung Hentrich, Nr. 17; L. Kraskowska. Roman Glass Vessels from Slovakia // JGS, 1981, vol. 23, p. 12, fig. 2; Recent Important Acquisitions // JGS, 1966, VIII, p. 128, no. 3

94.
ALABASTRON

Eastern Mediterranean or Alexandria (Egypt). 1st century BC

H remnant 16.3; D rim 1.8; GD 2.4
Received in 1902; bought from L.Gauhman as found in Olbia
E 810   ill. 52, 53

Spindle-shaped form, with sliced and melted rim, embossed band on upper section of body. Glass of interchanging stripes of various colours: wide semi-clear honey-brown and narrow dimmed white (veins); imitation of onyx.

Condition: Lower section of vessel lost; cracks; minor losses; surface iridescent, covered in silver film in places.

First ever publication

Analogies: Oliver 1967, p. 27, no. 1—5; Auth, no. 43; Fossing, p. 114, fig. 86; K.T.Luckner. Ancient Glass. Ancient Art at the Art Institute of Chicago. The Art Institute of Chicago Museum Studies, vol. 20, no.1, p. 87, ill. 62. Chicago, 1974

95.
FLASK

*Alexandria (Egypt) or Italy
First half of 1st century AD*

H 6; D: rim 2; GD 5; bottom 3.2; thickness of walls 0.2—0.3
Received in 1900 from A.Novikov collection; found on the territory of Pantikapaion necropolis
E698   ill. 65

Body in form of squeezed sphere; with cylindrical curved neck, flanged rim; flat bottom. Glass of stripes of various colours: wide of violet-blue, emerald-green and gold; narrow purple stripes and white veins, in imitation of stone.

Manufacturing technique mixed: Interglass gilding, mosaic and free blowing. Golden stripes are achieved by placing foil cracked when hot between two layers of clear colourless glass. Surface polished by buffing; circumferences of double grooves on shoulders and bottom, circumferences of single grooves on middle section of body.

Condition: Cracks and chips on lower section of body; surface iridescent in places.

Literature: Кунина 1970, c. 224—228, ил. 1

Analogies: Doppelfeld, Taf. 3; Oliver 1967, p. 24, fig. 16; p. 25, fig. 17, 18; Grose 1984, p. 33, fig. 11

96.
FLASK

*Alexandria (Egypt) or Italy
First half of 1st century AD*

H 7.4; D: rim 2; GD 4.4; bottom 2.4; thickness of walls 2—2.5
Received in 1915 from D.Tolstoy collection
E 1044   ill. 65

Pear-shaped biconical body; with distinctly modelled shoulders, cylindrical neck, flanged rim, flat bottom. Glass from

stripes of various colours: wide stripes of dark-blue, emerald-green and golden; narrow purple stripes and white veins in imitation of coloured stone.

Manufacturing technique mixed: Interglass gilding, mosaic and free blowing. Golden strips are made by placing foil cracked when hot between two layers of clear, colourless glass. Circumferences of double grooves on shoulders and bottom, circumferences of single grooves on lower section of body.

Condition: Good.

Literature: Художественное стекло, ил. 12, right; Кунина 1970, c. 224—228, ил. 2; Художественное ремесло, no. 274

Analogies: Saldern 1964, p. 42, no. 1; Oliver 1967, p. 24, fig. 14, 15; Recent Important Acquisitions // JGS, 1980, vol. 22, p. 88, no. 3; Sammlung Löffler, Nr. 30 (Farbtafel III); Smith Collection, no. 145; La Baume, Nr. M5, Taf. 52, *2*; Fitzwilliam Mus., no. 36; Glass of the Caesars, p. 41, № 17

97.
PYXIS

Alexandria (Egypt) or Italy. First half of 1st century AD

H 4.3; D: rim 5.5; bottom 4.7; thickness of walls 2.5
Received in 1883; found in 1883 in Pantikapaion necropolis (grave no. 6, below kurgan; together with cat. 185)
П.1883.6   ill. 65

Cylindrical form, with flange for lid and rounded transition to a flat bottom. Glass from stripes of various colours: wide dark-blue, emerald-green and golden; narrow white, in form of veins.

Manufacturing technique: Possible mould-pressing. Golden stripes are achieved by placing foil between two layers of clear colourless glass. Surface polished on both sides; circumference of doubled groove (D 3.6) on bottom.

Condition: Crack on lower section of body.

Literature: OAK for 1882—1888, c. XXV—XXVI; Художественное стекло, ил. 12 (left); Кунина 1970, c. 224—228, ill. 4

Analogies: Recent Important Acquisitions // JGS, 1962, vol. IV, p. 139, no. 4; p. 25, no. 1—9; Smith Collection, no. 143, 144; Oliver 1967, Glass of the Caesars, p. 42, no. 18 — in colour

98.
BOTTOM OF FLASK

*Alexandria, Egypt
First half of 1st century AD*

H remnant 3.1; GD 5.4; D bottom 2.7; thickness of walls 2.5—3.5
Received in 1848; found in 1843 in one of the Pantikapaion necropolis kurgans (together with cat. 204)
П.1843.38   ill. 64

Lower section of flask analogous to cat. 74 in form, glass colour, decoration and manufacturing technique. Double groove around bottom.

Literature: ДБК, I, с. LXVI, II, табл. LXXVII, 16, 16а; III, с. XXVII; ABC, pl. LXXVII, 16, 16а; Кунина 1970, с. 224—228, ил. 3

Analogies: See cat. 96

99.
FLASK

Eastern Mediterranean
First half of 1st century AD

H remnant 10; D rim 1.5; GD 8.3; bottom 2 Received in 1926 from S.Stroganov collection
E 1199   ill. 51

Body in form of squeezed sphere; with high conical neck; small, slightly concave bottom. Dark honey-yellow glass, with light-yellow patterns in imitation of agate. Decoration in form of vertical stripes lowering in loops from the neck and forming a five-petal "flower" on the shoulders. Stripes winded in spiral on bottom and lower section of body.

Manufacturing technique mixed: Mosaic and free blowing.

Condition: Upper section of neck with rim lost; surface heavily iridescent, with dimmed beige and silvery-lilac film; original colours retained on bottom.

First ever publication

Analogies: SH, П.1908.46; П.1908.47; Smith Collection, no. 156; La Baume, Nr. 15, 1, Taf. 57, 1; Matheson, no. 67, 70; Dusenbery 1967, p. 41, fig. 15, 16; Dusenbery 1971, p. 27, fig. 49; Fitzwilliam Mus., no. 58a; Sammlung Löffler, Nr. 45; Auth, no. 318, 319; Fremersdorf IX, Nr. 158

100.
FLASK

Eastern Mediterranean
First half of 1st century AD

H 8.5; D: rim 1.2; GD 5; bottom 2
Received in 1926 from S.Stroganov collection
E 1180   ill. 63

Spherical body, high conical neck with smooth outlines; sliced rim; small, slightly concave bottom. Clear honey-yellow glass, with opaque yellow and white patterns; in imitation of agate.

Manufacturing techique mixed: Mosaic and free blowing.

Condition: Cavities in places.

Literature: Glass, p.256, No. 235

Analogies: Compare: Sammlung Löffler, Nr. 45; Sammlung Oppenländer, Nr. 352; Matheson, no. 67, 71; compare with cat. 99

101.
FLASK

Eastern Mediterranean or Italy. First half of 1st century AD

H 8.6; D: rim 2.2; GD 6.5; bottom 2.9
Received in 1893 from J.Lemme' collection
E 495   ill. 59

Spherical body, with narrow cylindrical neck, "collar" rim; flat bottom. Semi-clear glass of blue and violet stripes, dimmed glass of white and light-blue stripes.

Manufacturing technique mixed: Mosaic and free blowing.

Condition: Cavities in places, top shining layer on most of surface lost.

First ever publication

Analogies: Matheson, no. 68; Sammlung Oppenländer, Nr. 346; Auth, no. 51, rim — no. 309

102.
FLASK

Eastern Mediterranean or Italy
First half of 1st century AD

H 11.5; D: rim 2.9; GD 7.3; bottom 4.6
Received in 1914 from AC; bought in 1912 in Parutino as coming from Olbia
Он.3830   ill. 58

Pear-shaped body; with cylindrical neck narrowing upwards, "collar" rim, slightly concave bottom. Glass from stripes of various colours: brown, light-blue, yellow, blue, descending from neck onto body in loop-like pattern and halting at bottom. Gold foil visible through one stripe on bottom.

Manufacturing technique mixed: Mosaic, free blowing, with interglass gold foil.

Condition: Glued back together again from pieces; unrecovered parts compensated by plaster.

First ever publication

Analogies: Auth, no. 309; compare: ibidem, no. 52; 313; Hayes, no. 80; Sammlung Oppenländer, Nr. 360; Matheson, no. 68; Sammlung Löffler, Nr. 51; Kisa I, S. 169, Abb. 84; compare: cat. 101

103.
BEADS

Alexandria, Egypt. 1st—2nd centuries AD

L necklace 5.7; beads: 0.9x0.7; 1.1x0.8; 1.1x0.9; 1.2x1; thickness 0.4—0.5
Received in 1854; found in 1853 in Pantikapaion necropolis (stone crypt)
П.1853.17   ill. 66

Necklace of forty six mosaic glass beads and one amber one. Glass beads in form of rectangular plaques with four types of intricate two-sided multi-coloured geo-metrical decoration. On three of them representations of human faces framed by squares, forming carpet ornamental design.

Condition: Three beads are broken; many heavily iridescent, their surfaces dulled.

Literature: Individual plaques: Алексеева 1971, с. 179, ил. 2, 19; с. 183; Алексеева 1982 (1), табл. 48:57; табл. 49:31, 43; 85, text с. 37 (E.Alexeyeva suggests that the necklace came from the one workshop and the similar plaques represent pieces of four rods)

Analogies: To certain types of pattern: Алексеева 1982 (1), табл. 49:82, 84

104.
BEAD

Alexandria, Egypt. Late 1st century BC — early 1st century AD

D2.1
Received in 1912; found in 1910 in Pantikapaion necropolis (grave no. 51/9/)
П.1910.62   ill. 66

Round, lens-shaped in slit, with orifice through it, into which bronze wire with ear for suspension has been passed. Dimmed greenish-blue glass; with intricate two-sided ornamentation. Representation of face in frame of green and white circumferences and septagon star with rays of minute white, red, yellow, dark-green and light-blue squares in centre. White face; purple eyebrows, pupils, mouth and outlines of eyes and nose; red outline of mouth. Top half of face outlined by lilac line; red rectangle above forehead.

Condition: Surface shabby; bronze oxidized.

Literature: ИАК, 1913, вып. 47, с. 61, grave 51 (9), с. 59, ил. 17; Алексеева 1971, с. 179, ил. 2, 20; Алексеева 1982 (1), табл. 48:52, с. 41, тип 456

105.
PLAQUE

Alexandria, Egypt. Late 1st century BC — early 1st century AD

H 1.5; W 1.4
Received in 1912; found in 1909 in Pantikapaion necropolis [grave no. 57 /4/]
П.1909.46   ill. 66

Rectangular form. Semi-clear turquoise glass. Representation of female head in complicated head-dress on both sides. White face; dark-purple eyebrows and outlines of eyes and nose; red mouth; locks of hair and pupils of clear amber-yellow glass. Dark-lilac head-dress, in form of hat with bow at top, hanging down across face and tied under chin; yellow meandering girdle above fore-

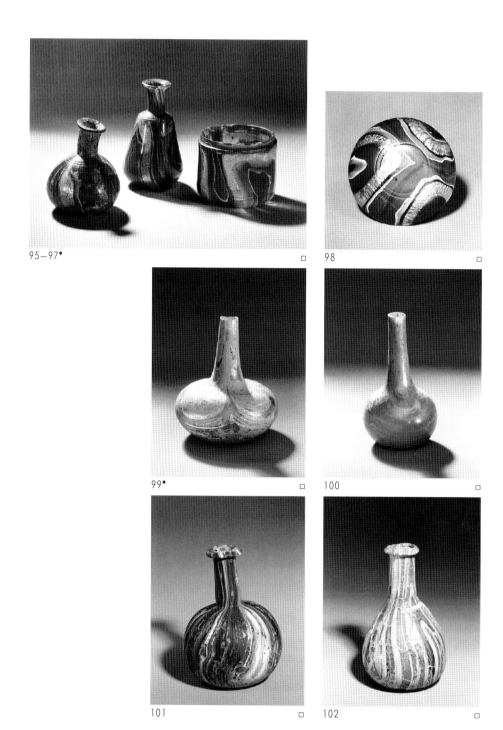

95–97*

98

99*

100

101

102

103–106

107, 108

108

head; small white squares with ovals inside at side ends of head-dress.

Condition: Upper corners of plaque lost. E.Alexeyeva (1971, с. 41, тип 455) suggests that the plaque had a bronze plate mounting with a loop for protecting; hence the absence of any aperture.

Literature: ИАК, 1913, вып. 47, с. 22, grave 57 (4), ил. 12; Алексеева 1971, с. 179, ил. 2, *5*; Алексеева 1982 (1), табл. 48:53

106.
BEAD

Alexandria, Egypt. 1st—2nd centuries AD

D 1.3
Received in 1924 from SAHMC; found in 1909 in Olbia necropolis (grave 12)
O.1909.46   ill. 67

Disc-shaped, with orifice through it. Dull light-green glass; representation of female face in frame of blue and red circumferences in centre on both sides. Light face, with white rectangular inset from eyebrows down to tip of nose; dark-lily eyebrows, pupils, hair and outlines of eyes and nose; red mouth.

Condition: Surface iridescent; colour, except of eyes, has lost its brightness.

Literature: Алексеева 1971, с. 179, ил. 2, *10*; Алексеева 1982 (1), табл. 48:41

Analogies: Compare with Алексеева 1982 (1), табл. 48:33—40, 42

107.
BEADS

Mediterranean or Alexandria (Egypt) 1st—3rd centuries AD

D. beads 1.2—1.5
Received in 1925 from Stieglitz Museum; bought in 1882 in Kertch from Ya.Buksil
E 1116   ill. 66

Necklace of ten spherical beads with intricate multi-coloured geometrical decoration.

Condition: Surface of seven beads iridescent to various degrees; colours have lost their brightness.

First ever publication

Analogies: Compare with Алексеева, 1982 (1), табл. 49:27, 35, 76—79

108.
BEADS

Mediterranean or Alexandria (Egypt) 1st—3rd centuries AD

D beads 2.1; 2.5; 2.7
Received in 1925 from Stieglitz Museum (together with cat. 107)
E 1116   ill. 66

Three large spherical beads with intricate multi-coloured geometrical patterns. Layer of mosaic glass enveloping turquoise core; decoration of middle section of each bead includes representation of female face: four faces on one bead, five on each of the other two. White faces, yellow hair; dark-lily eyebrows, pupils, outlines of eyes and nose and locks of hair; red mouth. On one of the beads the woman's head is set off by a red turban with rows of green rectangles.

Condition: Surface iridescent; on two beads colour has lost its brightness in many places.

First ever publication

Analogies: Compare with Sammlung Wolf, Nr. 149—151

109*   □   110*   □   111*   □   112*   □

113 а   □   113 б

114 а   114 б   114 в

115 а   115 б   □   116   □

PART 4.
MOULD-BLOWN GLASS
1st — 4th centuries AD

109.
AMPHORA

Master Ennion. Sidon, Syria
Early 1st century AD

H 17.7; D: rim 6.5; GD 10; bottom 5.7
Received in 1852; found in 1852 in
Pantikapaion necropolis
П.1852.54   ill. 68, 69

Barrel-shaped body; with wide neck, rim
in form of bolster, flat bottom. Elegant
vertical handles. Clear amber-brown glass.
Continuous relief ornamental design of
six tiers between relief girdles of hoops
and dots. Rows of elongated petals
(1 and 6) on neck and lower body;
stylized branches alternate with palmettes
(2) on shoulders; beneath them frieze of
network pattern (3), girdle of winding
branch and frame with two-line inscription
ЄΝΝΙΩΝ ЄΠΟΙЄΙ ("Ennion made") (4),
and tier of vine shoots (5) farther down.
Three relief concentric circumferences
with protuberance in centre on bottom.
Amphora is an early work by the master
Ennion and represents one of the only few
two-handled vessels with rich decoration
made by him.

Manufacturing technique: Blown in four-piece
mould (three for walls, one for bottom), judging
by the position of the vertical seams (two on
sides of front part with brand, one in middle of
opposite side).

Condition: Cracks on neck; silvery film of
iridescence on surface in places; surface
corroded and has almost totally lost its
brightness.

Literature: ДБК, табл. LXXVIII, 1—4; ABC,
pl. LXXVIII, 1—4; Kisa I, S. 167 (glass
mistakenly given as colourless), II, S. 657,
Abb. 274; Froehner, 1879, p. 65, 125 (6c);
АДЖ, с. 210; Harden, 1935, с. 168;
Шелковников, ил. 5; Кунина 1973,
с. 102—106, ил. 1—6; Качалов, с. 89, ил. 48

Analogies: Compare with Cypriot hexagonal
amphorae from Metropolitan Museum; Forbes

R.I.Studies in Ancient Technology. Vol. 5.
Leiden, 1966, p. 167, fig. 30 (identical brand);
compare with cat. 110—112

110.
OENOCHOE

Ennion's workshop (?). Sidon, Syria
First half of 1st century AD

H 17.9; D: neck 4—4.8; GD 10.2; bottom 5.6
Received in 1896; found in 1895 in
Pantikapaion necropolis ("Demetra's crypt";
together with cat. 111)
П.1896.32   ill. 71

Body narrowing downwards; with high
neck, curved rim; slightly concave bottom. Elegant handle, with flat protuberance at top. Clear light-green glass.
Continuous relief ornamental design of
four tiers between relief belts reminiscent
of decoration on Ennion's amphora (see
cat. 109). Rows of elongated petals on
neck and lower section of body, large
palmettos on shoulders, network pattern
in middle of body. Compressed circumference with protuberance in middle in
centre on bottom.

Manufacturing technology: Blown in three-piece
mould (two for walls with neck, one for lower
part with bottom), judging by the position of
the seams. M.Rostovtsev (АДЖ, p. 210, 514),
G.M.Richter (The Room of Ancient Glass,
Supplement to the Bulletin of the Metropolitan
Museum of Art, 1911, Lune, p. 16) and
D.B.Harden (Harden, 1935, p. 164) are
convinced that the unsigned oenochoae found
in the Pantikapaion necropolis (cat. 111, 112)
were created at Ennion's workshop.

Condition: Good.

Literature: АДЖ, с. 210, табл. LXI. 2; с. 514;
Кунина 1973, с. 106—111, ил. 7, 10—12;
Художественное ремесло, с. 65, no. 259
(ил. on с. 67)

Analogies: See cat. 111, 112; Smith Collection,
no. 68; compare with jugs with brand:
ЄΝΝΙΩΝ ЄΠΟΙЄΙ, ibidem, no. 67;
G.M.Richter. The Room of the Ancient Glass.
Supplement to the Bulletin of the Metropolitan

Museum of Art, 1911, June, p. 16, fig. 16;
Israeli, p. 35, fig. 1—3 and on frontispiece

111.
OENOCHOE

Ennion's workshop (?). Sidon, Syria
First half of 1st century AD

H 18.1; D: neck 4.4; GD 10.2; bottom 5.6
Received in 1896; found in 1895 in
Pantikapaion necropolis ("Demetra's crypt",
together with cat. 110)
П.1896.33   ill. 72

Indentical in shape to cat. 110. Clear
dark-blue glass; external decoration in
form of spots of dull white and yellow
glass. Continuous relief ornamental design identical to cat. 110 and reminiscent
of Ennion's amphora (cat. 109).

Manufacturing technique: See cat. 110; blown in
the same mould.

Condition: Handle and part of neck lost;
dent on shoulder.

Literature: АДЖ, с. 210, табл. LXI, 1;
Кунина 1973, с. 106—111, ил. 8

Analogies: See cat. 110

112.
OENOCHOE

Ennion's workshop (?). Sidon, Syria
First half of 1st century AD

H 18; D: neck 4.4—4.8; GD 10.3; bottom 5.4
Received in 1896 from V.Vyrubov collection
E 560   ill. 70

Identical in shape to cat. 110, 111. Clear
dark-blue glass; external decoration in
form of spots of dull white glass. Relief
ornamental design of four tiers identical
to cat. 110, 111 and reminiscent of
Ennion's amphora (cat. 109).

Manufacturing technique: See cat. 110, 111; blown
in the same mould.

Condition: Glued back together again from
pieces.

Literature: Кунина 1973, с. 106—111, ил. 9;
Художественное ремесло, с. 65, кат. 260

Analogies: See cat. 110

117 а   □   117 б   117 в   117 г

118   □   119   □   120   □

121, 122   □   123—125   □   126   □

127* а   127 б   128

113.
BEAKER

Syria. 1st century AD

H 6.6; D: rim 6.7; bottom 6.1
Received in 1924 from SAHMC; found in 1914
in the environs of Kertch (grave 1)
П.1914.17   ill. 73

Cylindrical form; with slightly flanged rim. Clear light-blue glass. Relief ornamental design of two horizontal tiers with garlands (six in each) and frieze with inscriptionλΑΒΕΤΗИΗΕΙΚΗΝ("Win a victory") between tiers. Tiers bordered by narrow girdles. Palm branches on walls conceal vertical seams from mould. Relief circumference with depression in centre on bottom.

Manufacturing technology: Blown in three-piece mould (two equal ones for walls, one for bottom). Rim faintly processed.

ΚΛΑΒΕ ΤΗИ ΚΝΕΙΚΗ Ν Κ

Condition: Glued back together again from pieces; losses to walls compensated by film.

Literature: Художественное стекло, ил. 8; Кунина 1968, с. 220 сл., ил. 1, *1*; 2, *1*; Кунина 1973, с. 133 сл., ил. 23

Analogies: Harden 1935, p. 178—179; Harden, 1944—1945, p. 92; Smith Collection, no. 96; Sammlung Oppenländer, Nr. 454

114.
BEAKER

Syria. 1st century AD

H 7.2; D: rim 7; bottom 4
Received in 1893 from J.Lemme' collection
E 403

Form narrowing downwards; with rounded walls, flat bottom. Clear yellow-green glass. Relief frieze of garlands with inscriptionλΑΒΕΤΗИΗΙΚΗΝ ("Win a victory" — two groups of six letters alternating with two pairs of wreaths) between two doubled girdles. Palm branches on sides betweengarlands conceal vertical seams from mould. Relief dot on outside bottom; relief border on lower section of body.

Manufacturing technique: Blown in three-piece mould (two equal ones for walls, one for bottom).

Condition: Surface heavily iridescent.

Literature: Кунина 1968, с. 222, ил. 1, *2*; 2, *2*; Художественное ремесло, кат. 290

Analogies: Marconi, p. 41, fig. 10

115.
BEAKER

Syria. 1st century AD

H 7.4; D: rim 7; bottom 6.8
Received in 1926 from S.Stroganov collection
E 1196   ill. 74

Cylindrical shape; with slightly flanged rim; flat bottom. Clear bluish-green glass. Relief ornamental design of alternating double girdles and horizontal stylized palm branches; frieze with inscription ΚΑΤΑΧΑΙΡΕΚΑΙΕΥΦΡΑΙΝΟΥ ("Be healthy and happy") in middle. Vertical palm branches divide decoration and inscription into two parts and conceal seams from mould. Two impressed concentric circumferences on outer bottom.

Manufacturing technique: Blown in three-piece mould (two equal ones for walls, one for bottom).

Κ ΚΑΤΑΙΧΑΙΡΕ Κ ΚΑΙΕΥΦΡΑΙΝΟΥ Κ

Condition: Rim glued back together again from pieces; damaged in places; surface heavily iridescent.

Literature: Кунина 1968, с. 224 сл., ил. 1, *3*; 2, *3*; Художественное ремесло, кат. 289

Analogies: Harden 1935, pl. XXV, a, b, c; Harden 1944—1945, pl. VIII, 3, 4; Smith Collection, no. 94; Israeli, p. 35, 36, fig. 4; other variant of inscription: ΚΑΤΑΧΑΙΡΕΚΑΙΕΥΦΡΑΙΝΟΥ. See: Sammlung Oppenländer, Nr. 453; Fitzwilliam Mus., no. 51

116.
BEAKER

Eastern Mediterranean or Italy
First half (?) of 1st century AD

H 7.2; D: rim 7.8; bottom 4.3
Date and circumstances of acquisition unknown
E 22   ill. 75

Cylindrical shape, walls tapered at bottom. Clear light-green glass. Relief ornamental design of three layers: laurel leaves under double girdle (1); rosettes between petals and circles (2); masks (from left to right) of Medusa, Mænades, lion, young satyr (3). Vertical tiers divide ornamental design into three equal parts and conceal seams from mould. Relief embossed circumference on bottom with dot in centre.

Manufacturing technique: Blown in four-piece mould (three for walls, one for bottom). Rim sliced off.

Condition: Cracks; losses along rim; surface iridescent.

First ever publication

Analogies: Compare with A.P. di Cesnola. Salaminia (Cyprus). London, 1882, p. 187, fig. 182

117.
BEAKER

Syria. First half of 1st century AD

H 12.5; D: rim 6.8; bottom 4.8
Received in 1875; bought in 1875 in Kertch
E 223   ill. 76

Almost cylindrical shape; with narrow lower section (pedestal of sorts). Clear yellow-green glass. Smooth wide stripe near rim and tapered lower section of walls; relief representations of figures of four gods facing each other in pairs (Jupiter and Bacchus, Sylvanus and Neptune) on body, fluted columns. Ionic capitals joined garlands of leaves. Three concentric circumferences (inner two compressed) on outside bottom.

Manufacturing technology: Blown in five-piece mould (four for walls, one for bottom), as the position of four seams partly concealed by columns indicates. Belongs to special group of mould-blown beakers with relief representations of four mythological characters, usually Neptune and Bacchus (the others without exact identification). See G.D.Weinberg, Mould-Blown Beakers with Mytholgical Scenes // JGS, 1972, vol. XIV, p. 26—47).

Condition: Cracks; piece of rim glued back on.

Литература: L.Stephani. Erklärung einiger im Jahre 1873 im südlichen Russland gefundenen Kunstwerke. C.R, 1874. St. Petersburg, 1877, p. 25 ff, pl. I, no. 9, 10; Kisa II, Abb. 271; Kisa III, S. 719, 720; Кунина 1973, с. 134—138, ил. 24 (on с. 134); Художественное ремесло, с. 70, 71, кат. 291; Glass, p. 255, no. 232

Аналогии: SH, E 644 (Кунина 1973, с. 134—138, ил. 25, on с. 136) identical to the published one; R.Lozar. Ein Glasbecher mit Göttfiguren aus Črnelo // Glasnik Muzejskoga društva za Sloveniju v Lublani. 1935, S. 103, fig. 1, pl. I, II; Berger, Taf. 8, Nr. 128; Cp. Hayward, p. 55, no. 9, fig. 11—14 (the figures of the gods stand on pedestals)

118.
BEAKER

Eastern Mediterranean or Northern Italy
Second half of 1st century AD

H 14.2; D: rim 7.1; bottom 4.6; thickness of walls 0.2—0.3
Received in 1931 from A.Bobrinsky collection
E 2222   ill. 77

Body gradually narrowing downwards; with walls vertical near rim. Clear light-blue glass. Continuous relief ornamental design of five rows of lotus buds arranged in chessboard fashion. Smooth walls near rim and narrow smooth stripe near bottom. Two relief concentric circumferences and one impressed one on bottom.

Manufacturing technique: Blown in four-piece mould (three for walls, one for bottom), as the position of seams indicates. Rim sliced off and crudely ground.

Condition: Glued back together again from pieces; chip along rim, holes in walls; surface iridescent in places.

First ever publication

Analogies: Smith Collection, no. 71, 72; Sammlung Oppenländer, Nr. 455; Hayes, no. 83; Auth, no. 78, 79; Matheson, no. 126; Masterpieces, no. 62; compare: Fogolari e Scarfi, Tav. 66; Сорокина 1962, с. 217, ил. 4; compare: Sammlung Cohn, Nr. 44 (relief points between buds); Fitzwilliam Mus., no. 56

119.
BEAKER

Syria. Late 1st century — first half of 2nd century AD

H 9; D: rim 5.9; bottom 3.7
Received in 1914; found in 1912 in
Pantikapaion necropolis (grave 30, together with cat. 218)
П.1912.15   ill. 78

Body narrowing downwards, with sharp bend of walls near top (shoulders of sorts) and smooth concave walls near rim. Clear bluish-green glass. Continuous relief ornamental design of diamonds, in imitation of pine-cone. Relief border along edge with dot in centre on outer bottom. Noted for its painstaking workmanship, perfection of details of ornamental design, thin walls and light glass.

Manufacturing technique: Blown in three-piece mould (two for part of walls with rim, one for bottom), as the position of seams indicates.

Condition: Cracks; dent along rim; surface iridescent.

Literature: ИАК, 1916, вып. 60, с. 15; Кунина, Сорокина, с. 163, ил. 8, *24*; Кунина 1973, с. 139, ил. 26; Художественное ремесло, кат. 292

Analogies: Compare: La Baume, Nr. 5 (Taf. 45, 2); Recent Important Acquisitions // JGS, 1970, vol. XII, p. 172, no. 7; Calvi 1968, tav. 16, 2 (cat. 250)

120.
BOWL

Eastern Mediterranean (Syria ?)
First half of 1st century AD

H 4.4; D: rim 11.8; bottom 4.2; inner omphalos 5.1
Received in 1870; presented by S.Tsibulsky
E 217   ill. 95

Semi-spherical form, with sharp bend of walls near top (shoulders of sorts) and concave walls near rim. Clear greenish glass. Close relief ribs along body, almost reaching rim. Bottom heavily pressed inwards (omphalos of sorts). Three relief concentric circumferences with dot in centre on outside bottom. Omphalos of semi-spherical form with flat top and dot in centre.

Manufacturing technique: Blown in three-piece mould (one for walls with bottom, two for upper section of walls with neck), as the position of seams, hardly visible near rim, indicates.

Condition: Surface, particlarly outside, iridescent.

First ever publication

Analogies: Sammlung Oppenländer, Nr. 451; compare with cat. 121, 122

121.
BOWL

Syria. Second quarter — mid 1st century AD

H 4.5; D: rim 6.5; bottom 3.6
Received in 1891; found in 1891 in
Pantikapaion necropolis
П.1891.820   ill. 93

Semi-spherical shape; with walls, slightly concave near rim and tapering towards bottom. Clear yellowish glass, with accidental stains. Close relief ribs along body, wide smooth frieze near rim. Distinct relief concentric circumferences with protuberance in centre on outside bottom.

Manufacturing technique: Blown in three-piece mould (one for walls with bottom, two for upper section of walls with rim), as the position of seams (hardly visible near rim) indicates.

Condition: Surface slightly iridescent.

Literature: Кунина 1973, с. 131, ил. 223, *3*

Analogies: SH, П.1902.140; E 681; cat. 122; Кунина 1973, с. 131, ил. 22, *1, 2, 4*; Сорокина 1965 (1), с. 185, ил. 1; № 3 (without ill. — SHM, 5533). All analogies found in towns of Bosporan Kingdom (5 in Pantikapaion, 1 in Nymphaion, 1 in Kepoi). Compare: Sammlung Oppenländer, Nr. 450; Berger, Taf. 9, 139 (Taf. 18, 37); Liepmann, Nr. 14; Benko, tabl. XXXVI, 4 (13/3) — other dimensions

122.
BOWL

Syria. Second quarter — mid 1st century AD

H 4.5; D: rim 6.5; bottom 3.6
Received in 1912; found in 1910 in
Pantikapaion necropolis (grave 47 /5/, together with cat. 38, 178)
П.1910.143   ill. 93

Identical in shape and ornamentation to cat. 121. Clear bluish-green glass.

Manufacturing technique: Identical to cat. 121, blown in the same mould.

Condition: Surface slightly iridescent.

Literature: ИАК, 1913, вып. 47, с. 57, 58; АДЖ, табл. LIX A, 4, 5; Сорокина, 1965 (1), с. 185, № 2 (without ill.); Кунина, Сорокина, с. 158, ил. 6, *12*; Кунина 1973, с. 131, ил. 22, *1*

Analogies: See cat. 121

123.
OENOCHOE

Syria. Second half of 1st century AD

H 11.3; D: rim 4.1; GD 7.8; bottom 3.8
Received in 1930 from Alexeyev collection
E 1900   ill. 80

Spherical body; with low neck. Narrow, smoothly curved handle, with looped protuberance at top. Clear violet glass; handle of clear pink glass. Three friezes of impressed ornamental design on body; double rows of small circles on shoulders and lower section; wide girdle of large intersecting rings with small circle in centre on bottom. Relief circumference with dot on bottom.

Manufacturing technique: Body blown in four-part mould (three for walls, one for bottom), as the position of seams (hardly visible, spaced at equal distances from each other) indicates.

Condition: Surface iridescent.

Literature: Художественное ремесло, кат. 261 (without ill.)

Analogies: See cat. 124, 125; compare body: with cat. 126; Сагинашвили, кат. 12; Hayes, no. 95; Auth, no. 83

124.
JUG

Syria. Second half of 1st century AD

H 12.2; D: rim 3.6; GD 7.8; bottom 3.8
Received in 1930 from Alexeyev collection
E 1901   ill. 80

Spherical body; with high neck, massive bolster-shaped rim, narrow spout. Handle with groove in middle, smoothly curved and slightly raised above rim. Clear honey-yellow glass; handle of opaque bluish-white glass. Impressed ornamental design, identical to cat 123, on body. Relief circumference with dot in centre on bottom.

Manufacturing technique: Body blown in the same mould as cat. 123, 125.

Condition: Surface iridescent.

First ever publication

Analogies: See cat. 123, 125

125.
OENOCHOE

Syria. Second half of 1st century AD

H 11.3; D: rim 4.8; GD 7.8; bottom 3.8
Received in 1949 from I.Tolstoy collection
E 2988   ill. 80

Spherical body; with low neck. Curved handle, with two external ribs and double looped protuberance at top. Clear violet glass. Impressed ornamental design, identical to cat. 123, 124, on body. Relief circumference with dot in centre on bottom.

Manufacturing technique: Blown in the same mould as cat. 123, 124.

Condition: Surface iridescent.

First ever publication

Analogies: See cat. 123

126.
FLASK

Syria. Second half of 1st century AD

H 17.1; D: rim 2.4; GD 8; bottom 3.7
Received in 1900 from A.Novikov collection; found on the territory of Nymphaion (probably in the necropolis)
E 642   ill. 79

Spherical body; with stepped shoulders, high narrow neck, muff-shaped rim; flat bottom. Clear light-blue glass. Impressed ornamenal design, identical to cat. 123—125, on body. Two close concentric circumferences with dot in the centre on bottom.

Manufacturing technique: Blown in three-piece mould (two of different sizes for body, one for bottom).

Condition: Surface iridescent.

Literature: Художественное ремесло, кат. 275 (without ill.)

Analogies: La Baume, Nr. C 23, Taf. 13, 3; compare ornamental design with cat. 123—125

127.
FLASK

Eastern Mediterranean. Second half of 1st century AD

H 16.2; D: rim 3; GD 9.5; bottom 4
Received in 1887; found in 1887 in Pantikapaion necropolis (grave 102)
П.1887.9

Body in form of slightly compressed (from the face side) sphere; with high narrow neck, muff-shaped rim; bottom of irregular (close to circumference) outlines, framed by bolster. Clear olive-green glass; lilac runs on neck. Relief ornamental design on facade sides of body in form of large six-petal rosette, framed by meander with swastikas: double petals on one; pointed leaves with vein in the middle of leaves on other; diamond shapes between ends of leaves.

Manufacturing technique: Body blown in two-piece mould, as the position of single relief seam in the middle of side parts and bottom indicates.

Condition: Surface iridescent and dulled in places.

First ever publication

Analogies: Dusenbery 1971, p. 14, fig. 9 (amongst the author's analogies is a vessel

from the Museum of Glass in Corning, see footnote 38a); E.Dillon. Glass. London, 1907, pl. VI (centre); compare ornamental design with cat. 128 and 11—12th century Iranian vessels (R.Hasson. Memorial Institute for Islamic Art, Spring 1979, p. 32, no. 60)

128.
FLASK

Syria. 1st century AD

H 11.5; D rim 2.9; W 8.2; bottom: 3 x 3.1
Received in 1893 from J.Lemme' collection
E 493

Body in form of heavily compressed (from the face side) sphere; with low neck, flanged irregular rim. Small, distinct square bottom. Vertical handles, curved near neck. Clear yellow glass. Relief ornamental design on facade sides of body in form of two concentric circumferences with six-petal rosette (within central one) and girdle of helixes (within outer one).

Manufacturing technique: Body blown in two-piece mould, as indicated by the position of the single relief seam.

Condition: Surface iridescent; silvery crust on one of the sides.

Literature: Художественное ремесло, кат. 278

Analogies: Сагинашвили, кат. 10; Israeli, p. 40, fig. 15; Dusenbery 1971, p. 14, fig 7; Sammlung Cohn, Nr. 43; Sammlung Oppenländer, Nr. 436; Auth, no. 67; Sammlung Löffler, Nr. 64; compare system of ornamental design with cat. 127

129.
AMPHORISKOS

Syria (Sidon ?). 1st century AD

H 8.9; D: rim 2; GD 4.4; bottom 2.5
Date of acquisition unknown; found in Pantikapaion necropolis
ПАН.586   ill. 94

Ovoid body; with low neck, thick bolster-shaped rim; flat bottom. Vertical handles, curved near rim. Clear greeny-blue glass. Continuous relief ornamental design, in imitation of wickerwork basket, with laurel wreathes round middle of body and noosed girdle under handles, on lower section of neck and on body.

Manufacturing technique: Body blown in two-piece mould. Painstakingly made.

Condition: Good.

Literature: Художественное стекло, ил. 9; Кунина 1973, с. 112, ил. 13

Analogies: Sammlung Oppenländer, Nr. 431; Auth, no. 63; Calvi 1968, tav. 16, 4 (cat. 246); Matheson, no. 128; compare: Israeli, p. 39, no. 8a, 8b, fig. 12, 13; R.Zahn, Sammlung. Baurat Schiller. Berlin, 1929, Taf. 9, Nr. 308

130.
SMALL JUG

Syria. 1st century AD

H 10.2; D: rim 3.1; bottom 2.4
Received in 1893 from J.Lemme' collection
E 498   ill. 85

Ovoid body; with low neck and slightly flanged rim. Narrow, curved handle, with looped protuberance rising above rim. White dull glass; handle of clear brown glass. Relief ornamental design of winding shoots with buds, divided by vertical lines into four equal parts, on body.

Manufacturing technique: Blown in two-piece mould, as the position of single relief seam, concealed on body by two of the vertical lines of the ornamental design, indicates.

Condition: Glued back together again; losses on walls; unrecovered parts of walls compensated by putty; surface iridescent.

Literature: Художественное ремесло, кат. 270 (without ill.)

Analogies: Israeli, p. 40, fig. 14 (with two handles)

131.
SMALL JUG

Syria (Sidon ?). 1st century AD

H 9.9; D: rim 2.7; bottom 3
Received in 1900 from A.Novikov collection; found on the territory of Nymphaion, probably in the necropolis
E 704

Hexagonal body; with rounded shoulders, cylindrical neck, bolster-shaped rim. Smoothly curved handle with groove in middle and double flat semi-circular protuberance at top. Clear greenish glass. Relief cane ornamental design on shoulders and lower section of body; wide frieze of six rectangular panel-facets, separated from each other by relief verticals, on middle section. Relief representation on each panel in following order: diagonal cross, oenochoe, amphora, reed-pipe, disc with circumference and protruding circle in centre, amphora. Three relief concentric circumferences with cavity in centre on bottom.

Manufacturing technique: Blown in multi-piece mould (two horizontal sections for lower sections of neck with shoulders and body with bottom; six horizontal ones for panels — seams coincide with edges. Apart from this, five vertical seams run in middle of each facet, with the exception of the one with the cross, starting from top and reaching the representation).

Condition: Glued back together again from pieces; losses on shoulders and bottom of body; surface iridescent in places.

Literature: Кунина 1973, с. 115 (without ill.); Художественное ремесло, кат. 269 (without ill.)

129*

130*

131

132, 133

134—136

137, 138

139—141

142—144

145*

146—148

149—151

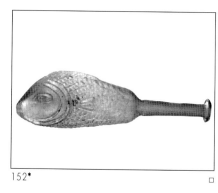

152*

Analogies: Smith Collection, no. 79; Hayes, no. 84; Sammlung Oppenländer, Nr. 443; Matheson, no. 123

132.
SMALL FLASK

Syria (Sidon ?). 1st century AD

H 7.3; D: rim 2.5; bottom 2.3
Received in 1931 from RAIC collection
E 2436

Figured body distinctly divided horizontally into three parts: rounded shoulders, hexagonal body and base with walls tapering sharply towards bottom (pedestal or pad-base of sorts). Borders of sections are distinctly modelled, silhouette altered by haut-relief. With strongly marked cylindrical neck, wide bolster-shaped rim. Semi-clear dark-violet glass. Indistinct relief ornamental design of six leaves, shoots of which join in arcs, on shoulders. Six bouquets, separated from each other by columns, in middle section of body. Haut-relief representations (one on each side) in the following order: bunch of grapes, pomegranate, cone; repeated in the same order on next three facets. Ornamental design of alternating leaves and buds at bottom.

Manufacturing technique: Blown in three-piece mould, as the positions of three seams, concealed by columns and dividing bottom into three equal sections, indicates.

Condition: Good.

Literature: Кунина 1973, с. 115, ил. 15, *4*; Художественное ремесло, кат. 276

Analogies: Cat. 133; Sammlung Oppenländer, Nr. 406, 407 (from dark-blue glass); compare with Auth, no. 65

133.
SMALL FLASK

Syria (Sidon ?). 1st century AD

H 7.3; D: rim 1.8; bottom 2.2
Received in 1926 from S.Stroganov collection
E 1224

Figured body (see cat. 131); with high separate cylindrical neck, flanged rim. Dull white glass. Decoration and manufacturing technique identical to cat 132.

Condition: Surface iridescent.

Literature: Кунина 1973, с. 115, ил. 15, *3*

Analogies: See cat. 132

134.
SMALL FLASK

Syria (Sidon ?). 1st century AD

H 8; D: rim 2.1; bottom 2.3
Received in 1915 from D.Tolstoy collection
E 1045

Almost ovoid body; with high neck widening slightly upwards, with narrow bolster-shaped rim, walls of base tapering towards bottom. Dull milky-white glass. Relief three-tier ornamental design. Six arcs with a bud in each in upper tier; six rectangular panels, separated from each other by columns with capital, base and pedestal, in middle section. Representation on each panels in the following order: crater with fruit, jug, hydria, oenochoe, kantharos with fruit, hydria. Pattern of twelve alternating leaves and cones on bottom.

Manufacturing technique: Body blown in three-piece mould, as the position of three seams concealed by columns and dividing bottom into three equal sections, indicates.

Condition: Surface iridescent; shine lost.

Literature: Кунина 1973, с. 115, ил. 15, *2*; Художественное ремесло, кат. 277

Analogies: See: cat. 135; Smith Collection, no. 77; Neuburg, pl. 41, 42; Cat. Damas, fig. 39; Стекло древней Армении, cat. 105; La Baume, Nr. C9, Taf. 9, 2; Sammlung Oppenländer, Nr. 401—405; Fitzwilliam Mus., no. 54 a,b; Matheson, no. 122; Auth, no. 328. Similar vessels from many museum and private collections were possibly manufactured in the one workshop, since usually only the combinations of elements in the ornamental design differ, as a result of the intersubstitution of standard sections of moulds.

135.
SMALL FLASK

Syria (Sidon ?). 1st century AD

H 8; D: rim 1.8; bottom 2.3
Received in 1930 from Alexeyev collection
E 1899

Ovoid body; with high neck narrowing upwards, with slightly flanged rim. Clear light-violet glass. Relief ornamental design similar to cat. 134, 136, but differs in suite and combination of vessels in rectangular panels — in following order: jug, crater with fruit, hydria, crater with fruit, jug, hydria.

Manufacturing technique: Identical to cat. 134

Condition: Surface iridescent.

Literature: Кунина 1973, с. 114, ил. 15, *1*; Smith Collection, no. 80

Analogies: See cat. 134

136.
SMALL FLASK

Syria (Sidon ?). 1st century AD

H 8.1; D: rim 2.4; bottom 2.4
Received in 1854; found in Pantikapaion necropolis
ПАН.599

Ovoid body; with low neck, collar rim. Relief ornamental design similar to cat.

134, 135, but differs in suite and combination of vessels in rectangular panels — in following order: crater with fruit, hydria, oenochoe, kantharos with fruit, oenochoe, oenochoe.

Manufacturing technique: Identical to cat. 134.

Condition: Hole on body; cracks on greater part of surface; original colour and shine lost.

Literature: ДБК, табл. LXXVII, 7; ABC, pl. LXXVII, 7; Кунина 1973, с. 113, ил. 14

Analogies: See cat. 134

137.
AMPHORISKOS

Syria. Second half of 1st century — early 2nd century AD

H 6.5; D: rim 2.5; GD 3.8
Received in 1893 from J.Lemme' collection
E 492

Four-sided body; with cut shoulders, low neck, collar rim; intricate body with wide facadal semi-spherical sides inserted in hexagon and narrow six-edged sides; conical bottom. Smoothly curved handles. Clear light-violet glass; handles of dimmed bluish-green glass, with violet runs. Relief ornamental design in form of two concentrical circumferences with dot in centre on each of facadal sides.

Manufacturing technique: Body blown in two-piece mould.

Condition: Rim glued back together again from pieces; small part of rim lost.

Literature: Кунина 1973, с. 124, ил. 19, *2*; Художественное ремесло, кат. 268 (without ill.)

Analogies: Кунина 1973, с. 124, ил. 19, *1* (SH, П.1903.169); Сагинашвили, кат. 7, 8; Стекло древней Армении, кат. 122—124; Smith Collection, no. 87, 88; Sammlung Oppenländer, Nr. 437; La Baume, Nr. C11; Taf. 9, 4; Auth, no. 68; Sammlung Löffler, Nr. 65; SH, E 1608; E 3219; Matheson, no. 130; Кунина 1974, с. 83, ил. 1, *3* (SH, E 3219); Богданова, с. 56, табл. XIX, 6

138.
AMPHORISKOS

Syria (Sidon ?). Second half of 1st century AD

H 6.3; D: rim 3; GD 4; bottom: 1 x 0.8
Received in 1891; bought in Kerch
E 310

Ovoid body; with high, almost cylindrical, neck, wide rim; rounded bottom. Vertical handles, curved near neck. Clear colourless glass; handles of clear light-violet glass. Relief ornamental design of long narrow petals (downwards from neck and upwards from bottom), divided by girdle with helixes, on body.

Manufacturing technique: Body blown in two-piece mould.

Condition: Surface iridescent.

Literature: Кунина 1973, с. 121, ил. 17, *3*;
Художественное ремесло, кат. 266

Analogies: SH, П.1871.53; П.1909.17;
П.1902.148; П.1902.102; E 1046; E 490;
cat. 140, 141; Кунина 1973, с. 119, ил. 16,
с. 121, ил. 17; Стекло древней Армении,
кат. 107—111; Сагинашвили, кат. 1, 2;
Dusenbery 1967, p. 40, fig. 14; Zouhdi, p. 53,
no. 63, fig. 40; Kern 1954, p. 38, 39, fig. 9;
Smith Collection, no. 75; Sammlung
Oppenländer, Nr. 413—415; Auth,
no. 66, 329; Sammlung Hentrich, Nr. 39;
Sammlung Löffler, Nr. 71

139.
FLASK

*Syria (?). Second half of 1st century — early
2nd century AD*

H 7.2; D: rim 2.6; GD 4.3; bottom: 1.4 x 1.7
Received before 1854; found in Kertch
(in Pantikapaion necropolis ?)
ПАН.590   ill. 84

Ovoid fluted body; with low distorted
neck, flanged rim. Thick, round handle.
Clear, light-violet glass; handle of semi-
clear, greenish glass.

Manufacturing technique: Blown in two-piece
mould. Seams do not join at bottom, therefore
jug cannot stand.

*Condition: Rim glued back together again
from pieces; loss of particle; surface
iridescent.*

Literature: ДБК, табл, LXXVII, 9; ABC, pl. LXXVII,
9; Кунина 1973, с. 123, ил. 18

Analogies: SH, E 313; E 418 (from J.Lemme'
collection, probably from Southern Russia);
SHM, 34405 (from Pantikapaion necropolis);
Богданова, с. 56, табл. XIX, 7 (from necropolis
near Zavetnoye, Crimea, grave 99); Marconi,
p. 39, fig. 37 (right); compare: Sammlung
Oppenländer, Nr. 426—428; Сагинашвили,
кат. 4—6; Стекло древней Армении,
кат. 116—118

140.
AMPHORISKOS

Syria (Sidon ?). Second half of 1st century AD

H 7.1; D: rim 2.8; GD 4.4; bottom 2
Received in 1924 from SAHMC; found in 1907
in Pantikapaion necropolis
П.1907.94   ill. 84

Ovoid body; with low neck, wide rim.
Small, smoothly curved handles. Clear
purple-violet glass; handles of semi-clear
yellow glass. Relief frieze of helixes between girdles on middle section of body;
continuous cane ornamental design on
upper and lower sections.

Manufacturing technique: Blown in two-piece
mould; joint of seams is inaccurate, therefore
one half of the vessel has slipped downwards
by 0.3 cm and horizontally by 0.1 cm.

Condition: Surface slightly iridescent.

Literature: Кунина 1973, с. 119, ил. 16, *3*

Analogies: See cat. 138; Кунина 1974, с. 83,
ил. 1, *3*

141.
FLASK

Syria (Sidon ?). Second half of 1st century AD

H 6.7; D: rim 2.3; GD 4.1; bottom 1.9
Received in 1904 from AC; found in 1903 in
Pantikapaion necropolis
П.1903/4.19

Ovoid body; with low neck, bolster-
shaped rim. Small, rounded handle. Clear
light-violet glass; handle of semi-clear
light-blue glass. Wide relief frieze of
helixes between double girdles on middle
part; continuous relief ornamental design
of narrow petals on upper and lower
sections.

Manufacturing technique: Blown in two-piece
mould; joint of seams is inaccurate, therefore
the lines of the ornamental design do not
converge, and bottom does not form a regular
circumference.

Condition: Surface slightly iridescent

Literature: Кунина 1973, с. 119, ил. 16, *1*

Analogies: See cat. 138, 140; SH, E 1046
(amphoriskos)

142.
AMPHORISKOS

Syria. Second half of 1st century AD

H 8.1; D: rim 3.2; GD 3.9
Received in 1893 from J.Lemme' collection
E 491

Ovoid body; with low neck, wide flanged
rim. Small, vertical, slightly curved handles. Clear light-violet glass; handle of
clear greenish glass. Continuous relief
ornamental design of girdle-ribs on the
body.

Condition: Surface iridescent.

Literature: Художественное ремесло, кат. 267
(without ill.); Кунина 1973, с. 127 (without ill.)

Analogies: SH, E 1233; Сагинашвили, кат. 9;
Стекло древней Армении, кат. 120; Spatz,
Nr. 37, Taf. 37; Sammlung Hentrich, Nr. 40;
Hayes, no. 85; Кунина 1974, с. 83, ил. 1, *2*
(SH, E 3220); compare also with cat. 143, 144

143.
AMPHORISKOS

Syria. Second half of 1st century AD

H 11.1; D: rim 2.3; GD 4.6; bottom 1.2
Received in 1903; found in 1903 in
Pantikapaion necropolis (grave 31)
П.1903.17

Ovoid body; with cylindrical neck, almost horizontal rim. Elegant, smoothly
curved handles. Clear yellow glass. Ornamental design on body and

manufacturing technique identical to
cat. 142, 144

Condition: Good.

Literature: ИАК 1905, вып. 17, с. 10, ил. 5;
Кунина 1973, с. 126, ил. 20

Analogies: SH, E 1233; cat. 142, 144;
Sammlung von Kirchner-Schwarz, Taf. 1,
Nr. 91; Smith Collection, no. 85; Стекло
древней Армении, кат. 119; Sammlung
Oppenländer, Nr. 418, 424; La Baume,
Nr. H 7 (Taf. 45, *4*); Sammlung Löffler, Nr. 63
(Taf. 7, *2*); Fitzwilliam Mus., no. 57; Auth,
no. 69, 333; Fremersdorf III, Taf. 32

144.
SMALL JUG

Syria. Second half of 1st century AD

H 7.5; D: rim 2.8; GD 3.8
Received in 1891; bought in Kertch
E 313

Ovoid body; with wide cylindrical neck,
bolster-shaped rim; pointed bottom. Thin,
smoothly curving handle, with protuberance on top. Clear light-violet glass. Ornamental design on body and manufacturing
technique identical to cat. 142, 143.

Manufacturing technique: Body blown in two-piece
mould, together with bottom.

*Condition: Neck and upper section of walls
glued together again from pieces; losses;
surface iridescent.*

First ever publication

Analogies: See cat. 142, 143

145.
SHELL FLASK

*Eastern Mediterranean (Syria ?)
1st century AD*

H 11.5; D: rim 3
Received in 1905 from AC; found in Olbia
E 917   ill. 92

Body in the shape of two-fold shell
(comb); with short neck widening slightly
upwards, flanged rim. Dull blue glass.
Continuous fan-shaped, grooved decoration on body follows the structure of
shell; modelled scroll-leaf at side.

Manufacturing technique: Blown in two-piece
mould.

*Condition: Surface iridescent; of dull lilac
shade.*

Literature: Художественное ремесло, кат. 307
(without ill.)

Analogies: Masterpieces, no. 65; compare:
Dusenbery 1971, p. 15, fig. 11; Calvi 1968,
Tav. 15, tav. 17, *1* (cat. 255)

146.
DATE FLASK

Syria. Mid 1st — mid 2nd centuries AD

H 8; D: rim 2.4
Received in 1931 from A.Bobrinsky collection
E 2156   ill. 91

Body in shape of date; with high cylindrical neck, wide flanged rim; rounded bottom. Clear violet glass. Embossed decoration on body in imitation of the uneven, bumpy surface of the dried fruit.

Manufacturing technique: Blown in two-part mould, seam concealed by relief.

Condition: Part of rim lost; surface slightly iridescent.

Literature: Кунина 1973, с. 129, ил. 21, *4*; Художественное ремесло, кат. 309

Analogies: See cat. 147, 148, SH, П.1909.6 (Кунина 1973, с. 129, ил. 21, *3*); ОЛ.46; Marconi, p. 39, fig. 7; Стекло древней Армении, кат. 127—129; Toll, pl. XLIV, no. 6; Zouhdi, no. 37; fig. 30; Neuburg, pl. XV, 50; Smith Collection, no. 256; Sammlung Oppenländer, Nr. 476—478; La Baume, Nr. H6, Taf. 45, 3; Spartz, Taf. 8, 36; Hayes, no. 87—89; Matheson, no. 139—148; Auth, no. 70, 344; Fitzwilliam Mus., no. 97a, b; Sammlung Löffler, Nr. 72; Sammlung Hentrich, Nr. 45, 46; compare with Calvi 1968, tav. 17, *3* (cat. 251)

147.
DATE FLASK

Syria. Second half of 1st century AD

H 6.3; D rim 1.6
Received in 1901; found in 1899 in Pantikapaion necropolis (grave 75)
П.1899.71   ill. 91

Body in shape of date; with short neck, flanged rim; rounded bottom. Semi-clear yellowy-brown glass. Decoration and manufacturing technology identical to cat. 146.

Condition: Part of rim lost; surface iridescent

Literature: ИАК, 1901, вып. 1, с. 92; Кунина 1973, с. 128, 129, ил. 21, *1*; Кунина, Сорокина, с. 167, ил. 10, *47*

Analogies: See cat. 146

148.
DATE FLASK

Syria. First half of 1st century AD

H 7.1; D rim 1.9
Received in 1866; found in 1866 in Pantikapaion necropolis (grave 1)
П.1866.32   ill. 91

Body in shape of date; with short neck, flanged rim; rounded bottom. Semi-clear yellowy-brown glass. Decoration and manufacturing technique identical to cat. 146, 147.

Condition: Silvery film of iridescence shot with lilac on surface in places.

Literature: Кунина 1973, с. 129, ил. 21, *2*

Analogies: See cat. 146

149.
GRAPE FLASK

*Eastern Mediterranean (Syria ?)
2nd century AD*

H 9.9; D: rim 5.1; GD 6.6 bottom 3.6
Received in 1928 from E.Shuvalova collection (bought in Italy ?)
E 1494   ill. 81

Ovoid body; with short wide neck widening upwards, bolster-shaped rim; thick modelled bolster along bottom of neck; base of body in shape of narrow ring-support; flat bottom. Clear brown glass. Continuous relief decoration of small semi-spheres on body, in imitation of the surface of a bunch of grapes. Smooth, pointed leaf on each of the two sides of shoulders. Four relief concentric circumferences on bottom.

Manufacturing technology: Blown in two-part mould; seam concealed by leaves.

Condition: Surface slightly iridescent.

Literature: Художественное ремесло, кат. 308; Glass, p. 254, no. 231

Analogies: Harden 1940, p. 103, fig. VI; compare La Baume, Nr. C18, Taf. 12, *2*; compare with cat. 150, 151

150.
GRAPE FLASK

*Eastern Mediterranean (Syria ?)
2nd century AD*

H 12.5; D: rim 2.8; GD 6.6; bottom 3.6
Received in 1928 from E.Shuvalova collection (bought in Italy ?)
E 1488   ill. 81

Ovoid body; with grooved waist round middle of stepped shoulders, high cylindrical neck smoothly turning into upper protecting section of shoulders, rim curving inwards; base of body in shape of thin ring-support. Small handles, carelessly made. Clear light green glass. Decoration of body and manufacturing technology identical to cat. 149 (blown in the one mould ?). Four feebly-marked embossed concentric circumferences on flat bottom, pontil-mark in centre.

Condition: Surface slightly iridescent.

Literature: Художественное стекло, ил. 17

Analogies: La Baume, Nr. C18, C19, Taf. 12, *2, 3*; Auth, no. 72, 335, 336; Matheson, no. 279; Smith Collection, no. 258; Dusenbery 1971, p. 14; fig. 10; Liepmann, S. 44, Nr. 18

151.
GRAPE FLASK

*Eastern Mediterranean (Syria ?)
2nd century AD*

H 12; D: rim 4; GD 6.6; bottom 3.6

Received in 1898 from M.Sivadjan collection; bought in Syria
E 1343   ill. 81

Ovoid body, identical to cat. 149, 150; with high cylindrical neck, massive collar-rim. Clear honey-brown glass. Decoration and manufacturing technology identical to cat. 149, 150 (blown in the one mould ?).

Condition: Surface slightly iridescent.

First ever publication

Analogies: See cat. 149

152.
BOTTLE

Eastern Mediterranean (?) 2nd – 3rd centuries AD

L 25; D rim 3
Received in 1926 from S.Stroganov collection
E 1203   ill. 82, 83

Flattened body in shape of fish with large head; long cylindrical neck with bolster-shaped rim. Clear light-green glass. Embossed decoration in imitation of scales, gills and fins on body; large eye outlined by relief bolster, with small circle in centre.

Manufacturing technique: Blown in two-part mould (joins at top and bottom of body).

Condition: Surface slightly iridescent.

Literature: Художественное ремесло, кат. 306 (without ill.)

Analogies: Compare: Masterpieces, no. 77; Recent Important Acquisitions // JGS, 1960, vol. II, p. 139, no. 7; Recent Important Acquisition // JGS, 1974, vol. XVI, p. 125, no. 4

153.
DIONYSUS

Eastern Mediterranean (Syria ?). Second half (?) of 2nd century AD

H remnant 12.1; GD 8.8; D bottom 5.1
Received in 1902; found in 1902 in Chersonesos necropolis (grave 1386)
X.1902.14   ill. 89

Body in shape of sculptured head of young Dionysus; with delicate facial features, slightly swollen lips, sunken pupils, dimple on chin. Clear glass. Coiffure of fine, wavy hair reaching down to neck; above forehead a headband with the attributes of Dionysus: two round fruits and large vine leaves. Free and wide modelling of face and hair at the front, symbolical and graphical at the back. The sliced end of the short neck forms the bottom with a sunken representation of the head of Medusa; the additional decoration on the bottom is fairly uncommon. The lively image, realistic execution and tender modelling put this work

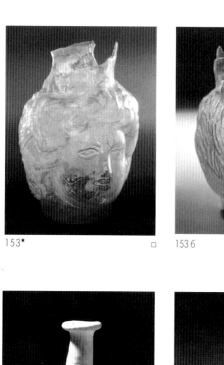

153*

153 б

153 в

154

155 а

155 б

156

157

158

159

amongst the best figure-vessels in the museums of the world.

Manufacturing technique: Blown in three-piece mould (two for the head, one for the bottom).

Condition: Glued together again from pieces; large part of neck, tip of nose and part of coiffure at back lost; milky-white deposit of iridescence on surface.

Literature: ОАК for 1902, с. 44, ил. 77a, 77б; ИАК, 1904, вып. 9, с. 13, ил. 6, 7; Качалов, с. 84, ил. 42; Сорокина 1968, с. 184, ил. 3, 7; Художественное ремесло, кат. 304 (without ill.); В.М.Зубарь. Некрополь Херсонеса Таврического I—IV вв. н. э. Киев, 1982, с. 92, ил. 60 (in centre); Соколов, № 146; Sokolow, Nr. 124

Analogies: Compare: Sammlung Cohn, Nr. 49; Bucovala, Nr. 237a, b; Sammlung Oppenländer, S. 161, Nr. 467, Farbtafel, also p. 171 (no information on the representation on the bottom of the vessel); compare with vessel in shape of head of young Dionysus from Kepoi necropolis: Сорокина, op. cit., с. 182, ил. 1, 2; Сорокина 1977, с. 134, ил. 5

154.
HEAD FLASK

Syria. Late 1st century — 2nd century AD

H 7.1; D: rim 2.1; bottom 2.2; GW 4.1
Received in 1926 from S.Stroganov collection
E 1221

Body with two-sided representation of sculptured head of Medusa; with high neck narrowing upwards, bolster-shaped carelessly made rim; with neck-base widening downwards. Dull white glass. Expressive face, clean-cut features, large nose, prominent chin, half-opened mouth (slit). Serpents framing face rendered in stylized manner.

Manufacturing technique: Blown in two-part mould (vertical seam along sides moves over onto bottom, dividing it into two sections).

Condition: Large part of surface damaged, has yellowy shade.

Literature: Художественное ремесло, кат. 281 (without ill.)

Analogies: Smith Collection, no. 286; La Baume, Nr. C13, Taf. 10, 2, 3; Sammlung Cohn, Nr. 48; Recent Important Acquisitions // JGS, 1964, vol. VI, p. 156, 157, no. 6; Sammlung Oppenländer, Nr. 461

155.
HEAD FLASK

Syria. Late 2nd century — early 3rd century AD

H 7.5
Received in 1900; found in 1897 in Chersonesos necropolis (crypt 982)
X.1897.61   ill. 86, 87

Body with two-sided representation in shape of sculptured head with two faces:

youth with headband on forehead (young Dionysus ?) and Medusa; with high cylindrical neck, bolster-shaped rim; small cylindrical neck-base. Dimmed white glass. The youth has a fine, elongated face, with narrow chin, wide-open eyes and sunken pupils. His hair is stylized, the curls along the cheeks are intertwined with ribbons. The face of Medusa is broad and coarse, with a flattened nose and evil smile. Serpents and hair are reproduced very schematically, in indistinct relief.

Manufacturing technique: Blown in two-piece mould.

Condition: Nose on the youth's face lost; patches of brown deposit on the surface.

Literature: ОАК for 1897, с. 126, ил. 242, 243; с. 30, ил. 92a, 92б; Художественное ремесло, кат. 302 (without ill.); Сорокина 1968, с. 187, ил. 3, 8, 9

Analogies: Sammlung Oppenländer, Nr. 460; Smith Collection, no. 280; Dusenberry 1971, p. 16, fig. 13, 14; Sammlung Cohn, Nr. 47; compare with La Baume, Nr. C13, Taf. 10, 2, 3 (face of Medusa)

156.
DOUBLE-HEAD FLASK

Syria. Late 2nd century — early 3rd century AD

H 8.3; D: rim 4; GD 5; D bottom 3.5
Received in 1931 from SAHMC; previously in A.Bobrinsky collection
E 2155   ill. 88

Spherical body with two-sided relief picture of two similar (?) child's faces; with high, almost cylindrical, neck, wide funnel-shaped rim; flat bottom. Clear yellow glass. Prominent pupils, curls in form of large relief spheres. Small relief cross on bottom. The relief on one of the faces is indistinct, hence it is impossible to attempt to say whether they are identical.

Manufacturing technique: Blown in three-part mould (two for the head, one for the bottom).

Condition: Surface iridescent.

First ever publication

Analogies: La Baume, Nr. C14, Taf. 10, 4; Hayes, no. 94; compare: Sammlung Oppenländer, Nr. 466; Sammlung Cohn, Nr. 51; Matheson, no. 191

157.
DOUBLE-HEAD JUG

Syria. Late 2nd century — early 3rd century AD

H 7.1; D: rim 2.2; GD 4.8; bottom 3.2
Received in 1891; bought in Kertch
E 312   ill. 88

Body with two-sided representation in shape of sculptured head with two similar

child's faces; with short neck, modelled rim; flat, smooth bottom of irregular outlines. Flat, sharply curving handle, touching forehead of one of the faces, fused into the rim. Clear honey-yellow glass. Sunken pupils, prominent eyebrows, spherical curls. Low, indistinct relief.

Manufacturing technique: Blown in three-part (?) mould (two parts for the faces, one for the bottom); side joins reach the bottom; carelessly made.

Condition: One side of vessel, rim and handle corroded.

Literature: Художественное ремесло, кат. 279 (without ill.)

Analogies: Dusenbery 1971, p. 17, fig. 15; Matheson, no. 191; Sammlung Oppenländer, Nr. 465; Sammlung Hentrich, Nr. 49; compare: Liepmann, Nr. 17; Auth, no. 74; La Baume, Nr. C 14, Taf. 10, 4; SH, E 1321

158.
DOUBLE-HEAD FLASK

Syria. Late 2nd century — early 3rd century AD

H 7.5; D: rim 2.7; GD 5.4; bottom 3.5
Received in 1909; presented by Grigory IV, Patriarch of Antioch
E 1402   ill. 88

Body with two-sided representation in shape of sculptured head with two similar child's faces; with narrow neck, constriction near base, wide rim; short and wide base/neck. Semi-clear glass, of bright-green, dirty-green, brown, yellow-green, yellow and red stripes. Indistinct relief. Three relief —shaped lines on bottom set in part of relief circumference which may be a part of misplaced and incompletely printed stamp (square in a circle).

Manufacturing technique: Blown in three-part mould (two for the walls, one for the bottom); side joins visible.

Condition: Surface iridescent in places.

Literature: Художественное ремесло, кат. 280 (without ill.)

Analogies: Smith Collection, no. 285; La Baume, Nr. C14, 4, Taf. 11, 1 and Nr. C 14, 5, Taf. 11, 2; Sammlung Oppenländer, Nr. 464; Matheson, no. 188

159.
BOY'S HEAD FLASK

Eastern Mediterranean (Syria ?) 3rd — early 4th centuries AD

H 16.6; D rim 5.5; GD 8.1; bottom: 4.8 x 5.2
Received in 1928 from E.Vinogradova collection
E 1441   ill. 90

Body in shape of sculptured head of boy; with high funnel-shaped, slightly deformed

160* □

161*

162

163

164

165 а □

165 б □

166 а □

166 б

167*а

167 б

168

169 □

170 а

170 б

neck, flat rim (sliced and melted); neck/base widening downwards; deformed, almost oval bottom. Clear greenish glass. Delicate facial features, swollen lips, large wide-open eyes, sunken pupils slightly raised up to eyelid; long hair in large soft locks, with forelock; wide ears. Interpretation of form is stylized, broad and large-scale.

Manufacturing technique: Blown in three-part mould (two for the walls, one for the bottom); side joins clearly seen and reach down to the bottom.

Condition: Crack on side; small loss behind left ear; surface iridescent.

Literature: Шелковников, ил. 3; Художественное стекло, ил. 19; Художественное ремесло, кат. 303

Analogies: Smith Collection, no. 279; A.Greifenhagen, Ancient Glass in the West-Berlin Museum // JGS, 1962, vol. IV, p. 64, no. 9; Recent Important Acquisitions // JGS, 1977, vol. XIX, p. 170, no. 7; D.Whitehouse, Glass of the Roman Empire. Corning, New York, 1988, p. 42, fig. 17

160.
PATERA

Northern Italy (?)
First half of 1st century AD

H 6.2; L with handle 29.6; D: rim 18.1; support 7.4
Received in 1894; found in 1894 in Pantikapaion necropolis (stone crypt; together with cat. 161)
П.1894.7   ill. 98

In shape of cup on stand; straight narrow thick walls, with high protuding profiled rim, cone-shaped pad-base in form of plate; rounded bottom. Straight, fluted handle, with sculptured stylized head of wolf or dog at end. Clear olive-green glass.

Manufacturing technique: Bowl blown in open mould; pad-base and handle subsequently applied.

Condition: Glued together from pieces; losses; surface iridescent; shine lost in places.

Literature: OAK for 1894, с. 44, ил. 67; Кунина 1964, с. 37—39, ил. 7; Художественное стекло, ил. 6; Художественное ремесло, кат. 301; Н.П.Сорокина, М.Ю.Трейстер. Две группы бронзовых зеркал из собрания Государственного Исторического музея // СА, 1983, № 4, с. 147, ил. 2, 7

Analogies: Compare with cat. 161; handles of the paterae with wolf (dog) heads: Smith Collection, no. 382; Froehner 1903, no. 1110, p. 153, pl. 192, 8; compare with animal heads on glass rhytons from Olbia and Aquilea: Ю.И.Козуб. Стеклянный ритон из Ольвии // История и культура античного мира. М., 1977, с. 71, ил. 2

161.
PATERA

Northern Italy (?). First half of 1st century AD

H 6.1; L with handle 30.4; D: rim 20; bottom 9.7
Received in 1894; found in 1894 in Pantikapaion necropolis (with cat. 160)
П.1894.6

In the shape of bowl on pad-base with handle; thick rounded, walls slanting downwards; with massive protecting profiled rim; pad-base in form of upset saucer, with rounded, convex sides and sliced, unground rim. Straight fluted handle with flattened sphere at end.

Manufacturing technique: Bowl blown in open mould; pad-base and handle attached to it.

Condition: Cracks; part of walls with rim and handle glued back on again.

Literature: OAK for 1896, с. 43, 44; Кунина 1964, с. 37—39, ил. 6; Н.П.Сорокина, М.Ю.Трейстер. Две группы бронзовых зеркал из собрания Государственного Исторического музея // СА, 1983, № 4, с. 147, ил. 2, 6

Analogies: Compare with cat. 160. The shape imitates that of metal vessels; the polished rim is borrowed from early Roman Empire clay vessels.

162.
HEXAGONAL JUG

Eastern Mediterranean (?)
Circa mid — 1st century AD

H 17.1; D: rim 3.9; bottom 8.1; W of sides varies, 4.1—4.6 down near bottom
Received in 1872; found in 1872 in Pantikapaion necropolis (grave 4; together with cat. 360)
П.1872.108

Hexagonal body with straight walls; sloping shoulders, distinct construction near neck, bolster-shaped rim; flat bottom. Tape-shaped handle with three external ribs, curved at right angle and loop-shaped curve under rim. Clear bluish glass.

Manufacturing technique: Body blown in open mould; pontil-mark (D 2.3) on bottom.
Condition: Surface dulled in places.

Literature: OAK for 1872, с. XXII—XXIII; Кунина, Сорокина, с. 149, ил. 2, 3; Художественное ремесло, кат. 254

Analogies: Auth, no. 344; Стекло древней Армении, кат. 136; Fremersdorf IV, Taf. 127; Doppelfeld, Taf. 60, 61; Vanderhoeven, no. 128; compare with Vetri Romani, no. 131

163.
RECTANGULAR JUG

Eastern Mediterranean (?). 40s—70s AD

H 21.6; D: rim 5.6; W side 9.8
Received in 1872; found in 1872 in

Pantikapaion necropolis (grave 3; together with cat. 63, 213, 298)
П.1872.95

Massive rectangular body; with broad flat shoulders separated from short neck by distinct constriction; muff-shaped rim; flat bottom. Tape-shaped handle with groove in middle, curved almost at right angle. Clear aquamarine glass.

Manufacturing technique: Body blown in open mould.

Condition: Surface iridescent and dulled in places.

Literature: OAK for 1872, с. XXII

Analogies: Сорокина 1957, табл. 12, 4, compare: Кунина, Сорокина, с. 155, ил. 5, 27; Cadik, pl. 10 (from Southern Russia)

164.
RECTANGULAR JUG

Eastern Mediterranean. Mid — third quarter of 1st century AD

H 16; D rim 4.3; W each side (near bottom) 6.3
Received in 1872; found in 1872 in Pantikapaion necropolis (grave 5; together with cat. 187)
П.1872.118

Prismatic body; with sloping shoulders separated from low cylindrical neck by distinct intake; muff-shaped rim; slightly concave bottom. Tape-shaped handle with wide groove in middle, curved at right angle. Clear aquamarine glass.

Manufacturing technique: Body blown in open mould.

Condition: Good.

Literature: OAK for 1872, с. XXIII

Analogies: Cat. 165; SH, П.1900.11 (Кунина, Сорокина, с. 155, ил. 5, 28); ННФ.66.4 (Кунина 1982, с. 120, ил. 1); Сорокина 1965 (2), с. 230, ил. 12, 19, 20; Cadik, pl. 10, a; compare also Liepmann, Nr. 23 (rim of jug is flat)

165.
RECTANGULAR JUG (WITH BRAND)

Eastern Mediterranean. Second half of 1st century AD

H 17.6; D rim 3.9; W each side (near bottom) 6.7
Received in 1912; found in 1909 in Pantikapaion necropolis (grave 38)
П.1909.20   ill. 96, 97

Prismatic body; with sloping shoulders separated from short cylindrical neck by distinct intake, with muff-shaped rim; flat bottom. Massive tape-shaped handle with groove in middle, curved at right angle. Clear aquamarine glass. Five relief circumferences with dot in centre on bottom: one in middle (D 1.9) and one in each corner (D 1).

171

172*

173

174

175* a

175 б

176

177 * a

177 * б

Manufacturing technique: Body blown in open mould.

Condition: Cracks on shoulders; surface iridescent.

Literature: ИАК, 1913, вып. 47, с. 12

Analogies: See cat. 164

166.
RECTANGULAR JUG (WITH BRAND)

Rhineland (Cologne ?). Third quarter of 1st century AD

H: 11.7; body 8.8; D rim 3.4; bottom: 7 x 7
Received in 1909; found in 1906 in Pantikapaion necropolis (grave 65/11/; together with cat. 346)
П.1906.81   ill. 100

Almost cubic body; with short cylindrical neck, as if sunken into sloping shoulders; with collar-shaped rim; flat bottom. Massive, short, wide, tape-shaped handle, curved almost at right angle. Clear aquamarine glass. Relief brand on bottom: two concentric circumferences with dot in centre and one small one in each corner.

Manufacturing technique: Blown in open mould.

Condition: Surface iridescent.

Literature: ИАК, 1909, вып. 30, с. 73; Кунина, Сорокина, с. 162, ил. 7, *23*

Analogies: Fremersdorf IV, Taf. 116, 117; Kisa I, S. 127, Abb. 64; brand: Сорокина 1965 (2), с. 231, ил. 12, *8*; Кунина 1982, с. 120, ил. 1

167.
RECTANGULAR JUG (WITH BRAND)

Eastern Mediterranean. Second half of 1st century — early 2nd century AD

H: 9.3; body 6.4; D rim 3.3; bottom: 6.2 x 6.2
Received in 1924 from SAHMC;
found in 1914 in Pantikapaion necropolis
П.1914.67

Almost cubic body; with sloping shoulders, cylindrical neck, muff-shaped collar-shaped rim; flat bottom. Wide, tape-shaped handle. Clear light-aquamarine glass. Brand on bottom: one relief circumference in centre (D 2.2) and one in each corner (D 1.1).

Manufacturing technology: Blown in open mould.

Condition: Surface faintly slightly iridescent.

First ever publication

Analogies: Сорокина 1965 (2), с. 231, ил. 12, *16*; without brand: Vessberg 1952, pl. VI, 5; compare brand with cat. 165; Сорокина, op. cit., ил. 12, *17—20*

168.
RECTANGULAR JUG (WITH BRAND)

Rhineland (Cologne ?)
Late 1st century — early 2nd century AD

H: 22; body 16.2; D rim 4.5; bottom: 5.5 x 5.5
Received in 1974; found in 1974 in Nymphaion necropolis (crypt 24, grave 2)
ННФ.74.454

High rectangular body narrowing slightly downwards; with flat shoulders, distinctly protuberant short cylindrical neck, wide rim; flat bottom. Wide tape-shaped handle, with eleven closely set external ribs, curved almost at right angle. Clear bright-blue glass. Brand of two concentric circumferences intersected by diagonal cross with a dot in the centre and rounded protuberances at the ends (D 0.4) on bottom.

Manufacturing technique: Blown in open mould; rim compressed from above.

Condition: Glued together again from many pieces; parts of body lost; many cracks on neck and bottom.

Literature: Кунина 1982, с. 121, ил. 2

Analogies: In shape: Vanderhoeven, no. 69, 70; D.Charlesworth. Roman Square Bottles // JGS, 1966, vol. VIII, p. 35, fig. 18; Vessberg 1952, pl. VI, 4; Fitzwilliam Mus., no. 67a, 68; compare brand with Liepmann, Nr. 22

169.
SMALL RECTANGULAR JUG (WITH TWO COMPARTMENTS)

Rhineland or Gaul. 1st—2nd centuries AD

H: 11.5; body 8.1; bottom 7.7; rim: 2 x 2.2; thickness at top of neck 0.4
Received in 1854; found in 1852 in Pantikapaion necropolis (grave 26)
П.1852.8   ill. 99

Cubic body; with sloping shoulders, short cylindrical neck, flat rim (sliced and melted), slightly concave thick walls; flat bottom. Narrow, tape-shaped handle with

groove in middle, curved at right angle. Clear aquamarine glass. Divided into two sections from rim down to bottom by vertical partition.

Manufacturing technique: Blown in open mould.
Condition: Small crack on shoulders; hole in partition; surface iridescent in places.

Literature: Извлечение, с. 182, ил. 75; ЗООИД, 1859, т. III, с. 545

Analogies: Morin-Jean, p. 66, fig. 47B

170.
SMALL RECTANGULAR FLASK (WITH BRAND)

Eastern Mediterranean. Mid — third quarter of 1st century AD

H 9.2; D rim 2.8; bottom: 3.5 x 3.5
Received in 1912; found in 1909 in the environs of Kertch (grave 97/8/)
П.1909.115

Prismatic body; with sloping shoulders, high wide neck widening slightly downwards, bolster-shaped rim, flat bottom. Clear aquamarine glass. Relief indistinct three-lined brand from Greek letters on bottom.

Manufacturing technique: Blown in open mould.

Condition: Thick silvery film of iridescence on surface.

First ever publication

Literature: ИАК, 1913, вып. 47, с. 33; Кунина, Сорокина, с. 153, ил. 6, *58*

Analogies: Compare shape: Vessberg 1952, pl. VI, 3; Liepmann, Nr. 24

171.
RECTANGULAR FLASK

Rhineland or Gaul. Second half of 2nd century AD

H 12.6; D: rim 2.3; neck 1.2; bottom: 3.4x3.4
Received in 1911; found in 1908 in Pantikapaion necropolis (grave 45/8/)
П.1908.107

Prismatic body; with flat shoulders, very high neck clearly distinct from shoulders, flat wide rim, slightly concave walls; slightly concave bottom. Clear glass, with shades of light yellow.

Manufacturing technique: Blown in open mould (or formed by tools ?); hardly discernable pontil-mark (D 1) on bottom.

Condition: Surface iridescent.

Literature: ИАК, 1911, вып. 40, с. 89; Кунина 1984, с. 155, № 16, табл. III, 16

Analogies: Dusenbery 1967, p. 43, fig. 29;

Morin-Jean, p. 71, fig. 59, 60; Benko.
tabl. XIII, 3 (2n/2); compare with Vessberg
1952, pl. IX, 13

172.
CYLINDRICAL JUG (WITH BRAND)

Master Frontinus. Gaul. 3rd—4th centuries AD

H with handle 17.8; D: rim 3.7; bottom 8.4
Received in 1914; bought from I.Edlis;
accidental discovery at Olbia
E 859   ill. 101

Cylindrical body; with horizontal shoulders,
short narrow neck widening downwards,
flat rim; flat bottom. Tape-shaped handle,
curved almost at right angle, with ribs.
Clear light-blue glass. Six relief hoops on
both upper and lower sections of body;
two relief concentric circumferences with
small circle in centre on bottom; two relief
brands with Latin letters FROTI along edge
of bottom occupying about one-third of
circumference; carelessly made, with uneven gaps between letters. Made at Frontinus's workshop (judging by brand and
shape).

Manufacturing technique: Blown in three-piece
mould (two similar ones for walls with
shoulders and one for the bottom).

Condition: Surface iridescent in places.

Literature: Художественное ремесло, кат. 257;
Кунина 1981, с. 44, 45, ил. на с. 45

Analogies: In shape: Morin-Jean, p. 169,
fig. 223, p. 173, fig. 228; Isings, Form 89;
Kisa I, S. 115, Abb. 57 (left); Sammlung
Hentrich, Nr. 53, 54; two-handled: Isings,
Form 128; Smith Collection, no. 263; Kisa III,
S. 802, Abb. 324 (with other version of
the same master's brand: S. 803, Abb. 324a);
Kisa I, S. 115, Abb. 57 (right); Doppelfeld,
Taf. 52; Spartz, Nr. 99, Taf. 24, 99;
brand: Froehner 1879, p. 130, no. 74; Kisa III,
S. 944, Nr. 41

173.
FLASK

Bosporos' (?). 4th century AD

H 18; D: rim 7; GD 10.3; bottom 5.5
Found in Southern Russia (in Kertch ?)
ПАН.593   ill. 104

Spherical body; with wide, narrowing
neck, funnel-shaped orifice, wide bolster-
shaped distorted rim; concave bottom.
Clear greenish glass. Diagonal spiral
grooving on body.

Manufacturing technique: Blown in open
grooved mould, with rotation; pontil-mark
(D 1.2) on bottom.

Condition: Surface iridescent; heavily corroded.
First ever publication

Analogies: See cat. 175; compare also:
Сорокина 1971, с. 96, ил. 5, *1* (pear-shaped
body); Benko tabl. XXI, 2 (5/3) (squat body);
Сорокина 1963, с. 139, ил. 2, *3* (without
grooving); Скалон 1973, с. 50, ил. 1 (without
grooving). Retort-shaped vessels from greenish
glass are often to be found in 4th—5th
centuries Bosporan necropoleis (usually without
grooving); according to К.Скалон (see p. 51),
they represent works by Bosporan masters;
compare shape with Hayes, no. 202; compare
diagonal spiral grooving: Sammlung
Oppenläner, Nr. 491; Liepmann, Nr. 33;
Harden 1936, pl. XVIII, 612; Hayes,
no. 282, 306; Sammlung Cohn, Nr. 67;
Sammlung Hentrich, Nr. 59—61; Auth, no. 152

174.
FLASK

Bosporos' (?). 4th century AD

H 28.8; D: rim 8.4; GD 17.6; bottom 9.1
Received in 1900 from A.Novikov collection;
found in Kertch (in Pantikapaion necropolis ?)
E 637   ill. 102

Spherical body; with small, narrow neck,
funnel-shaped orifice, flat rim (melted);
concave bottom. Clear greenish glass.
Diagonal spiral grooving on body.

Manufacturing technique: Similar to cat. 173;
note high quality. Pontil-mark (D 2.5) on bottom.

Condition: Cracks on body; surface iridescent.

First ever publication

Analogies: SH, E 2189 (in shape and
dimensions, though not in decoration);
see also cat. 173

175.
JUG (WITH LION'S MASK)

South-eastern Mediterranean (Egypt ?)
4th century AD

H 30; D: rim 8.5; GD 12.3; pad-base 6.9
Received in 1931 from LILI; found in Kertch
(earthen crypt; together with cat. 400)
1820/1042   ill. 103

Ovoid body; shoulderless, with neck
ending in funnel, rim curved inside; with
profiled, massive pad-base. Tape-shaped
handle, with groove in middle, curved at
right angle, with ornamental triangular
modelled protuberance at top. Clear
light-green glass. Spiral grooving on body;
modelled relief lion mask under handle,
thread girdle on neck.

Manufacturing technique: Body blown in grooved
mould (upper boundary distinct at transfer to
neck), with buffing.

*Condition: Part of handle protuberance lost;
surface iridescent.*

Literature: OAK for 1913—1915, с. 101, ил. 168;
Художественное стекло, ил. 23; Скалон

1974, с. 44—48, ил. 4, 5; Искусство
Византии, с. 76, 77, № 94; Засецкая 1993,
с. 92, 93, кат. 368, табл. № 368

Analogies: Kisa I, S. 187, Abb. 93; medallions
with lion masks: Edgar, pl. X, no. 32.768;
Hayes, pl. 37, no. 605 (identical) and no. 606

176.
JUG

Syria. 4th century AD

H 18.1; D: rim 7.2; bottom 5.4
Received in 1884 from M.Sivadjan collection;
found in Syria
E 1334   ill. 105

Cylindrical body; with protruding bolster-shaped shoulders, wide high neck
widening downards; funnel-shaped
stepped orifice; flat bottom. Thick, braid-
shaped, smoothly curved handle. Close-
set vertical ribs with grooving, on body
in imitation of basket weaving. Thick
border and spiral super-imposed thread
on neck. Light-aquamarine glass; handle
and spiral thread of olive-green glass.

Manufacturing technique: Blown in open grooved
mould; pontil-mark on bottom.

Condition: Surface iridescent on one side.

First ever publication

Analogies: SH, E 2599 (shape of body,
ornamental design); Sammlung Cohn, Nr. 60,
61, 68; Sammlung Hentrich, Nr. 71, 72;
Liepmann, Nr. 20; compare ornamental design
with Auth, no. 84, 346

177.
FLASK

Syria. 4th century AD

H 19.5; D: rim 4.5; shoulders 8.1; bottom 6.6
Received in 1900 from A.Novikov collection;
found in Kertch (in Pantikapaion necropolis ?)
E 632   ill. 106

Figured body with four prismatic protuberances, in line with the cross-shaped
bottom; with sloping (bolster-shaped)
shoulders, high narrow neck widening
into a funnel, with protruding rim. Rounded, thick handles, with pinches. Clear
olive-green glass. Thick applied braid
under rim. Diagonal grooving on body.
Impressed honeycomb ornamental design on bottom. The form of the vessel is
unique and is possibly linked to the
spread of Christianity in the Bosporan
Kingdom in the 4th century.

Manufacturing technique: Body blown in open
grooved mould with honeycomb ornamental
design on bottom, with rotation; after this the
body was given the form of a cross.

Condition: Cracks on neck.

First ever publication

Analogies: Compare handles with Sammlung
Hentrich, Nr. 206; compare honeycomb
ornamental design with Auth, no. 91

PART 5.
FREE-BLOWN GLASS
1st—5th centuries AD

178.
AMPHORA (WITH PAINTED DESIGN)

Northern Italy. First half of 1st century AD

H 30; D: rim 4.8; shoulders 8.6; bottom 5.1
Received in 1912; found in 1910 in Pantikapaion
necropolis (grave 47/5/; together with cat. 38, 122)
П.1910.38   ill.107,108

Body widening broadly upwards; with
rounded shoulders, short wide neck,
bolster-shaped rim, small curve of
walls near base; flat bottom. Flat
handles with two ribs, curved at right
angle. Continuous painted plant ornamental design of shoots with vine and
ivy leaves, with birds sitting on them,
on body. Green, yellow, red, light-
blue and white enamel (with subsequent firing) used for shoots; red and
yellow for the birds. Yellow olive branch
between yellow girdles on shoulders.
A unique example of ancient glass-
work; one more painted amphora
(sharp-ended) has been found in Cyprus, as well as several cups.

*Condition: Surface iridescent; painted
design has lost its original colouring on
one side*

Literature: ИАК, 1913, вып. 47, табл. I.
с. 57, сл.; М.И.Ростовцев. Стеклянные расписные
вазы поздне-эллинистического времени
и история декоративной живописи
// ИАК, 1914, вып. 54, табл. IV, 3; АДЖ,
табл. LIX, A, *4, 5;* Шелковников, ил. 4;
Художественное стекло, ил. 14;
Художественное ремесло, кат. 251 (col. ill.);
Silvestrini p. 438, fig. 11; Кунина,
Сорокина, с. 158, ил. 6, *5;* Соколов,
№ 121; Sokolow, Nr. 102; Качалов, с. 88,
цв. ил. 47; D.Battle, S.Cottle. Sotheby's
Concise Encyclopaedia of Glass. London,
1991, ill. on p. 36 (right); Glass, p. 257, no. 237

Analogies: Amphora: Smith Collection, no. 346;
cups: Silvestrini, p. 435, fig. 5, 6; p. 437,
fig. 9; Heron de Vilefosse, Verres antiques
trouvés en Algérie. Revue Archéologique.
Nouvelle serie, XXVII, 1874, p. 281, left,
pl. IX; Smith Collection, no. 169

179.
AMPHORA

*Eastern Mediterranean or Egypt. Second
half of 1st century AD*

H 28.5; D: rim 5.1; shoulders 12.3; bottom 8
Found in 1846 in Pantikapaion necropolis
(kurgan X, grave 3)
П.1846.42   ill.109

Body widening broadly upwards; with
rounded shoulders; high, slightly swollen neck (with intake near body), muff-
shaped rim, small curve of walls near
base, concave bottom. Narrow handles curved almost at right angle, with
wide groove in middle. Clear yellow-
green glass. Three thin engraved girdles alternate with two ground ones
(W 0.3 and 0.5) on body.

*Condition: Neck with handles glued on;
surface iridescent.*

Literature: ДБК, табл. LXXVII, 14; ABC,
pl. LXXVII, 14

Analogies: Compare one-handled jugs: Edgar,
pl. V, 32.540; Кунина, Сорокина, с. 167,
ил. 10, *4, 5;* Auth, no. 131; Sammlung Löffler,
Nr. 99, Taf. 12, *3;* compare shape with
cat. 178

180.
BOWL (WITH PAINTED DESIGN)

*Northern Italy. Second quarter of 1st
century AD*

H 7; D: rim 8.5; GD 9.5; bottom 4
Received in 1914 from AC; bought in 1913;
found in Olbia
Ол.18180   ill.110—112

Semi-spherical shape. Clear colourless
glass. All outer surface of vessel, including
bottom, covered in enamel-painted design (with subsequent firing). The figure of
an antelope, painted in red-brown, black
and white colours with chiaroscuro modelling, runs towards the left amongst green
shrubbery. To its left two ducks hang
projecting by their feet, their heads downwards; to the right of the antelope a duck

(with a branch under it) swims towards the
right amongst thickets. The ducks are
painted in red, black, blue, yellow and
brown colours. On the opposite side three
garlands of flowers, made to look as if
they are hung on ribbons from the upper
edge of the vessel, are tied in a fancy knot.
The two side ribbons (yellow and blue-
white), attached at both ends, form two
loops; the red one in the middle hangs
limply. Apart from flowers, three green
leaves are entwined in each garland on
both sides. On the bottom is a rosette of
eight pointed leaves, red and blue in
alternation, with a blue dot in the centre;
around it is a thin rim of large dark-green
dots. A unique example of ancient glass-
work amongst the very few works on
similar subjects.

*Condition: Glued together again from
pieces; lost parts substituted by film.*

Literature: М.И.Ростовцев. Стеклянные
расписные вазы позднеэллинистического
времени и история декоративной живописи
// ИАК, 1914, вып. 54, с. 1—26, ил. 1;
табл. I, *1, 2;* табл. II; АДЖ, табл. LIX A, *1, 2;*
Художественное стекло, ил. 15; K.Gorbunova
and I.Saverkina. Greek and Roman Antiquities in
the Hermitage. Leningrad, 1975, no. 109;
Соколов, № 125; Sokolow, Nr. 101

Analogies: Sammlung Oppenländer, Nr. 397;
Сорокина 1978, ил. 2, *1;* Silvestrini,
p. 439—441, fig. 12—14; ibid p. 436, fig. 7,
p. 437, fig. 9; Heron de Vilefosse. Verres
antiques trouvés en Algérie. Revue
Archéologique. Nouvelle serie, XXVII, 1874,
p. 281, pl. VIII, IX; Masterpieces, no. 68; Smith
Collection, no. 167—169; fragment of cup with
representation of cockerel: SH, O.1910
(М.И.Ростовцев, op cit.; ИАК, 1914, вып. 54,
табл. 1, *3)*

181.
PAINTED PYXIS (WITH LID)

Egypt (Alexandria) or Syria. 1st century BC

H pyxis 3.1; D rim 13.3; W rim 1.1; D lid 14.4

178*

179

180* a

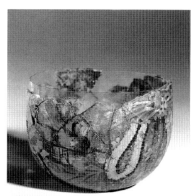

180 б

181* a

181 б

182* a

182 б

182 в

Received in 1900 from G.Kallo collection; found in Olbia

E 805   ill. on p.13

In shape of shallow cup; rounded, thick walls; horizontal, unevenly cut, rim; round bottom. Lid in shape of plate with flat bottom, horizontal shoulders and uneven rim (curving inwards). Clear colourless glass. Ornamental painted design on inside of bottom and from inside of lid across shoulders and rim. Pale trace of golden flower visible on bottom. Painted design on lid of three circular friezes between golden girdles: golden laurel wreath on blue background, intertwined with red tape rendered by diagonal lines with golden edges (central frieze, on shoulders); golden stick ornamental design on red background (middle frieze, in the zone of transition from shoulders to base); row of vertical golden diamonds on red background (outer frieze, along the rim). When observed from above, through the clear glass of the lid, the golden ornamental design stands out distinctively against the red and blue backgrounds and, together with the golden ornamental design on the bottom, creates a bright decorative effect.

Manufacturing technique: Traces of polishing by buffing on outsides of lid and bottom. Design made with size paints (without firing) in sequence: golden ornamental design, red backgrounds, blue background.

Condition: Glued together from many pieces; losses at three places on lid; surface heavily iridescent and dulled on both sides. Painted design damaged: decoration on cup and blue and red colours of friezes almost totally lost. M.I.Rostovtsev in 1914 noticed remnants of gold on the bottom and the presence of four small plaster circles applied at regular intervals on the blue background of the lid, possibly "with the aim...of preventing the colours of the border from coming into contact with the border of the cup".

Literature: М.И.Ростовцев. Стеклянные расписные вазы поздне-эллинистического времени и история декоративной живописи // ИАК, 1914, вып. 54, с. 22—24, табл. VIII

Analogies: Smith Collection, no. 347; compare also: M.Cristofani. La coppa di Tresilico // Klearchos, Anno VIII, no. 29—32. Reggio Calabria, 1966, p. 63—79, fig. 6, 7; compare ornamental design motifs with cat. 48

182.
PYXIS (WITH PAINTED LID)

Cyprus. First half of 1st century AD

H: (with lid) 8.1; pyxis 7.7; D: rim 8.2; GD 9.7; bottom 3.5; lid 8.6
Received in 1926 from S.Stroganov collection
E 1218

Biconical body widening downwards; with narrow, slightly flanged rim, curved walls of body; slightly concave bottom. Lid with smooth concave at top, narrow rounded shoulders, curved inner edge. Clear aquamarine glass (good quality); aquamarine. Doubled engraved girdle on groove, separating rim from body; two engraved girdles (0.2 apart) on lower section of walls. Inside of lid features black (dark brown ?) colour drawing (intended to be seen from outside) of boy Eros running towards the right, his head turned backwards to the left, with a whip in his hands (the handle in his right hand; the rope in his left), with a fine head of hair almost reaching his shoulders, eyes wide open, half-open mouth, large wings (right one visible near base). Folds of cloak and the soil are represented by three parallel strokes.

Condition: Small part of rim of lid broken off; surface of pyxis iridescent in places; part of lines in drawing erased.

Literature: Кунина 1987, с. 36—38; с. 37, ил. 1, 2

Analogies: In form: SH, Ол.1904; Vessberg 1952, pl. III, 17; Vessberg links such vessels (p. 119, typ. A. II, pl. III, 9—18) with painted lids analogous to the Hermitage one in shape and drawing (p. 149, pl. X, 3—5; pl. XXI), considering them to be the produce of Cypriot workshops. The representation of a single person, in most cases Aphrodite and Eros, was typical. Eros was, as a rule, drawn in motion with a bunch of grapes in his hands: see M.Ohnefalsch-Richter, Kypros. Die Bibel und Homer. Berlin, 1893, Tafel-Band, Taf. LXVI, 4; Masterpieces, no. 69; Recent Important Acquisitions // JGS, 1974, vol. XVI, p. 125, no. 6. The lid of the Hermitage pyxis (Eros with a short whip) represents a new version of the subject.

183. KRATERISKOS

Northern Italy. First half of 1st century AD

H 15; D: rim 13.9; GD 10.4; foot 7.4; thickness of walls 0.3—0.4; ribs 0.3; ribs protrude by 0.6
Received in 1854; found in 1852 in environs of Kertch (grave 107)
П.1852.64   ill.113

Figured body: with high walls widening upwards, semi-spherical lower section of body (with ribs); with bolster-shaped rim; conical foot, with thin rim serving as base. Clear bluish glass (good quality). Reminiscent in its elegant outlines, distinctive shape and detailed execution to the silver and red varnished goblets made during the reign of Caesar Augustus.
Condition: Good.

Literature: Извлечение, с. 182, ил. 75; Кунина 1984, с. 153, № 10; табл. I, 10 (с. 149)

Analogies: Compare: Calvi, 1965, p.15, 16, fig. 12 (blown in mould); compare also Berger, S. 39, Nr. 83; Taf. 5, *83* (Taf. 18, *44*)

184. KRATERISKOS

Northern Italy. 1st century AD

H 14.6; D: rim 1.5; GD 12.7; foot 7.3
Received in 1893 from J.Lemme' collection
E 357   ill.116

Figured body; high double-curved walls of upper section of body projecting over rounded base; slightly protruding edge. Small, decorative handles (near lower curve of body). Conical foot, on round, slightly concave base. Clear blue glass; with outside entirely covered in little spots of dull white, red and yellow glass (in imitation of jasper). Handles of clear blue glass. White outlining along rim.

Manufacturing technique: Body possibly blown in open mould.

Condition: Surface heavily iridescent on both sides; original colour of decoration survives on part of foot.

Literature: Glass, p. 256, no. 236

Analogies: A. von Saldern, Ancient Glass in the Museum of Fine Arts, Boston. Boston, 1968, no. 21; Petru 1972, tabl. XVIII, 15; Kern 1956, Taf. XXII, 1, 2; Benko, tabl. XXXIX, 6 (15/3); Recent Important Acquisitions // JGS, 1966, vol. VIII, p. 128, no. 69 (Corning Museum of Glass, no. 64.1.3); Matheson, no. 110; for the "multi-coloured spotted surface" see Fremersdorf 1938, S. 118 ff; for shape see cat. 183

185.
MODIOLUS

Northern Italy. Early 1st century AD

H 12.1; D: rim 13.4; pad-base 7.8
Received in 1883; found in 1883 in Pantikapaion necropolis (grave 6; beneath kurgan, together with cat. 97)
П.1883.8   ill.115

Conical body with wide base formed by lower sections of walls; with protuberant, profiled stepped rim; concave bottom. Short, loop-shaped handle. Clear cobalt-blue glass; outside entirely covered in little spots of dull yellow and white glass. Pontil-mark (D 2.9) on bottom.
Condition: Outer surface of pad-base slightly iridescent.

Literature: OAK for 1882, с. XXV, XXVI; Художественное стекло, ил. 13; Haevernick 1978, S. 9, Nr. 91; Кунина 1984, с. 147, № 2, с. 149, табл. I, 2

Analogies: Kern 1956, tav. 22, *3*; Petru 1972, Nr. 353, S. 135, tabl. C IV, 16; Sammlung Oppenländer, Nr. 390; compare form with clear glass modioli: Benko, tabl. XXXVIII (14d/3); Sorokina 1977, p. 131, ill. 4, *2*; Haevernick

183*

184*

185*

186

187—189

190—192

193, 194

195—197

198

199

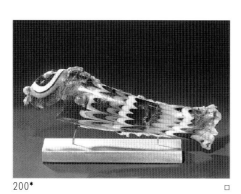

200*

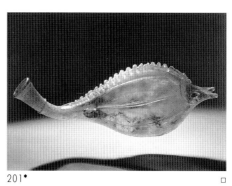

201*

1978, S. 329, Bild 3c, e; Сорокина 1962, с. 219, ил. 6, *1*, *2*; Kern 1963, Taf. 2; Auth, no. 107; Bucovala 1968, nr. 20

186.
MODIOLUS

Western territory of the Roman Empire or Italy. 1st century AD

H 20.4; D: rim 24.7; pad-base 12.4
Received in 1910 from AC; bought in 1909; found on territory of Olbia
On.1901   ill.114

Conical body with wide, massive base formed by lower sections of walls; with bolster-shaped rim; concave bottom. Wide, tape-shaped handle curved in a loop. Clear colourless glass. Embossed girdle under rim (2.7 lower).

Condition: Glued together again from many pieces; losses; silvery film of iridescence on surface.

Literature: ИАК, 1906, вып. 13, с. 125, ил. 65

Analogies: Compare: Haevernick 1978, S. 328, Bild 1; Sammlung Cohn, Nr. 115

187.
AMPHORISKOS

Northern Italy. Mid — 3rd quarter of 1st century AD

H 12.7; D: rim 3.3; GD 6.8; bottom 3
Received in 1872; found in 1872 in Pantikapaion necropolis (grave 5; together with cat. 164)
П.1872.120   ill.117

Ovoid body; with conical neck, bolster-shaped rim; concave bottom. Thin, curved, asymmetrical handles with groove in middle, attached low down to neck. Clear blue glass; with outside covered in little spots of dull white glass; one spot yellow; blue handles.

Condition: Glued together again from pieces; surface iridescent in places; colour of spots changed.

Literature: OAK for 1872, с. XXIII; Кунина 1984, с. 151, № 4; с. 148, табл. I, 4

Analogies: SH, E 686 — blue glass with white spots (A.Novikov collection, Nymphaion); Sammlung Oppenländer, Nr. 392, 393; Fremersdorf 1938, Taf. 14, *4*; Sammlung Löffler, Farbtafel III, 17; compare: Simonett, Taf. 11, *3* (left)

188.
AMPHORISKOS

Northern Italy. 1st century AD

H 12.6; D: rim 2.9; GD 6.9; bottom 3.5
Received in 1875; found in 1875 in Pantikapaion necropolis (grave 1)
П.1875.423   ill.117

Ovoid body; with high neck smoothly turning into body, irregular bolster-shaped rim; concave bottom. Smoothly curving, asymmetric handles with groove in middle, attached low down to neck. Clear light-violet glass; with outside entirely covered in little spots of dull blue and white glass. Clear light-aquamarine handles.

Condition: Glued together again from three pieces; surface iridescent in places.

Literature: OAK for 1875, с. XXII—XXIII; Художественное ремесло, кат. 265 (without ill.), Кунина 1984, с. 151, № 5; с. 148, табл. I, 5

Analogies: See cat. 190; Одесский археологический музей АН УССР. Киев, 1983, с. 61, ил. 106, с. 174, № 106 (found in Pantikapaion); compare also: Sammlung Oppenländer, Nr. 391

189.
AMPHORISKOS

Northern Italy. First half of 1st century AD

H 11.9; D: rim 3; GD 6.9; bottom 3.6
Received in 1911; found in 1908 in Pantikapaion necropolis (grave 23)
П.1908.124   ill.117

Ovoid body; with cylindrical neck, with bolster-shaped rim; concave bottom. Thin, smoothly curved handles. Clear brown glass; with outside entirely covered in little spots of dull white and blue glass. Clear cobalt-blue glass.

Condition: Glued together again from pieces; surface iridescent; several spots peeled off from brown glass or changed colour.

Literature: ИАК, 1911, вып. 40, с. 74, 75, ил. 12; Кунина 1984, с. 151, № 3, с. 148, табл. I, 3

Analogies: In shape cat. 189; Сорокина 1978, с. 268, ил. 1, *1*; Auth, no. 55; compare Sammlung Oppenländer, Nr. 392

190. AMPHORISKOS

Northern Italy. 1st century AD

H 11.2; D: rim 3.3; GD 6.1; bottom 3.5
Received in 1931 from SAHMC; previously in A.Bobrinsky collection
E 2224   ill.118

Analogous in form, colour of glass and ornamentation to cat. 188. Made at the same workshop (?).

Condition: Glued together again from several pieces; surface iridescent in places; colour patches dulled.

First ever publication

Analogies: Compare with cat. 188

191.
AMPHORISKOS

Eastern Mediterranean. 1st century AD

H 10; D: rim 2.2; GD 5.6; bottom 2.4
Received in 1875; found in 1875 in Pantikapaion necropolis (grave 7)
П.1875.442   ill.118

Ovoid body; with cylindrical neck, slightly flanged rim; slightly concave bottom. Thin, smoothly curved handles. Clear dark-blue glass; handles of dull white glass, with shades of light-blue. Rim separated by groove on inside.

Condition: Silvery film of iridescence on surface in places; shine lost.

Literature: OAK for 1875, с. XXVIII

Analogies: Compare shape with amphoriskoæ from multi-coloured glass: cat. 187, 189; Čadik pl. 13 (right); Toll, pl. LX (tomb 55, no. 23); Sammlung Oppenländer, Nr. 545; Hayes, no. 128; SH, E 687 (from cobalt-blue glass)

192. AMPHORISKOS

Eastern Mediterranean or Northern Italy 1st century AD

H 11.8; D: rim 2.9; GD 6.1; bottom 3.1
Found in 1847 in Pantikapaion necropolis
П.1847.25   ill.118

Pear-shaped body; with cylindrical base formed by narrowed lower section of body; with cylindrical, slightly swollen neck, bolster-shaped rim; slightly convex bottom. Thin, smoothly curving handles. Clear light-aquamarine glass.

Condition: Surface iridescent; shine lost in places.

First ever publication

Analogies: Isings, Form 15; Calvi 1968, cat. 1, tav 1, *7*; Vessberg 1952, pl. VI, 25; Fitzwilliam Mus., no. 61c; La Baume, Nr. 11, Taf. 55, *3*; Smith Collection, no. 62; Simonett, Taf. 10, *5* (left); compare: cat. 338; Auth, no. 353

193.
SMALL FLASK

Northern Italy. First half of 1st century AD

H 7.8; D: rim 1.8; GD 3.6; bottom 1.9
Received in 1893 from J.Lemme' collection
E 450   ill.120

Spherical body; with high cylindrical neck, small bolster-shaped rim; flat bottom. Clear blue glass; outside entirely covered in little spots of dull white, red, light-blue and yellow glass.

Condition: Part of rim lost; surface iridescent.

First ever publication

194.
SMALL FLASK

Northern Italy. First half of 1st century AD

H 7.4; D: rim 2; GD 3.5; bottom 1.8
Received in 1893 from J.Lemme' collection
E 449   ill.120

Pear-shaped body; with short neck, small flanged rim; flat bottom. Clear greenish glass; outside entirely covered in little spots of dull white, red and yellow glass.

Condition: Surface iridescent.

First ever publication

195.
SMALL FLASK

Eastern Mediterranean or Northern Italy. First half of 1st century AD

H 5.3; D: rim 1.8; GD 4.8; bottom 2.1
Received in 1893 from J.Lemme' collection
E 465

Biconical body; with cylindrical neck, wide rim; flat bottom. Clear colourless glass. Rows of winding threads of dull white glass on body and bottom.

Condition: Silver film of iridescence on surface.

First ever publication

196.
SMALL FLASK

Eastern Mediterranean. First half of 1st century AD

H 7.7; D: rim 1.5; GD 4.1; bottom 2.7
Received in 1893 from J.Lemme' collection
E 453

Pear-shaped body; with high, almost cylindrical neck, small bolster-shaped rim; slightly concave bottom. Clear light-blue glass. Rows of spiral threads of dull white glass on body and bottom.

Condition: Cracks on body and upper neck; surface iridescent.

First ever publication

Analogies: Sammlung Oppenländer, Nr. 648; compare: Auth, no. 357; Hayes, no. 111; Dusenbery 1971, p. 27, no. 50; Dusenbery 1967, p. 41, no. 16, fig. 17; compare with cat. 198

197.
SMALL FLASK

Eastern Mediterranean. First half of 1st century AD

H 8.4; D: rim 1.1; GD 3; bottom 0.8
Received in 1928 from Gaman-Gamon collection
E 1592

Raindrop-shaped body; with high, cylindrical neck with intake near body; small rim; flat bottom. Clear honey-yellow glass. Rows of spiral threads of dull light-blue glass on body and bottom.

Condition: Part of rim lost; cracks on body.

First ever publication

Analogies: Sammlung Cohn, Nr. 82

198.
FLASK

Eastern Mediterranean. First half of 1st century AD

H 11.5; D: rim 2.6; GD 6.8; bottom 2.5
Received in 1926 from S.Stroganov collection
E 1208   ill.119

Spherical body; with narrow, conical neck, small flanged rim. Clear light-violet glass. Spiral rows of thread of dull blue glass across entire surface.

Condition: Surface iridescent.

Literature: Художественное ремесло, кат. 287 (withont ill.)

Analogies: Кунина, Сорокина, с. 170, ил. 11, *11*; La Baume, Nr. D18, Taf. 19, *1*; Sammlung Oppenländer, Nr. 646, 648; Dusenbery 1967, p. 41, fig. 17, 18; Dusenbery 1971, p. 27, no. 51, fig. 50; Matheson, no. 74; Auth, no. 95; Fitzwilliam Mus., no. 93c; Myres, p. 511, no. 5737

199.
FLASK

Eastern Mediterranean. 1st century AD

H 11.1; D: rim 2.9; GD 8.1; bottom 2.8
Received in 1926 from S.Stroganov collection
E 1198   ill.129

Body in shape of sphere slightly flattened at top; with eleven external ribs, high neck widening downwards, bolster-shaped rim. Clear glass, colour of body of various intensities (from pale-pink to light-violet on opposite sides and dark-violet on ribs).

Condition: Silvery film of iridescence on surface in places.

Literature: Художественное ремесло, кат. 273 (without ill.)

Analogies: G.M.Young. Excavations at Siphnos. Annual of the British School at Athens. 44, 1949, pl. 32, p. 39; Smith Collection, no. 152; Fitzwilliam Mus., no. 58c; Vessberg 1952, pl. VII, 16; compare: Sammlung Hentrich, Nr. 116

200.
FISH VESSEL

Eastern Mediterranean. 2nd century AD

L 17.3; GH 4.7
Received in 1903; found in 1903 in Chersonesos necropolis (grave 1492)
X.1903.9   ill.123,124

Body in shape of fish; wide, smooth contours, with wide trapezoid tail, large round head and large modelled lips. Multi-coloured glass, corresponding to forms and parts of body: clear violet-pink glass for the body; clear dark-cherry glass for the upper head; stripes of dull white and yellow glass for the gills; dull white, yellow and red-brown

glass for the scales. Mouth, eyes, spine and side ribs are made in relief from clear, bright, turquoise glass, lower fin is made from orange-yellow glass. One of the best examples from the limited series of such ornamented vessels.

Manufacturing technique: Original combination of free blowing with ancient technique of ornamentation from threads of coloured glass by "combing" (see technique for sandy-earthenware cores).

Condition: Glued together again from many pieces; part of head, body, tail and one eye (trace visible) lost.

Literature: ИАК, 1905, вып. 16, табл. VI, с. 94 сл.; Художественное стекло, ил. 11; Художественное ремесло, кат. 305; Соколов, № 149; Sokolow, Nr. 100

Analogies: Compare with Smith Collection, no. 334

201.
FISH VESSEL

Eastern Mediterranean (Syria ?)
2nd — 4th centuries AD

L 23.5; GH 8.5; orifice: 2.5x3.9
Received in 1898 from M.Sivadjan collection; bought in Syria
E 1359   ill.121,122

Body in shape of fish; with flat body, curved tail turning into funnel-shaped orifice. Clear bluish-green glass. Thin rim of applied thread on orifice; ball-shaped eyes; thin embossed stripe for gills, modelled cylinder with pinched dorsal fin, loop-shaped applied mouldings for side ribs. Embossed ribs (three at one side, four on the other) along body and (one) on lower section.

Condition: One eye lost (trace visible); surface iridescent.

Literature: Художественное стекло, с. 8 (without ill.)

Analogies: Smith Collection, no. 335; Sammlung Oppenländer, Nr. 697; Recent Important Acquisitions // JGS, 1969, vol. XI, p. 110, no. 6; JGS, 1973, vol. XV, p. 188, no. 9; Cat. Damas, p. 105, no. C.1436, fig. 40

202.
TRULLA

Eastern Mediterranean or Italy
1st century AD

H 8; D: rim 10.3; pad-base 4.4; L handle 6.4
Received in 1926 from SAHMC; found in 1910 in Olbia necropolis (grave 33; together with cat. 247)
O.1910.132

Spherical body; with slightly raised and flanged rim, conical support. Long, flat handle, narrowing in the middle. Clear colourless glass. Bolster below inner and outer sides of rim. Form typical of earlier metal scoops.

Condition: Glued together again from many pieces; parts of body lost; surface iridescent.

First ever publication

Analogies: Одесский археологический музей. Путеводитель. Одесса, 1970, ил. on с. 24; Сорокина 1978, с. 270, ил. 2, 6; Sammlung Oppenländer, Nr. 557; Vessberg 1952, pl. II, 21; Recent Important Acquisitions // JGS, 1974, vol. XVI, p. 125, no. 5; Bucovala 1968, p. 36, nr. 27; SH, E 2598

203.
DISH

Eastern Mediterranean. 1st century AD

H 2.8; D: rim 18.8; pad-base 14.5; thickness of pad-base 0.6
Received in 1926 from S.Stroganov collection
E 1211   ill.128

Short walls; with slightly flanged rim, short flat pad-base (protruding by 0.2 from bottom). Clear yellow glass. Two appliedmoulded festooned braids against one another on rim; protuberance on inside of bottom, pontil-mark (D 2.5) in centre on outside.

Condition: Surface iridescent in places.

First ever publication

Analogies: Compare: Vessberg 1952, pl. I, no. 11, 16; Sammlung Cohn, Nr. 136; Hayes, no. 195; Isings, Form 43; Matheson, no. 108

204.
RIBBED BOWL
("ZARTE RIPPENSCHALE")

Northern Italy. First half of 1st century AD

H 7; D: rim 7.2; neck 7; GD 9.1; thickness of walls 0.1; ribs 0.1
Found in 1847 in kurgan of Pantikapaion necropolis (together with cat. 98)
П.1843.39   ill.126

Spherical body; with thin outer ribs, concave neck; slightly flanged rim; flat bottom. Dull milky-white glass. Rows of spiral light-blue thread on body ending with a curl at the bottom. Rim sliced off and ground at top.

Condition: Surface has almost totally changed its colour; pieces of rim lost.

Literature: ДБК, табл. LXXVII, 6; ABC, pl. LXXVII, 6; Бларамберг, с. 318; Haevernick 1967, S. 161, Nr. 5; Сорокина 1969, с. 218, ил. 1, 5а, с. 220, табл. I; Кунина 1984, с. 152, № 6, табл. I, 6

Analogies: Despite the large number (more than 500) of "Zarte Rippenschalen", cups made from dull white glass are fairly uncommon: no more than 10 in all are known; see, for example, Sammlung Oppenländer, Nr. 263; Pfeffer und Haevernick, S. 81, Nr. 4; Matheson, no. 101

205.
RIBBED BOWL
("ZARTE RIPPENSCHALE")

Northern Italy. Second—third quarters of 1st century AD

H 7; D: rim 8.1; neck 8.1; GD 9.4; thickness of walls 0.2; ribs 0.4
Received in 1893 from J.Lemme' collection
E 376   ill.125

Semi-spherical body; with sparse thick outer ribs, high concave neck, slightly flanged rim; flat bottom. Clear blue glass. Rim sliced off and ground at top.

Condition: Cracks on walls; surface iridescent.

First ever publication

Analogies: Compare form: Sammlung Oppenländer, Nr. 264; Fitzwilliam Mus., no. 60a; colour (blue glass without ornamental design) ibid., no. 60b; SH, П.1913.6 (Кунина 1984, с. 153, № 7, табл. I, 7); cat. 211

206.
RIBBED BOWL
("ZARTE RIPPENSCHALE")

Northern Italy. Second—third quarters of 1st century AD

H 5.5; D: rim 7.4; neck 7.3; GD 8.6; thickness of walls 0.1; ribs 0.2
Received in 1931 from SAHMC; previously in A.Bobrinsky collection; bought in Kertch
E 2163   ill. on p.40

Semi-spherical body; with thick outer ribs, short concave neck, flanged rim; flat bottom. Clear, cobalt-blue glass. Rows of spiral dull white thread on body. Rim sliced off and ground at top.

Condition: Surface iridescent (especially outside); traces of white thread on ribs.

Literature: Художественное ремесло, кат. 296 (without ill.); Кунина 1984, с. 153, № 9, табл. I, 9

Analogies: La Baume, Nr. N1, Taf. 53, 1; Sammlung Oppenländer, Nr. 262; Haevernick 1970, S. 156—164

207.
RIBBED BOWL
("ZARTE RIPPENSCHALE")

Northern Italy. Second—third quarters of 1st century AD

H 5; D: rim 7.3; neck 7.1; GD 8.7; thickness of walls 0.2; ribs 0.1
Received in 1893 from J.Lemme' collection
E 377   ill. on p.40

Semi-spherical body; with thin dense outer ribs, extremely concave neck, flanged protruding rim; flat bottom. Clear violet glass. Rows of white thread from dull glass on body, forming five-circuit curl on bottom. Rim sliced off.

Condition: Glued together again from pieces; piece of rim and part of walls lost; remnants of thread in places on shoulders, ribs and bottom; surface iridescent.

First ever publication

Analogies: Sammlung Oppenländer, Nr. 260; Haevernick 1970, S. 159—165; Fogolari e Scarfi, tav. 63, 1

208.
RIBBED BOWL
("ZARTE RIPPENSCHALE").

Northern Italy. Second—third quarters of 1st century AD

H 5.8; D: rim 7.7; GD 8.7; neck 7.3; thickness of walls 0.3; ribs 0.2
Received in 1908; bought from Yatrinas
E 821   ill. on p.40

Semi-spherical body; with ribs flattened at lower sections, concave neck, slightly flanged rim; flat bottom. Clear honey-yellow glass. Rim sliced off and ground at top.

Condition: Part of rim lost; surface iridescent.

First ever publication

Analogies: Compare shape with cat. 211 (blue glass)

209. RIBBED BOWL
("ZARTE RIPPENSCHALE")

Northern Italy. Second—third quarters of 1st century AD

H 5; D: rim 7.2; neck 7.1; GD 9.1; thickness of walls 0.2; ribs 0.1
Received in 1893 from J.Lemme' collection
E 378   ill.127

Analogous in form, colour, ornamentation and manufacturing technique to cat. 207 (exception: three-circuit spiral on bottom with white spot in centre).

Condition: Part of rim lost; surface iridescent; white thread surviving in places, best of all on bottom.

First ever publication

Analogies: Cat. 207

210.
RIBBED BOWL
("ZARTE RIPPENSCHALE")

Northern Italy. First half of 1st century AD

H 4.6; D: rim 7; neck 6.6; GD 7.6; thickness of walls 0.1; ribs 0.2
Received in 1908; found in 1905 in Pantikapaion necropolis (grave 147/39/; together with cat. 338)
П.1905.154   ill.127

Semi-spherical body; with thick outer ribs, concave neck, flanged rim; flat bottom. Clear bluish glass. Rim sliced off.

Condition: Part of rim glued on, piece lost; surface iridescent in places.

202

203   □

204   □

205   □

206—208   □

209—211   □

212   □

213

214

215   □

216   □

217

Literature: ИАК, 1909, вып. 30, с. 42, 43; Кунина 1984, с. 153, № 8, табл. I, 8

Analogies: Haevernick 1970, S. 156; Hayes, no. 636; compare Dusenbery, 1967, p. 45, fig. 33, 34

211.
RIBBED BOWL ("ZARTE RIPPENSCHALE")

Northern Italy. Second—third quarters of 1st century AD

H 6.1; D: rim 8; neck 8; GD 8.9; thickness of walls 0.2; ribs 0.2—0.3
Received in 1898; bought from L.Gauhman; from Olbia (?)
E 574   ill.127

Semi-spherical body; with distinctive vertical outer ribs, concave neck, slightly flanged rim; flat bottom. Clear blue glass. Rim sliced off and ground.

Condition: Surface iridescent; original shine lost in many places.

Literature: Haevernick 1970, S. 161

Analogies: Sammlung Hentrich, Nr. 36; compare shape with Sammlung Oppenländer, Nr. 265 (brown glass)

212.
FLASK

Eastern Mediterranean. 1st century AD

H 17.1; D: rim 2.9; GD 10; bottom 3.5
Received in 1893 from J.Lemme' collection
E 386   ill.130

Spherical body; shoulderless, with high conical neck, small slightly flanged rim; flat bottom. Clear honey-yellow glass. Rim sliced off and melted at top.

Condition: Part of rim glued on, piece lost; surface heavily iridescent; with silver crust in places; lilac-iridescent shade acquired in places.

First ever publication

Analogies: Hayes, no. 114, 115; compare: Fitzwilliam Mus., no. 63 (with handle); Smith Collection, no. 319 (with ornamental design from thread)

213.
BOTTLE

Eastern Mediterranean. 40s—70s AD

H 17; D: rim 3.9; GD 8.1; bottom 3
Received in 1872; found in 1872 in Pantikapaion necropolis (grave 3; together with cat. 63, 163, 299)
П.1872.96

Pear-shaped body; with high cylindrical neck with intake below, flat horizontal rim; small, flat bottom. Clear bluish glass; bright on protuberance on bottom.

Condition: Good.

Literature: OAK for 1872, c. XXII

Analogies: Compare: Dusenbery 1967, p. 42, fig. 22 (shorter neck); Spartz, Nr. 54, Taf. 15, *54*; Ю.И.Козуб. Стеклянные бальзамарии из некрополя Ольвии // Античная культура Северного Причерноморья в первые века нашей эры. Киев, 1988, с. 44, ил. 2 (right); type I, 1б)

214.
BOTTLE

Eastern Mediterranean (Cyprus ?) Second half of 1st century AD

H 18.5; D: rim 5.3; GD 12.7; bottom 5.7
Received in 1894; found in 1894 in Pantikapaion necropolis (crypt with four recesses /northern recess/; together with cat. 377)
П.1894.24

Spherical body; with high cylindrical neck, muff-shaped profiled rim; slightly concave bottom. Eight engraved girdles of several close thin lines on body.

Condition: Surface dulled in places.

Literature: OAK for 1894, c. 45

Analogies: Cat. 215, 216; Сагинашвили, кат. 47; Vessberg 1963, pl. 58, *110*; Bucovala 1968, nr. 144; La Baume, Nr. E1, Taf. 43, *1*; Sammlung Löfler, Nr. 109, Taf. 13, *3*; Hayes, no. 146; Sammlung Niessen, Band II, Taf. L II, 1061

215.
FLASK

Eastern Mediterranean (Cyprus ?). Second half of 1st century AD

H 18.4; D: rim 4.5; GD 12.8; bottom 5
Received in 1904; found in 1903 in Pantikapaion necropolis (grave 100; together with cat. 305)
П.1903.67   ill.132

Analogous in form to cat. 214. Clear yellow glass. Engraved girdles of close thin lines: three on the middle section and two on both top and on lower section of body.

Condition: Surface iridescent.

Literature: ИАК, 1906, вып. 17, с. 25

Analogies: Compare with cat. 214

216.
FLASK

Eastern Mediterranean. Second half of 1st century AD

H 12.9; D: rim 4; GD 9.8; bottom 5.6
Received in 1862; found in 1862 in Pantikapaion necropolis (grave 54; together with cat. 239)
П.1862.25   ill.131

Analogous in form to cat. 214, 215. Clear yellow glass. Four engraved girdles on body.

Condition: Surface iridescent.

First ever publication

Analogies: Cat. 214, 215 (large dimensions); Isings, Form 70; Vessberg 1963, pl. 58, *110*

217.
BOTTLE

Eastern Mediterranean. Second half of 1st century AD

H 17.3; L neck 9.3; D: rim 3; GD 8.7; bottom 3.4
Found in 1846 in Pantikapaion necropolis (kurgan XIII, grave 1)
П.1846.50

Spherical body; with very high narrow, almost cylindrical, neck; massive, muff-shaped rim; small, flat bottom. Clear olive-green glass. Intersecting ground grooves (W 0.3) on body; three engraved girdles of thin lines on neck.

Condition: Surface iridescent.

First ever publication

Analogies: Smith Collection, no. 374; Bucovala, 1968, nr. 144; Filarska, Nr. 94, tabl. XIX, 3; G.M.Young. Excavations in Siphnos // Annual of the British School at Athens. 44, 1949, p. 89, pl. 32, *5*; compare form, dimensions and colour of glass with cat. 127, form and dimensions: cat. 126

218.
BOTTLE

Syro-Palestinian region. Late 1st century — early 2nd century AD

H 20.9; L neck 9.4; D: rim 2.5; bottom 5.8
Received in 1914; found in 1912 in Pantikapaion necropolis (grave 30; together with cat. 119)
П.1912.16

Cone-shaped body; very high narrow, cylindrical neck with constriction below; massive, muff-shaped rim; slightly concave bottom. Clear bluish glass. Engraved girdles of thin lines: three on the middle section and two on both top and on lower section of body.

Condition: Surface iridescent.

Literature: ИАК, 1916, вып. 60, с. 15; Кунина, Сорокина, с. 163, ил. 8, *26*

Analogies: Filarska, nr. 121, tabl. XXVII, 1; Hayes, no. 145

219.
FLASK

Syria. First half of 2nd century AD

H 19; D: rim 7.1; top of neck 4.3; shoulders 10.2; GD 15; bottom 12
Received in 1924 from SAHMC; found in 1912 in Pantikapaion necropolis (grave 39)
П.1912.22   ill.133

Squat, trapezoid body; with high, wide neck narrowing upwards, with intake at bottom, bolster-shaped rim; concave bottom. Clear greenish glass.

218

219 □

220

221 □

222

223*

224

225

226* □

227 □

Condition: Surface iridescent.

Literature: ИАК, 1916, вып. 60, с. 16

Analogies: SH, П.1903.97; Basserman-Jordan, Taf. VI, 58; Edgar, pl. VII, 32.634; Filarska, Nr. 204, tabl. XLIII, 2; Vessberg 1952, pl. VIII, 24; compare: Fremersdorf IX, Nr. 117; Benko, tabl. V, 4 (2a/13a)

220.
UNGUENTARIUM

Eastern Mediterranean (Syria ?). Second half of 1st century AD

H 36.2; L neck 28.9; D rim 3.2; GD 9.2; bottom 5
Found in 1840 or 1841 in Kertch or its environs
П.1840/41.2

Small, spherical body; very high cylindrical neck with constriction below; massive muff-shaped rim; slightly concave bottom. Clear light-blue glass. Two engraved girdles on upper and on lower sections of body, three on middle section.

Condition: Part of body glued together again from pieces; hole; surface iridescent.

Literature: ДБК, табл. LXXVII, 13; ABC, pl. LXXVII, 13

Analogies: Compare: cat. 221 (height considerably smaller); Hayes, no. 144; Sammlung Hentrich, Nr. 192

221.
UNGUENTARIUM

Eastern Mediterranean. Late 1st century AD

H 21.3; L neck 14; D: rim 2.1; GD 8.5; bottom 3.8
Received in 1901; found in 1900 in
Pantikapaion necropolis (grave 63)
П.1900.40   ill.138

Spherical body; with very high neck widening downwards; small, bolster-shaped rim; flat bottom. Clear bluish glass.

Condition: Surface iridescent.

Literature: ИАК, 1902, вып. 2, с. 52; Кунина, Сорокина, с. 167, ил. 10, *11*

Analogies: Cat. 219; Vessberg 1952, pl. IX, 5, 6

222.
FLASK

Rhineland or Gaul. Second half of 2nd century — early 3rd century AD

H 12.2; D: rim 3.1; GD 8; bottom 3.3
Received in 1904; found in 1903 in
Pantikapaion necropolis (grave 49; together with cat. 332, 371)
П.1903.45

Spherical body; with elegant figured neck, with constriction and small swelling at bottom, funnel-shaped at top; slightly concave below. Clear colourless glass. Thin engraved girdle under rim. Rim sliced off and ground.

Condition: Surface iridescent.

Literature: ИАК, 1905, вып. 17, с. 15; Кунина 1984, с. 157, № 18; с. 156, табл. III, 18

Analogies: Isings, Form 92; compare: Morin-Jean, fig. 109; Benko, tabl. VI, 2 (2e/16)

223.
FLASK

Rhineland (Cologne ?). 3rd century AD

H 10.6; D: rim 2; GD 11.7; pad-base 4.5
Received in 1928 from E.Vinogradova collection
E 1440

Lens-shaped body; with concave swelling and constriction at neck, neck widening upwards, on short circular pad-base. Clear colourless glass. Eleven deep cavities on body. Rim sliced off and ground.

Condition: One cavity with hole; surface iridescent.

Literature: Художественное ремесло, кат. 282

Analogies: Doppelfeld, Taf. 98, 99; Saldern, 1964, p. 45, no. 8; compare with Sammlung Löffler, Nr. 142 (without cavity)

224.
FLASK

Eastern Mediterranean. 3rd century AD

H 11.5; D: rim 4.2; GD 9.7; pad-base 4.5
Received in 1909; found in 1904 in
Pantikapaion necropolis (grave 199/19/)
П.1904.84

Almost biconical body; with smooth silhouette, funnel-shaped orifice; bolster-shaped rim, on short circular pad-base; concave bottom. Clear greenish glass. Girdle of applied thread on neck. Pontil-mark (D 1.3) on bottom.

Condition: Glued together again from pieces; part of body lost; iridescent film of rainbow colours on surface.

Literature: ИАК, 1907, вып. 25, с. 62

Analogies: Auth, no. 154; Spartz, Nr. 86, Taf. 19, *86*; Vessberg 1952, pl. VIII, 2; Bucovala, nr. 85—88; compare with Benko, tabl. IV, 2 (2b/4); Hayes, no. 201

225.
FLASK

Rhineland or Gaul. Second half of 3rd century AD

H 12.1; D: rim 1.8; GD 8.1; bottom 2.5
Received in 1873; found in 1873 in
Pantikapaion necropolis (grave 12)
П.1873.70

Spherical body; with neck narrowing markedly upwards, with distinct constriction below; small concave bottom. Clear colourless glass. Rim sliced off

and melted. Pontil-mark (D 0.8) on bottom.

Condition: Cracks on body; piece of body lost; milky-iridescent film on surface.

Literature: Кунина 1984, с. 158, № 19, с. 156, табл. III, 19

Analogies: SH, П.1907.86 (Кунина 1984, с. 158, № 20; с. 156, табл. III, 20); Isings, Form 103; Spartz, Nr. 103, Taf. 25, *103*; Morin-Jean, p. 95, fig. 110; p. 96, fig. 111; Vanderhoeven, pl. XXVIII, no. 122; Fremersdorf IX, Nr. 89—100

226.
FLASK

*Eastern Mediterranean
Second half of 4th century AD*

H remnant 16.2; D: neck 3.5;
estimated H neck 3.5—5; GD 15.5; bottom 5.5;
thickness of walls 0.4
Received in 1893; found in 1892 in Chersonesos necropolis (grave 266)
X.1892.65   ill.134

Spherical body; with neck narrowing slightly upwards; concave bottom. Clear colourless glass. Engraved ornamental design of intersecting circumferences on body.

Condition: Glued together from pieces; upper part of neck lost; surface iridescent.

Literature: OAK for 1892, с. 116, № 266

Analogies: Matheson, no. 203; Doppelfeld, Taf. 154; Benko, tabl. VIII, 1 (2g/10); Sammlung Cohn, Nr. 76; Sammlung Löffler, Nr. 250, Taf. 36, *3*; A.B.Follman-Schultz. Die römischen Gläser aus Bonn. Köln, 1988, Taf. 7, *88*; S. 38

227.
FLASK

*Eastern Mediterranean (Syria ?)
2nd — 4th centuries AD*

H 14.5; W body 10.7; thickness of body 2.6;
bottom: 3.6x2.3
Received in 1912; bought from Osman-Sherif Nuri-Bey
E 874   ill.137

Flattened, almost oval body; with short tulip-shaped neck, with constriction below; reinforced rim; small, oval, slightly concave bottom. Clear greenish glass. Diagonal rows of spiral applied thread on body, becoming less projected the further down it goes.

Condition: Surface iridescent.

First ever publication

Analogies: Hayes, no. 171; Abdul-Hak, p. 29, fig. 5; compare: Sammlung Hentrich, Nr. 185, 186; Sammlung Cohn, Nr. 134; Fremersdorf IV, Taf. 86; Auth, no. 170, 455, 456; Hayes, no. 199

228   □ 229   □ 230   □ 231

232   □ 233   □ 234

235—237   238   239

240   □ 241   □ 242—244   □ 245

228.
ARYBALLOS

Eastern Mediterranean. Second half of 1st century — early 2nd century AD

H 11.5; D: rim 5; GD 11.2
Received in 1931; found in 1860 in Pantikapaion necropolis (grave 44)
П.1860.18   ill.139

Spherical body; with short neck, massive muff-shaped profiled rim. Small, wide, thick handles. Thick semi-clear dark-aquamarine glass. Three engraved girdles alternate with two wide ones on body.

Condition: Golden film of iridescence across almost entire surface.

First ever publication

Analogies: Aryballoe of such dimensions are fairly uncommon, see Sammlung Cohn, Nr. 129; Sammlung Hentrich, Nr. 264; compare also: Bucovala 1968, nr. 129

229.
AMPHORA

Eastern Mediterranean. Second half of 1st century AD

H 12.7; D: rim 6.4; GD 12.1; bottom 5.8
Received in 1885; found in 1884 in Pantikapaion necropolis (grave 17)
П.1884.11   ill.136

Spherical body; with short cylindrical neck, muff-shaped horizontal rim; slightly concave bottom. Tape-shaped, smoothly curving handles. Clear bluish glass. Two close engraved girdles on upper and lower sections of body, one on middle section.

Condition: Surface slightly iridescent in places.

Literature: Glass, p. 258, no. 239

Analogies: Filarska, nr. 149, tabl. XXXIII, 2; Sammlung Oppenländer, Nr. 564

230.
JUG

Eastern Mediterranean (Cyprus). Mid—third quarter of 1st century AD

H 14.2; D: rim 5.7; GD 15.6; bottom 7.6
Found in Pantikapion necropolis (kurgan III, grave 1; together with cat. 287, 296, 361, 362)
П.1842.69   ill.173

Wide, almost cylindrical body; with rounded shoulders, wide neck narrowing upwards, with constriction below, muff-shaped profiled rim; concave bottom. Wide, flat handle with four ribs, bent almost at right angle. Clear bluish glass. Pontil-mark (D 1.2) on bottom.

Condition: Glued together from pieces; parts of walls lost; surface dulled.

Literature: ЗООИД, 1844, т. I, с. 616 сл.; Спасский, с. 144; Кунина, Сорокина, с. 152, ил. 4, *13*

Analogies: Vessberg 1952, pl. V, 21, 22; Bucovala, p. 29, nr. 11; jugs of similar shape are very often found in the necropoleis of the Bosporan Kingdom, most of them in graves dating back to the second half of the 1st century AD: see Кунина, Сорокина, с. 152, ил. 4, *13*, с. 155, ил. 5, *10, 35*, с. 162, ил. 7, *19*; Сорокина 1977, с. 121, ил. 2, *1, 2*; Сорокина 1978, с. 268, ил. 1, *10*

231.
JUG

Eastern Mediterranean (Cyprus ?). Mid—second half of 1st century AD

H 14.4; D: rim 6.9; GD 14.1; bottom 11
Received in 1872; found in 1872 in Pantikapaion necropolis (grave I; together with cat. 240, 300)
П.1872.83

Wide, cylindrical body; with short cylindrical neck, with distinct constriction below, muff-shaped profiled rim; slightly concave bottom. Flat, wide handle with ribs, bent at right angle. Clear light-blue glass, bright-aquamarine where reinforced. Seven double and single engraved girdles alternate on body.

Condition: Good.

Literature: OAK for 1872, c. XXI—XXII

Analogies: See cat. 230

232.
JUG

Eastern Mediterranean Second half of 1st century AD

H 14.4; D: rim 5.6; GD 12.5; bottom 7.5
Received in 1874; found in 1874 in Pantikapaion necropolis (grave 2; together with cat. 348)
П.1874.89   ill.142

Wide, cylindrical body; with short, almost cylindrical neck, with constriction below, muff-shaped rim; slightly concave bottom. Flat, wide handle, with twelve ribs only visible below, bent at right angle. Clear greenish-yellow glass. Two close engraved girdles on upper and lower sections of body; one wide girdle of six thin lines on middle section.

Condition: Crack under handle; surface iridescent in places.

First ever publication

Analogies: See cat. 230

233.
JUG

Eastern Mediterranean (Cyprus ?). Second half of 1st century — first half of second century AD

H 22; D: rim 13.9; body 19.5—21; bottom 16.5

Received in 1931 from A.Bobrinsky collection
E 2234   ill.141

Wide, cylindrical body; with rounded shoulders, with very short neck, with constriction below, muff-shaped profiled rim, horizontally flanged rim; slightly concave bottom. Wide, flat handle with dense ribs, bent at right angle. Clear light-blue glass. Three engraved girdles alternate with two ground ones on body.

Condition: Surface slightly iridescent.

First ever publication

Analogies: Vessberg 1952, pl. V, 21, 22 (smaller dimensions); Алексеева 1982 (2), с. 91, ил. 52 (H. 16.2); Сорокина 1978, с. 268, ил. 1, *10* (smaller dimensions)

234.
JUG

Eastern Mediterranean Second half of 1st century AD

H 11.5; D: rim 10; GD 17.7; bottom 12
Received in 1877; found in 1877 in Pantikapaion necropolis (grave 71)
П.1877.66

Squat, wide body; with very short wide neck, massive muff-shaped rim; slightly concave bottom. Wide handle with eleven ribs, bent almost at right angle. Clear blue glass. Double thin ground girdles on shoulders and one on lower body, one wide girdle between two narrow ones in middle section.

Condition: Cracks on body; surface iridescent in places.

First ever publication

Analogies: See cat. 230—233; only proportions are different

235.
JUG

Eastern Mediterranean. Third quarter — late 1st century AD

H 16.3; D: rim 3.3; shoulders 7; bottom 4.5
Received in 1904; found in 1903 in Pantikapaion necropolis (grave 233/110/)
П.1903.110

Elongated body narrowing downwards; with rounded shoulders, short cylindrical neck, muff-shaped rim; concave bottom. Tape-shaped handle with three ribs, bent almost at right angle. Clear light-blue glass; bright-aquamarine on rim and handles.

Condition: Surface iridescent; shine lost in many places.

Literature: ИАК, 1905, вып. 17, с. 49; Кунина, Сорокина, с. 162, ил. 7, *27*

Analogies: See cat. 236, 237; SH E 2206; П.1903.51; П.1903.13; Sammlung Löffler,

Nr. 100, Taf. 12, *4*; compare with jugs with engraved girdles: Сорокина 1978, с. 268, ил. 1, *9*; Fortuna 1969, p. 25, fig. 27; Hayes, no. 147; Edgar, pl. V, 32.540; Кунина, Сорокина, с. 167, ил. 10, *4, 5*; Sammlung Löffler, Nr. 99, Taf. 12, *3*

236.
JUG

Eastern Mediterranean. Second half of 1st century AD

H 18; D: rim 3.8; shoulders 7.1; bottom 6
Received in 1901; found in 1899 in Pantikapaion necropolis (grave 57)
П.1899.69

Elongated, almost cylindrical body; with short neck, muff-shaped rim; concave bottom. Tape-shaped, curved handle with four ribs. Clear blue glass; handle made of clear olive-yellow glass.

Condition: Surface iridescent

Literature: ИАК, 1901, вып. 1, с. 88; Кунина, Сорокина, с. 155, ил. 5, *16*

Analogies: See cat. 235

237.
JUG

Eastern Mediterranean. Second half of 1st century AD

H 16.2; D: rim 3.5; shoulders 6.7; bottom 4.9
Received in 1925; found in 1900 in Pantikapaion necropolis (grave 33)
П.1900.13

Analogous in form and colour to cat. 236; only differences are very short neck and small handle with five ribs.

Condition: Surface iridescent.

Literature: ИАК, 1902, вып. 2, с. 46, ил. 6

Analogies: See cat. 235

238.
JUG

Eastern Mediterranean (Syria ?). Second half of 1st century AD

H 20; D: rim 5.3; bottom 9
Received in 1894; found in 1894 in Pantikapaion necropolis (crypt with four recesses /southern recess/; together with cat. 214, 377)
П.1894.45

High, cylindrical body; with horizontal shoulders; cylindrical neck, with constriction below, wide horizontal rim; slightly concave bottom. Wide, tape-shaped, curved handle. Clear, slightly greenish glass. Two engraved girdles on both upper and lower sections of body; one on middle section.

Condition: Surface heavily iridescent and corroded

Literature: OAK for 1894, с. 45

Analogies: Hayes, no. 208; Fitzwilliam Mus., p. 40, no. 77b; compare: Auth, no. 132

239.
JUG

*Eastern Mediterranean
Second half of 1st century AD*

H 14.3; D: rim 6.5; bottom 16
Received in 1862; found in 1862 in Pantikapaion necropolis (grave 54; together with cat. 216)
П.1862.33

Cone-shaped body; with short cylindrical neck, wide profiled rim; flat bottom. Wide, tape-shaped handle curved at right angle. Clear colourless glass, with bubbles. Seven engraved girdles of several thin lines on body.

Condition: Inner surface dulled in places.

First ever publication

Analogies: Сорокина 1978, с. 268, ил. 1, *4*; Spartz, Nr. 52, Taf. 14, *52*; Sammlung Löffler, Nr. 110

240.
JUG

*Eastern Mediterranean
Mid — second half of 1st century AD*

H 19.5; D: rim 4.6; GD 11.9; bottom 7
Received in 1872; found in 1872 in Pantikapaion necropolis (grave I; together with cat. 230, 301)
П.1872.85   ill.144

Pear-shaped body; with short neck, muff-shaped profiled rim; slightly concave bottom. Tape-shaped handle with three ribs, bent almost at right angle. Clear bluish glass. Seven engraved girdles of varying numbers of thin lines on body.

Condition: Surface iridescent; golden-iridescent film in places.

Literature: OAK for 1872, с. XXI—XXII

Analogies: Such jugs are often found in 1st and 2nd century graves of the Bosporan Kingdom, see SH, П.1903.150; П.1910.19; cat. 241; E 610; E 1891; Кунина, Сорокина, с. 151, ил. 3, *8*, с. 167, ил. 10, *8*; Bucovala, p. 27, nr. 6, 7

241.
JUG

Eastern Mediterranean. Second half of 2nd century AD

H 26; D: rim 4.7; GD 14.3; bottom 5.6
Received in 1875; found in 1875 in Pantikapaion necropolis (grave 6; together with cat. 371, 372, 373)
П.1875.441   ill.140

Massive, pear-shaped body; with short cylindrical neck, muff-shaped rim; small, slightly concave bottom. Tape-shaped

handle with three thick ribs, bent at right angle. Clear greenish-blue glass.

Condition: Surface iridescent; shine lost in places.

Literature: OAK for 1875, с. XXVIII; Кунина, Сорокина, с. 165, ил. 9, *43*

Analogies: See cat. 240

242.
SMALL JUG

Cyprus. Second half of 1st century AD

H 8.5; D: rim 2.6; GD 5.8; bottom 2.9
Found in Kertch
ПАН.588   ill.145

Pear-shaped body; with short cylindrical neck, muff-shaped rim; flat bottom. Narrow handle, smoothly curved, with flat semi-circular protuberance at top. Clear bluish glass. Embossed, comb-shaped tape on body under handle.

Condition: Cracks on lower section of body; surface iridescent.

Literature: ДБК, табл. LXXVII, 8; ABC, pl. LXXVII, 8

Analogies: Cat. 243, 244; SH, П.1910.51; П.1914.66; X.1895.17; Vessberg 1952, pl. V, 18; A.P. di Cesnola. Salaminia (Cyprus). London, 1882, pl. XVIII, 32; Myres, p. 511, no. 5410; Dusenbery 1967, p. 48, fig. 47; Liepmann, Nr. 68; compare: Isings, Form 55b

243.
JUG

Cyprus. Second half of 1st century AD

H 14; D: rim 3.4; GD 8.6; bottom 5
Received in 1847; found in 1847 in Pantikapaion necropolis
П.1847.30   ill.145

Pear-shaped body, with circular pad-base formed by lower sections of walls; with short cylindrical neck, muff-shaped rim; slightly concave bottom. Tape-shaped handle with flat, semi-circular protuberance at top. Clear yellowy-greenish glass; handle and ornamentation from clear bluish glass. Embossed, comb-shaped tape on body under handle.

Condition: Surface iridescent.

Literature: ДБК, табл. LXXVII, 5; ABC, pl. LXXVII, 5

Analogies: See cat. 242; SH, E 609

244.
JUG

Cyprus. Second half of 1st century AD

H 13.5; D: rim 3.5; GD 7.6; bottom 4
Found in Kertch
ПАН.827   ill.145

Analogous in form and ornamentation to cat. 243; differs by its wide rim. Clear bluish glass.

Condition: Surface iridescent.

Literature: Художественное ремесло, кат. 271 (without ill.)

Analogies: See cat. 242

245.
SMALL JUG

Eastern Mediterranean (Cyprus ?)
1st century AD

H 9.5; D: rim 2.7; bottom 4
Received in 1924 in SAHMC; bought in
Parutino as coming from Olbia
Ол. 4656

Pear-shaped body; with cylindrical neck; distorted, bolster-shaped rim; flat bottom. Narrow curved handle with three ribs and flat semi-circular protuberance at top. Clear yellowish glass.

Condition: Crack on neck; surface iridescent.

First ever publication

Analogies: Compare: Liepmann, Nr. 68;
Fitzwilliam Mus., no. 102b; Vessberg 1952,
pl. V, 15; compare also with cat. 244

246.
SMALL JUG

Eastern Mediterranean. 1st century AD

H (without handle) 12.7; rim: 3.4x5.7; GD 9.7;
bottom 4.1
Received in 1879; found in 1879 in
Pantikapaion necropolis (grave 47)
П.1879.35   ill.135

Spherical body with short cylindrical pad-base formed by lower sections of walls; with cylindrical neck, profiled rim with stretched and slightly raised lip. Narrow handle curving sharply above rim. Clear light-blue glass. Two engraved girdles on both upper and lower sections of body; three on middle section.

Condition: Surface iridescent in places.

First ever publication

Analogies: Cat. 247; SH, П.1906.165;
Сорокина 1978, с. 268, ил. 1, 5; Fortuna 1969,
p. 25, fig. 26; Bucovala 1984, p. 60, fig. 2

247.
SMALL JUG

Eastern Mediterranean. 1st century AD

H (without handle) 12.7; D: rim 2.7; GD 9.5; bottom 4.8
Received in 1926 from SAHMC; found in
1910 in Olbia necropolis (grave 33; together
with cat. 202)
O.1910.134

Spherical body; with cylindrical support formed by lower sections of walls; with high, almost cylindrical neck, profiled rim with stretched and slightly raised lip.

Narrow handle curving smoothly above rim. Clear yellowy-greenish glass.

Condition: Glued together from many pieces; losses; surface iridescent.

First ever publication

Analogies: Cat. 246; SH, П.1906.165; E 2211;
Сорокина 1978, с. 268, ил. 1, 5; Fortuna 1969,
p. 25, fig. 26 (short neck)

248.
SMALL JUG

Eastern Mediterranean. Second half of 1st century — early 2nd century AD

H (without handle) 12.5; rim: 3.9x5.1; GD 8.7;
D bottom 3.5
Received in 1884; found in 1884 in
Pantikapaion necropolis (grave 35)
П.1884.43   ill.146

Almost spherical body; with small pad-base formed by lower sections of walls; with high neck widening downwards, flanged rim with narrow lip; concave bottom. Narrow handle curving smoothly above rim. Clear light-blue glass (good quality). Pontil-mark (D 1.6) on outside of bottom.

Condition: Faint iridescence of rainbow colorous on inner surface.

Literature: Художественное ремесло, кат. 272
(without ill.); Glass, p. 258, no. 238

Analogies: Compare with cat. 246

249.
OENOCHOE

Roman Empire. 1st century AD

H (without handle) 18.4; D: rim 7.3; GD 12.9;
bottom 1.6; H support 1.6; D support 7.3
Received in 1854; found in 1853 in
Chersonesos necropolis
X.1853.8   ill.148

Spherical body; with short, slightly swollen neck, with distinct intake below, with thin pad-base widening downwards. Flat, wide handle with dense ribs, curved in loop shape. Clear colourless glass. Flat tape with horizontal curls on body and lower end of handle. Pad-base painstakingly made. Pontil-mark (D 1.6) on bottom.

Condition: Hole under handle; surface iridescent.

Literature: Извлечение, с. 154, ил. 62

250.
JUG

Eastern Mediterranean. 1st century AD

H 19; D: rim 4.4; GD 12.4; D pad-base 6.8
Received in 1900 from A.Novikov collection;
found on territory of Nymphaion, probably
in necropolis
E 684   ill.147

Body in shape of sphere flattened at top with small circular support from lower sections of walls; shoulderless, with high neck narrowing upwards, massive flanged rim; concave bottom. Flat ribbed handle, curving smoothly, with flat protuberance at top; attached way below rim. Clear cobalt-blue glass.

Condition: Surface heavily iridescent.

Literature: Художественное ремесло, кат. 256
(without ill.); Glass, p. 259, no. 240

Analogies: Vessberg 1952, pl. VI, 11; Morin-
Jean, p. 101, fig. 119; Matheson, no. 92, 93;
Berger, Nr. 89, Taf. 6, *89*; Taf. 20, *76* (89);
compare: Simonett, S. 80, Abb. 62, *32*; S. 108,
Abb. 88, *9*, S. 162, Abb. 138, *42*; Кунина,
Сорокина, с. 151, ил. 3, *25*; Sammlung Löffler,
S. 47, Nr. 125 (ill. on dust-jacket)

251.
JUG

Eastern Mediterranean
Late 1st century — early 2nd century AD

H 17.1; D: rim 5.3; GD 13.6; bottom 7
Received in 1909; found in 1906 in
Pantikapaion necropolis (grave 59—60/5—6/Б)
П.1906.74

Body in shape of sphere flattened at top; with shoulders, high neck narrowing upwards, flanged rim; concave bottom, with semi-spherical protuberance. Wide handle with four ribs curved at right angle; and loop-shaped protuberance above rim. Clear light-aquamarine glass. Pontil-mark (D 2) on bottom.

Condition: Cracks on walls; parts of body lost; surface iridescent.

Literature: ИАК, 1909, вып. 30, с. 71 сл.;
Кунина, Сорокина, с. 167, ил. 10, *13*

Analogies: Compare with cat. 250

252.
JUG

Eastern Mediterranean (?)
Late 1st century — 2nd century AD

H 19.1; D: rim 6.9; GD 12.1; bottom 6.9
Received in 1925 from SAHMC; bought in 1903
in Parutino as coming from Olbia
Ол. 4672

Body narrowing downwards with narrow support formed by lower sections of walls, with sloping shoulders, neck widening downwards; flanged rim; concave bottom. Vertical, distorted handle with three outer ribs. Clear bluish glass. Pontil-mark (D 2.7) on bottom.

Condition: Surface heavily iridescent.

First ever publication

Analogies: Compare: Filarska, Nr. 143, tabl. XXXI, 5
(handle above rim); Hayes, no. 125 (blue glass)

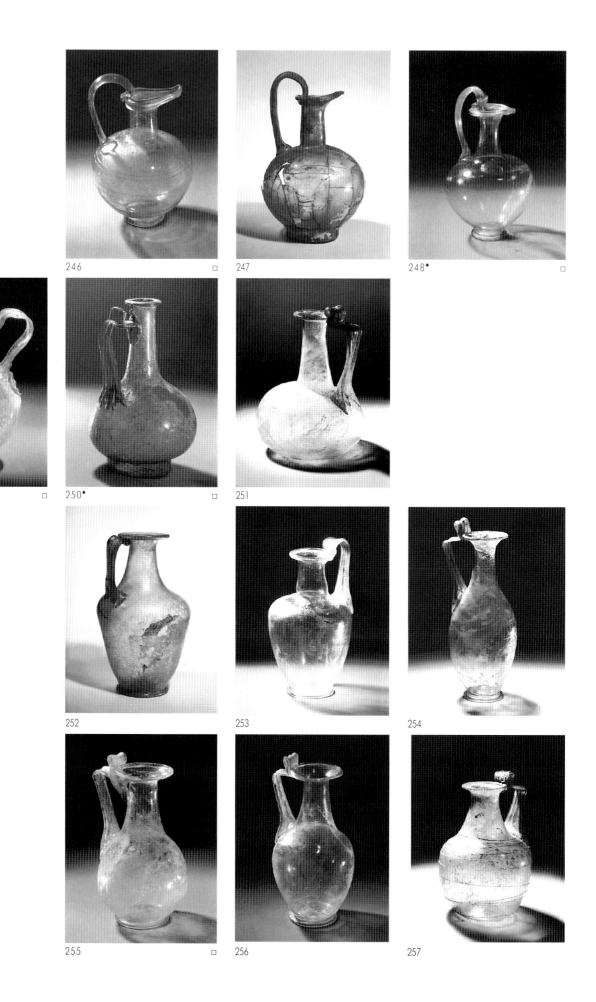

246   □

247

248*   □

249*   □

250*   □

251

252

253

254

255   □

256

257

253.
JUG

Roman Empire. 1st—2nd centuries AD

H (without handle) 16.2; D: rim 5.5; GD 10.3; pad-base 6
Received in 1900 from A.Novikov collection; found on territory of Nymphaion
E 606

Ovoid body with narrow support from lower sections of walls; with broad, almost horizontal shoulders, neck slightly swollen at bottom, with distinct constriction at bottom; curved bolster-shaped rim. Tape-shaped handle with four ribs, slightly raised above rim. Clear colourless glass. Pontil-mark (D 2.6) on bottom.

Condition:

First ever publication

Analogies: Compare quality of glass and handle with cat. 249

254.
JUG

Bosporan Kingdom (Pantikapaion ?). Late 1st century — early 2nd century AD

H 20.6; D: rim 5.7; GD 8.6; bottom 5
Received in 1912; found in 1909 in environs of Kertch (grave 98/9/; together with cat. 368)
П.1909.118

Ovoid body with wide pad-base formed by lower sections of walls; with neck widening downwards, funnel-shaped orifice, flanged bolster-shaped rim; concave bottom. Flat handle with four ribs, bent almost at right angle, with loop-shaped protuberance above rim. Clear light-aquamarine glass, with small bubbles. Pontil-mark (D 2) on bottom.

Condition: Crack on orifice; surface iridescent in places.

Literature: ИАК, 1913, вып. 47, с. 33; Кунина, Сорокина, с. 167, ил. 10, *25*; Кунина 1997, с. 52, № 1, с. 53, рис. 24

Analogies: SH, П.1904.21; П.1911.25; Кунина, Сорокина, с. 163, ил. 8, *9*; В.П.Азарова. Один из участков пантикапейского некрополя // Археология и история Боспора. Сборник статей. II. Симферополь, 1962, с. 325, ил. 7; Алексеева 1982 (2), с. 47, ил. 25

255.
SMALL JUG

Eastern Mediterranean or Bosporan Kingdom. Late 1st century — early 2nd century AD

H 12.7; D: rim 4.7; GD 7.6; pad-base 4.6
Received in 1975 from private collection; found in Olbia (?)
E 3245   ill.143

Spherical body, with neck widening downwards, wide funnel-shaped orifice, flanged rim, short circular pad-base; flat bottom. Tape-shaped handle curved at angle, with loop-shaped protuberance above rim. Clear bluish glass. Faint mark (of pontil (?); D 1.8) on bottom.

Condition: Surface iridescent.

First ever publication

Analogies: Compare with SH, П.1914.75 (larger)

256.
JUG

Bosporan Kingdom (Pantikapaion ?). Late 1st century — early 2nd century AD

H 17.8; D: rim 5.9; GD 9.1; pad-base 5.8
Received in 1915; found in 1911 in Pantikapaion necropolis (grave 38/13)
П.1911.25

Ovoid body with pad-base formed by lower sections of walls; with neck widening downwards, funnel-shaped orifice, flanged rim; concave bottom. Narrow, tape-shaped handle with three ribs, bent at right angle, with loop-shaped protuberance above rim. Clear light-aquamarine glass. Girdle of spiral applied thread (one and a half circuits) on body near base.

Condition: Surface iridescent and dulled.

Literature: ИАК, 1914, вып. 56, с. 14; Кунина 1997, с. 48, № 2, с. 49, рис. 16

Analogies: Compare with cat. 254

257.
JUG

*Bosporan Kingdom (?)
Late 1st century — early 2nd century AD*

H 16.5; D: rim 5.6; GD 11.8; bottom 6
Received in 1931; found in 1914 in Pantikapaion necropolis
П.1914.97

Almost spherical body; with neck sharply widening downwards, funnel-shaped orifice, flanged rim; concave bottom. Tape-shaped handle with four ribs, bent at right angle, with loop-shaped protuberance above rim. Clear light-aquamarine glass, with large quantity of bubbles. Rows of spiral applied thread across entire surface (with transition to bottom). Pontil-mark (D 2.2) on bottom.

Condition: Spiral thread on neck only partially intact; surface iridescent.

First ever publication

Analogies: Compare: Fremersdorf, Taf. 29; SH, П.1914.95 (smaller, spherical body) and cat. 258 (without decoration)

258.
JUG

Bosporan Kingdom (Pantikapaion ?). Second half of 1st century AD

H 13; D: rim 4.5; GD 8.6; bottom 4.6
Received in 1906; found in 1900 in Pantikapaion necropolis (grave 69; together with cat. 363)
П.1900.46

Body narrowing slightly downwards; with sloping shoulders, short neck widening downwards, flanged rim; concave bottom. Wide handle with four ribs, bent almost at right angle, with loop-shaped protuberance above rim. Clear light-aquamarine glass, with small bubbles. Pontil-mark (D 2.2) on bottom.

Condition: Surface iridescent; dulled in many places.

Literature: ИАК, 1902, вып. 2, с. 53; Кунина, Сорокина, с. 152, ил. 4, *31*; Кунина 1997, с. 43, № 3, с. 44, рис. 3

Analogies: Cat. 257; SH, П.1903.64; П.1900.14; Кунина, Сорокина, с. 163, ил. 8, *18*; La Baume, Nr. D71, Taf. 32, *4* (from Southern Russia)

259.
JUG

Bosporan Kingdom (Pantikapaion ?). Second half — late 1st century AD

H 14.5; D: rim 4.3; GD 8.6; pad-base 4.7
Received in 1904; found in 1903 in Pantikapaion necropolis (grave 184/61/)
П.1903.96

Biconical body with protuding wide circular pad-base formed by lower sections of walls; with neck widening downwards; flanged rim; concave (with pad-base) bottom. Tape-shaped handle with three ribs, with loop-shaped protuberance over rim. Clear light-aquamarine glass, with small bubbles. Pontil-mark (D 1.9) on pad-base.

Condition: Surface iridescent.

Literature: ИАК, 1905, вып. 17, с. 40; могила 184 (61); Кунина 1997, с. 45, № 2, с. 46, рис. 7

Analogies: Such small jugs are often found in the graves of Bosporan towns: see SH, П.1914.48; П.1900.15; П.1903.91; Čadik, pl. 6 (left) from Southern Russia; В.Ф.Гайдукевич. Некрополи некоторых боспорских городов // МИА, 1959, № 69, с. 193, ил. 62, *1*

260.
JUG

Bosporan Kingdom (?). Third quarter — late 1st century AD

H 25.9; D: rim 9; GD 12.8; pad-base 8.2
Received in 1904; found in 1903 in

258

259

260

261 □

262

263 □

264

265

266

267

Pantikapaion necropolis (grave 210/87/)
П.1903.105

Body narrowing downwards; with circular pad-base formed by lower sections of walls; with horizontal shoulders, neck widening downwards, overhanging profiled rim; concave bottom. Tape-shaped handle with distinct curve, four ribs, loop-shaped protuberance above rim. Clear aquamarine glass. Pontil-mark (D 3) on bottom.

Condition: Glued together from pieces; parts of walls lost; surface heavily iridescent.

Literature: ИАК, 1904, вып. 9, с. 64, ил. 3; Кунина, Сорокина, с. 163, ил. 8, *31*; Кунина 1997, с. 51, № 10, с. 50, рис. 22

Analogies: Compare with cat. 259

261.
JUG

Bosporan Kingdom. Late 1st century — early 2nd century AD

H 22.6; D: rim 7.2; GD 12.1; pad-base 6.5
Received in 1931 from SAHMC; previously in A.Bobrinsky collection
E 2236   ill.149

Ovoid body with circular pad-base formed by lower sections of walls; with neck widening downwards, funnel-shaped orifice, flanged rim; concave bottom. Tape-shaped, curved handle, with four ribs and loop-shaped protuberance above rim. Clear aquamarine glass. Pontil-mark (D 2.2) on bottom.

Condition: Surface slightly iridescent in places.

Literature: Кунина 1997, с. 50, № 5, с. 49, рис. 19

Analogies: Кунина, Сорокина, с. 163, ил. 8; *11*; Сорокина 1978, с. 268, ил. 1, *7*

262.
JUG

*Bosporan Kingdom (?)
Late 1st century — early 2nd century AD*

H 20.1; D: rim 5.5; GD 10.6; bottom 5.6
Received in 1893 from J.Lemme' collection
E 387   ill.151

Body narrowing downwards; with neck narrowing downwards, wide flattened rim; concave bottom. Flat, smoothly curved handle, with thin, close ribs and loop-shaped protuberance above rim. Pink-violet glass. Pontil-mark (D 2.2) on bottom.

Condition: Silvery film of iridescence on surface in many places.

First ever publication

Analogies: cat. 259; SH, E 417 (with pad-bases); П.1900.14 (smaller) — all from colourless glass

263.
JUG

Bosporan Kingdom (Pantikapaion ?). First half of 2nd century AD

H 22.1; D: rim 6.5; GD 9.8; bottom 6.5
Received in 1912; found in 1909 in environs of Kertch (grave 106/17/; together with cat. 369)
П.1909.136

Stretched body narrowing downwards; with sloping shoulders, with neck widening downwards, funnel-shaped orifice, bolster-shaped rim; concave bottom. Narrow, tape-shaped handle, bent at almost right angle with flat loop-shaped protuberance above rim. Clear colourless glass; with shades of green on handle. Pontil-mark (D 2.2) on bottom; dent from tongs on neck.

Condition: Rim glued together from pieces; two holes on orifice; milky-white film of iridescence on surface.

Literature: ИАК, 1913, вып. 47, с. 35, 36; Кунина, Сорокина, с. 167, ил. 10, *34*; Кунина 1997, с. 57, № 13, с. 58, рис. 36

Analogies: Jugs of similar shape are often found in the necropoleis of 2nd century Bosporan towns — see cat. 265, 266; SH, П.1912.44; П.1903.131; E 397; Сорокина 1977, с. 130, ил. 3; compare with Кобылина, с. 80, ил. 117

264.
JUG

Eastern Mediterranean or Bosporan Kingdom (?). 2nd century AD

H 21.5; D: rim 5.8; GD 9.5; bottom 5.7
Received in 1900 from A.Novikov collection, probably in Pantikapaion necropolis
E 603   ill on p.39

Ovoid body with walls narrowing towards base; with almost cylindrical neck, funnel-shaped orifice, flanged rim; concave bottom. Handle bent at angle, with double protuberance above rim. Clear slightly yellowish-green glass. Rows of diagonally spiralled applied thread on body. Pontil-mark (D 2.1) on bottom.

Condition: Surface iridescent.

Literature: Шелковников, ил. 2 (right); Художественное ремесло кат. 255 (without ill.); Glass, p. 259, no. 241

Analogies: In shape typical of the output of the Bosporan workshop, only decorated with thread and double protuberance on handle — compare: SH, П.1910.87; П.1907.57, П.1903.31; compare with cat. 267

265.
JUG

Bosporan Kingdom. 2nd century AD

H 18.8; D: rim 5.5; GD 8.8; bottom 6

Received in 1908; bought from S.Nikonova
E 836

Body narrowing downwards; with sloping shoulders, short neck widening downwards, funnel-shaped orifice, flanged rim; concave bottom. Narrow, tape-shaped handle, curved at right angle, with loop-shaped protuberance over rim. Clear light-blue glass. Pontil-mark (D 2.5) on bottom.

Condition: Surface iridescent.

Literature: Кунина 1997, с. 59, № 18, с. 58, рис. 39

Analogies: Сорокина 1977, с. 130, ил. 3; see cat. 263, 266

266.
JUG

Bosporan Kingdom. Second half of 2nd century AD

H 20.2; D: rim 6.1; GD 8; bottom 6
Received in 1925; found in 1900 in Pantikapaion necropolis (grave 17; together with cat. 326, 375)
П.1900.4

Stretched, almost ovoid body; with neck widening downwards, funnel-shaped orifice, flanged rim; concave bottom. Narrow, tape-shaped handle, bent almost at right angle, with loop-shaped protuberance above rim. Clear, almost colourless glass, with shades of green, with many bubbles. Pontil-mark (D 2.3) on bottom.

Condition: Glued together from pieces; hole in wall; cracks; surface heavily iridescent.

Literature: ИАК, 1902, вып. 2, с. 43; Кунина, Сорокина, с. 165, ил. 9, *46*; Кунина 1997, с. 59, № 14, с. 58, рис. 37

Analogies: See cat. 263

267.
JUG

Bosporan Kingdom. Second half of 2nd century — first half of 3rd century AD

H 20.8; D: rim 6.8; GD 10; bottom 7.3
Received in 1931 from A.Bobrinsky collection
E 2237

Figured body: spherical at top, cylindrical near base, with slight curve where they merge; with sloping shoulders, neck widening downwards, wide funnel-shaped orifice, profiled rim; concave bottom. Wide, tape-shaped handle bent almost at right angle; with protuberance in form of flat loop above rim. Clear bluish-green glass. Five parallel double engraved girdles on body. Pontil-mark (D 1.9) on bottom.

Condition: Surface mechanically damaged and iridescent in places.

268

269*

270

271 □

272

273

274

275 □

276, 277* □

278, 279 □

280 □

281

Literature: Кунина 1997, с. 63, № 4, с. 62, рис. 43

Analogies: SH, П.1914.96; П.1908.16; П.1841/42.25; Кобылина, с. 80; ил. 117: compare with cat. 264

268.
JUG

Bosporan Kingdom (Pantikapaion ?). Early 4th century AD (?)

H (without handle) 18.9; D: rim 5.5; GD 8.4; bottom 5
Received in 1912; found in 1910 in
Pantikapaion necropolis (grave 83/11/)
П.1910.91

Elegant body, rounded at top, narrowing sharply downwards; with sloping shoulders, high neck widening downwards, funnel-shaped orifice, flattened rim curving inwards; concave bottom. Wide, tape-shaped handle curved above rim. Clear greenish glass, with many small bubbles; stripe of dark-violet glass along outside of handle; unintentional stain of violet glass on body. Neck slightly distorted at top; pontil-mark (D 2) on bottom.

Condition: Glued together from pieces; hole in body; surface heavily iridescent.

Literature: ИАК, 1913, вып. 47, с. 69, могила 83/11/, Кунина 1997

Analogies: SH, П.1902.174; П.1909.4; П.1910.87 (elegant handle with protuberance above rim); П.1910.91 (quite possibly the oldest such jug among Bosporan workshops' output; found with 4th century bronze fibula)

269.
OENOCHOE

Eastern Mediterranean. 1st century AD

H 13.7; rim: 5x5.3; GD 7.2; D pad-base 5
Received in 1873; found in 1873 in
Pantikapaion necropolis (grave 22)
П.1873.97

Ovoid body; with short neck, bolster-shaped rim, with flattened, circular pad-base. Narrow, vertical handle making a round curve above rim. Clear light-blue glass. Pontil-mark (D 2) on bottom.

Condition: Scratch on body; surface dulled in places.

Literature: OAK for 1873, с. VI

Analogies: Compare: SH, П.1903.94 (with narrower neck); La Baume, Nr. D 28, Taf. 21, *3*

270.
OENOCHOE

Eastern Mediterranean or Bosporan Kingdom Third quarter — late 1st century AD

H 23; rim: 7.6x7.6; GD 9; D foot 9.3;
thickness of walls 0.3—0.4
Received in 1908; found in 1905 in
Pantikapaion necropolis (grave 110/2/)
П.1905.86

Ovoid body; with wide neck, thick rim curving inwards; slightly concave bottom, large wide foot. Wide handle with three ribs, smoothly curved, with massive loop-shaped protuberance above rim. Clear aquamarine glass. Foot made separately and fastened onto bottom; pontil-mark (D 2) on foot.

Condition: Surface iridescent.

Literature: ИАК, 1909, вып. 30, с. 33; Кунина, Сорокина, с. 163, ил. 8, *20*

Analogies: Compare with cat. 269

271.
OENOCHOE

Eastern Mediterranean. 1st century AD

H 12.2; rim: 4.3x4.4; GD 9.2; D bottom 5.3
Received in 1875; found in 1875 in
Pantikapaion necropolis (the first from two adjacent stone graves)
П.1875.377   ill.150

Spherical body; with short neck widening downwards; bolster-shaped rim; slightly concave bottom. Narrow vertical handle with protuberance in shape of flat loop over rim. Clear light-blue glass, with opal patterns and many large bubbles.

Condition: Cracks on lower section of body; piece of wall glued back on again; minor loss.

Literature: OAK for 1875, с. XVIII

Analogies: Compare: SH, П.1862.30; П.1914.95 (with applied thread), П.1914.45 (higher neck)

272.
OENOCHOE

Eastern Mediterranean. Second half of 2nd century AD

H 10.1; rim: 4.7x4.7; GD 8.5; D bottom 4
Received in 1874; found in 1874 in Pantikapaion necropolis (grave 5; together with cat. 322, 323, 374)
П.1874.116

Figured body: spherical, with constriction below, walls narrowing towards base; with short neck widening downwards, narrow rim; slightly concave bottom. Narrow handle curving slightly over rim. Clear bluish glass, with large bubbles.

Condition: Surface iridescent in places.

Literature: OAK for 1874, с. XI; Кунина, Сорокина, с. 165, ил. 9, *56*

Analogies: Compare: Spartz, Nr. 90; Isings, Form 88b

273.
OENOCHOE

Eastern Mediterranean. 2nd century AD

H 7.9; rim: 3.8x4.3; GD 7.2; D bottom 3.6
Received in 1924 from SAHMC; found in 1913 in Olbia necropolis (grave 56)
O.1913.146

Spherical body; with short cylindrical neck, bolster-shaped rim; slightly concave bottom. Flat, slightly curving handle, with flat semi-circular protuberance over rim. Clear bluish glass.

Condition: Surface iridescent.

Literature: OAK for 1913—1915, с. 45, ил. 67

Analogies: SH, П.1902.103; cat. 274—277; Одесский археологический музей АН УССР. Киев, 1983, с. 61, № 107 (ил.); с. 174, № 107 (found in Kertch); Sammlung Niessen, Band II, Taf. XXXI, 518, 519

274.
SMALL JUG (WITH LIP)

Eastern Mediterranean. First half of 2nd century AD

H 11.4; rim: 4.5x6; GD 9; D bottom 4
Received in 1901; found in 1900 in
Pantikapaion necropolis (grave 35)
П.1900.16

Squat body, in form of globe flattened at top; with short, widening neck, funnel-shaped orifice, bolster-shaped rim with narrow, slightly raised lip; slightly concave bottom. Wide tape-shaped handle, with wide groove in middle, bent at angle, with flat double protuberance near rim. Clear slightly yellowish glass. Two thin engraved girdles on upper section of body, girdle of eight thin lines on lower part, two thin engraved girdles, hardly visible, around bottom.

Condition: Whitish and golden-iridescent spots of iridescence.

Literature: ИАК, 1902, вып. 2, с. 46; Кунина, Сорокина, с. 167, ил. 10, *29*

Analogies: See cat. 273, 275—277

275.
SMALL JUG (WITH LIP)

Eastern Mediterranean. 2nd century AD

H 14.2; rim: 5.5x7.5; GD 11.2; D bottom 5.1
Received in 1854; found in 1853 in
Pantikapaion necropolis
П.1853.62   ill.155

Spherical body; with narrow short neck slightly sunk into shoulders, wide funnel-shaped orifice, profiled rim with slightly raised lip; concave bottom. Flat handle, with three, barely visible ribs, bent at an angle, with flat protuberances at base and rim. Clear aquamarine glass. Pontil-mark (D 1.8) on bottom.

Condition: Surface iridescent and shine almost totally lost.

Literature: Извлечение, с. 182, ил. 75

Analogies: SH, П.1902.103; cat. 273, 274, 276, 277

276.
SMALL JUG (WITH LIP)
Eastern Mediterranean. 2nd century AD

H 10.6; D: rim 5; GD 8.8; bottom 3.6
Received in 1902; found in 1899 in Chersonesos
necropolis (crypt 1013; together with cat. 277)
X.1899.36   ill.153

Body in form of globe flattened at top;
with neck widening slightly downwards,
funnel-shaped orifice, bolster-shaped
rim with slightly raised lip; slightly concave bottom. Handle bent at angle, with
three-horned protuberance above rim
(fastened by side horn-shaped protection). Clear light-violet glass. Embossed
ornamental design, much run, in shape
of net with large meshes on body.
Handle carelessly made.

Condition: Surface iridescent.

Literature: ИАК, 1901, вып. 1, с. 16, ил. 14;
Г.Д.Белов. Римские приставные склепы
№№ 1013—1014 // Херсонесский сборник,
вып. II. Севастополь, 1927, с. 122, ил. 15

Analogies: SH, П.1902.103; cat. 273—275, 277

277.
SMALL JUG (WITH LIP)
Eastern Mediterranean. 2nd century AD

H 10.3; D: rim 4.4; GD 8.6; bottom 4.3
Received in 1902; found in 1899 in Chersonesos
necropolis (crypt 1013; together with cat. 276)
X.1899.35   ill.153

Spherical body; with short neck widening downwards, funnel-shaped orifice,
narrow bolster-shaped rim with slightly
raised lip; slightly concave bottom. Wide
handle, with groove in middle, curving
smoothly with loop-shaped protuberance and two flat protuberances at
sides above rim. Clear colourless glass;
bubbles lengthwise on neck. Rows of
applied diagonally spiralled thread on
body, becoming gradually less projected towards the bottom.

*Condition: Spot of silvery-white iridiscent
film on surface.*

Literature: ИАК, 1901, вып. 1, с. 16, ил. 15;
Г.Д.Белов. Римские приставные склепы
№№ 1013—1014 // Херсонесский сборник,
вып. II. Севастополь, 1927, с. 122, ил. 16

Analogies: See cat. 273—276

278.
JUG
Bosporan Kingdom. 3rd century AD

H 12.4; D: rim 5.3; GD 11.1; bottom 8.3

Received in 1909; found in 1904 in
Pantikapaion necropolis (grave 198/181/)
П.1904.83   ill.154

Pear-shaped body; with protruding profiled rim; flat bottom. Thick handle in
shape of braid, bending sharply, with
loop-shaped protuberance near base.
Clear light-aquamarine glass. Rim sliced
at top.

*Condition: Cracks on walls; silvery-
iridescent film on surface.*

Literature: ИАК, 1907, вып. 15, с. 62; Кунина
1997, с. 73, № 2, рис. 55

Analogies: Cat. 279; SH, E 611 (with ground
ornament); Сорокина 1965 (2), с. 218, ил. 9, 2;
with ground ornament: p. 213, ill. 7, 6; с. 218,
ill. 9, 1, 3 — in all 14 jugs from the Northern
Black Sea coast (10 of them from Pantikapaion
and Tanais); N.Sorokina suggests the Bosporan
production of the vessels; compare: JGS, 1966,
vol. VIII, ill. on cover (jug from Corning Museum
of Glass, USA)

279.
SMALL JUG
Bosporan Kingdom. 3rd century AD

H 10.5; D: rim 5.2; GD 8.4; bottom 5
Received in 1904; found in 1903 in Pantikapaion
necropolis (grave 159/36/; together with cat. 318)
П.1903.93   ill.154

Pear-shaped body; with very short neck,
flanged rim; flat bottom. Handle in
shape of braid, curving smoothly. Clear
aquamarine glass, with large amount of
bubbles. Pontil-mark on bottom.

*Condition: Silvery-iridescent film on surface
in places.*

Literature: ИАК, 1905, вып. 17, с. 35; Кунина
1997, с. 72, № 1, с. 73, рис. 54

Analogies: See cat. 278

280.
JUG
*Bosporan Kingdom. Late 3rd century —
early 4th century AD*

H 18; D: rim 6.4; GD 11; bottom 6.5
Received in 1935; found in 1902 in
Pantikapaion necropolis (grave 181/3/)
П.1902.160   ill.152

Pear-shaped body; with high neck
widening downwards, funnel-shaped
orifice, rim curving inwards; concave
bottom. Tape-shaped handle, with three
ribs, smoothly curved under rim. Clear
olive-greenish glass, with many small
and occasional large bubbles. Pontil-
mark (D 3.2) on bottom.

*Condition: Inner surface slightly dimmed in
places.*

Literature: ИАК, 1904, вып. 9, с. 107

Analogies: Often encountered in late 3rd century
and 4th century Bosporan graves; see Скалон
1973, с. 51, ил. 3; Сорокина 1963, с. 139,
ил. 2, 5; Сорокина 1971, с. 98, ил. 6, 1

281.
JUG
*Bosporan Kingdom. Late 3rd century —
early 4th century AD*

H 15.4; D: rim 6; GD 9.2; bottom 5
Received in 1953 from I.Tolstoy collection
E 3091

Spherical body; with high, almost cylindrical, neck, funnel-shaped orifice, bolster-shaped rim; concave bottom. Wide
flat handle with barely visible ribs,
slightly flanged at rim. Clear light-
aquamarine glass with many small bubbles. Pontil-mark (D 2.9) on bottom.

Condition: Surface iridescent.

First ever publication

Analogies: Typical for late 3rd and 4th century
Bosporan graves; see Скалон 1973, с. 50, ил. 1;
Сорокина 1963, с. 139, ил. 2, 3

282.
SKYPHOS
Italy or Syria. 1st century AD

H 5; D: rim 7.5; GD 8; pad-base 4
Received in 1900 from A.Novikov collection,
found in Kertch, probably in Pantikapaion necropolis
E 665   ill.156

Body widening downwards; with curved
rim, flattened pad-base in form of
shallow plate. Rounded handles, with
flat round protuberances above and
below (tong marks can be seen). Clear
greenish-blue glass.

Condition: Surface iridescent in places.

Literature: Художественное ремесло, кат. 295
(without ill.)

Analogies: Isings, Form 39; La Baume, Nr. L4,
Taf. 49, 4. Flat platforms on upper protuberances
of handles were often intended for a brand
bearing the master's name, which would be
applied with the aid of tongs so that the name
of the master and the town would be
simultaneously printed on both its outer and
inner surfaces — in Greek characters on one
side, and in Latin on the other. The Sidon
master Artas often made such bilingual stamps:
see Fremersdorf 1938, S. 117, Abb. 1; Smith
Collection, no. 165 a, b, c; also SH, Ж 120;
Ж 121 (two protuberances of handles from
beakers of clear blue and honey-yellow glass
with the bilingual stamps of this master)

283.
KANTHAROS
Egypt (Alexandria) or Italy. 1st century AD

H 5; D: rim 7; bottom 5.8

Received in 1872; found in 1872 in Pantikapaion necropolis (child's grave)
П.1872.65

Body widening slightly downwards; with flat rim; flat bottom. Narrow, round handles attached 1cm below rim. Clear olive-greenish glass. Rim carefully polished.

Condition: Surface iridescent in places.

First ever publication

Analogies: Compare shape with ceramic kantharoe from the times of Caesar Augustus; compare handles: Isings, Form 38; compare shape of body: Masterpieces, no. 68; Simonett, Taf. 6

284.
TWO-HANDLED BOWL

Eastern Mediterranean or Italy. (First half of ?) 1st century AD

H 4.8; D: rim 12.1; pad-base 4.5
Received from SAHMC; previously in A.Bobrinsky collection, acquired in Kerch
E 2178   ill.157

With rounded walls; smoothly curved rim, with low ring-shaped pad-base in shape of small plate. Narrow handles, in shape of braid, rounded, elevated over rim. Clear light-bluish glass. Pad-base made separately and affixed to vessel. Pontil-mark (D 2) on bottom. Noteable for its laconic form and elegant proportions.

Condition: Good.

First ever publication

Analogies: Form imitates that of silver vessels; compare with K.Pernice und F.Winter. Der Hildesheimer Silberfund. Berlin, 1901, S. 36, fig. 13

285.
BOWL

Eastern Mediterranean. 1st century AD
H 6.5; D: rim 10.2; pad-base 4.7
Received in 1893 from J.Lemme' collection
E 380   ill.158

With rounded walls; with high profiled overhanging rim, protruding massive flat pad-base. Clear dark-aquamarine glass. Shallow round cavity (D 1) on inner bottom. Pad-base made separately. Repeats form of earthenware red-lacquer bowls.

Condition: Film of silvery iridescence on parts of surface.

First ever publication

Analogies: Cat. 286; Isings, Form 69a; Vessberg 1952, pl. IX, 40, 41; La Baume, Nr. D5, Taf. 16, *1*; Sammlung Oppenländer, Nr. 295, 296; Auth, no. 97; Liepmann, Nr. 71; Matheson, no. 106, 107

286.
BOWL

Eastern Mediterranean. 1st century AD
H 6.4; D: rim 11; pad-base 4.5
Received in 1904 from Kertch
П.1903/4.8   ill.159

With rounded walls; massive high profiled protecting rim, flat pad-base. Clear cobalt-blue glass. Spherical protuberance on inner bottom; depression on outside of pad-base (D 0.9).
Condition: Surface iridescent in places.

First ever publication

Analogies: See cat. 285

287.
BOWL

Eastern Mediterranean. Mid — third quarter of 1st century AD

H 6.4; D: rim 11; pad-base 6.7
Found in 1842 in Pantikapaion necropolis (kurgan III, grave 1; together with cat. 230, 296, 340, 361, 362)
П.1842.67   ill.173

Almost vertical walls, narrowing downwards; profiled, protecting rim; with narrow, hollow, ring base; concave bottom. Clear bluish glass. Pontil-mark (D 2.1) on bottom.

Condition: Surface slightly iridescent.

Literature: ЗООИД, 1844, т. I, с. 616, сл.; Спасский, с. 144; Кунина, Сорокина, с. 152, ил. 4, *14*

Analogies: Spartz, Nr. 45, Taf. 11, *45*; Auth, no. 102

288.
BOWL

Eastern Mediterranean (Syria ?) 1st century AD

H 8.9; D: rim 13.2; pad-base 5.6
Received in 1927 from SAHMC; bought in Parutino, Nikolaevskaya Region as coming from Olbia
Ол. 3576

With high rounded, walls; with high, almost vertical, protecting rim; hollow ring-base; concave bottom. Clear bluish glass. Pontil-mark (D 2) on bottom.

Condition: Glued together from many pieces; losses; surface iridescent.

First ever publication

Analogies: Petru 1969, p. 167, tabl. 1, *10*, compare: Fitzwilliam Mus., no. 62; Vessberg 1952, pl. IX, 40; Auth, no. 361; Isings, Form 69a

289.
BOWL

Eastern Mediterranean. Three quarter of 1st century — early 2nd century AD

H 4.5; D: rim 10.2; pad-base 4.5
Received in 1854; found in 1852 (1853 ?) in the environs of Kerch
П.1852/53.24

Semi-spherical form; with flanged, slightly profiled rim; on low, thick ring-base; concave bottom. Clear bluish glass. Pontil-mark (D 2.7) on bottom.

Condition: Good.

First ever publication

Analogies: Vessberg 1952, pl. I, 29; Fitzwilliam Mus., no. 77c; compare with Hayes, no. 296

290.
BOWL

Eastern Mediterranean Late 1st century — early 2nd century AD

H 5.6; D: rim 13.2; pad-base 6.1
Received in 1873; found in 1873 in Pantikapaion necropolis
П.1873.146

Semi-spherical shape; with smoothly flanged rim; on low ring-base; slightly concave bottom (coned in centre). Clear bluish glass. Pontil-mark (D 2.1) on bottom.

Condition: Film of silvery iridescence on outer surface in places.

First ever publication

Analogies: Simonett, S. 167, Abb. 142, *17b, 17c, 33*; Isings, Form 42a; La Baume, Nr. D2, Taf. 15, *2*; compare with Auth, no. 364

291.
BEAKER (PYXIS ?)

Eastern Mediterranean (Cyprus ?). First half of 1st century AD

H 6; D: rim 8.1; GD 9.3; bottom 4; thickness of walls 0.15
Received in 1864; found in 1863 in Pantikapaion necropolis (grave 96)
П.1863.33   ill.162

Biconical form; thick walls, slightly protecting over base; slightly flanged rim; slightly concave bottom. Clear cobalt-blue glass. One hardly discernable thin engraved girdle on body below rim, doubled at bottom below curve of walls. Rim sliced off and polished. Judging by the type of rim, cup might have been provided with lid.

Condition: Film of silvery iridescence on surface in places.

Literature: CR for 1863, 1864, p. XIII

Analogies: See cat. 182, 292; Vessberg 1952, pl. III, no. 15, 16; compare: Petru 1972, tabl. IV, 4; tabl. LXXXIV, 8, 9; Spartz, Nr. 31, Taf. 7; Fremersdorf IV, Taf. 76, 77

282

283

284*

285

286

287

288

289

290

291

292

293

294

292.
BEAKER (PYXIS ?)

Eastern Mediterranean (Cyprus ?)
First half of 1st century AD

H 7.3; D: rim 6.8; GD 8.8; bottom 4.5
Received in 1926 from S.Stroganov collection
E 1202   ill.161

Biconical form; with high walls, slightly flanged rim; concave bottom. Clear colourless glass, with small spherical bubbles. Three equidistant thin engraved girdles below neck, in middle section and at foot of body. Rim sliced off. The shape of rim suggests that the cup might have been provided with lid.

Condition: Thick film of silvery iridescence on inner surface.

First ever publication

Analogies: Compare: cat. 182, 291; Vessberg 1952, pl. III, 9; Petru 1972, tabl. IV, 4, tabl. LXXXIV, 8, 9; Auth, no. 351; Benko, tabl. XXVIII, 4 (12b/21)

293.
BEAKER

Eastern Mediterranean. Second half of 1st century AD

H 11.2; D rim 10.6; GD: 11.4; bottom 5.8; thickness of walls 0.2
Received in 1904; found in 1903 in Pantikapaion necropolis (grave 278/155/; together with cat. 308)
П.1903.151

High, almost cylindrical body, narrowing slightly upwards and near base; slightly concave bottom. Clear aquamarine glass. Three wide polished girdles and three thin engraved girdles in alternation on body.

Condition: Surface heavily iridescent; shine lost in places.

Literature: ИАК, 1905, вып. 17, с. 57; Кунина, Сорокина, с. 151, ил. 3, *11*

Analogies: Кунина, Сорокина, с. 158, ил. 6, *38, 54*; Сорокина 1962, с. 224, ил. 9, *7*; Auth, no. 367; Fremersdorf IV, Taf. 74; compare with Sammlung Hentrich, Nr. 245

294.
CUP

Eastern Mediterranean or Italy. Second quarter — mid 1st century AD

H 7; D: rim 7.1; bottom 3; thickness of walls 0.2
Received in 1854; found in 1852 (1853 ?) in the environs of Kertch
П.1852/53.27

Body sharply narrowing downwards; with rounded, thick walls; flat bottom. Dull dark-blue glass. Relief girdles on body under rim and near base; polished groove on middle section.

Manufacturing technique: Traces of polishing by buffing on inside and outside. Made in mould (?).

Condition: Surface heavily iridescent on both sides; upper layer of glass partially lost; colour has changed.

First ever publication

Analogies: Berger, Taf. 6, *94* (Taf. 19, *48*); E.Ritterling. Das frührömische Lager bet Hofheim im Taunus. Annalen des Vereins für Nassauische Altertumskunde und Geschichtforschung. Bd. 40, 1912, Taf. XXXVIII, 3A; compare: Recent Important Acquisitions // JGS, 1978, vol. 20, p.120, no. 7; compare shape with cat.144

295.
BEAKER

Syro-Palestinian region. Second — third quarter of 1st century AD

H 11.7; D: rim 7.3; pad-base 4.3; thickness of walls 0.3
Received in 1854; found in 1852 (1853 ?) in the environs of Kertch
П.1852/53.23   ill.169

High body narrowing sharply downwards, with rounded walls; with slightly flanged rim, massive flat pad-base; concave semispherical bottom. Clear aquamarine glass. Wide polished groove between two engraved lines on centre of body; at equal distances both above and below; engraved girdles; a similar girdle under rim. Rim sliced off and polished.

Condition: Good.

First ever publication

Analogies: Vessberg 1952, pl. IV, 6; Isings, Form 34; Sammlung Hentrich, Nr. 247; compare with cat. 296

296.
BEAKER

Syro-Palestinian region. Mid — third quarter of 1st century AD

H 11.4; D: rim 6.4; pad-base 4.3
Found in 1842 in Pantikapaion necropolis (kurgan III, grave 1; together with cat. 230, 287, 340, 361, 362)
П.1842.68   ill.173

Analogous in form and decoration to cat. 295; difference lies in position of decorations: one engraved girdle under rim and one on lower part of body, wide polished girdle between two engraved ones at top. Clear aquamarine glass.

Condition: Surface iridescent in places.

Literature: ЗООИД, 1844, т. I, с. 616 сл.; Спасский, с. 144; Кунина, Сорокина, с. 152, ил. 4, *15*

Analogies: SH, П.1903.19 (compare also with cat. 295); Vessberg 1952, pl. IV, 6; Dusenbery, 1967, p. 47, fig. 41; Dusenbery, 1971, p. 21, fig. 29; Hayes, no. 133; Кунина, Сорокина, с. 158, ил. 6, *55*; Isings, Form 34; Сорокина 1977, с. 136, ил. 6, *3*; Алексеева 1982 (2),

с. 59, ил. 33, *6*; compare: cat. 297; Sammlung Hentrich, Nr. 246

297.
BEAKER

Eastern Mediterranean
Mid—third quarter of 1st century AD

H 13.1; D: rim 7.4; pad-base 3.5
Received in 1880; found in 1880 in Pantikapaion necropolis (submound grave 50)
П.1880.14   ill.164

Very high, cone-shaped body; with slightly flanged rim, small flat pad-base; slightly concave bottom. Clear cobalt-blue glass. Polished groove between two engraved girdles on upper part of body, one engraved girdle under rim and one at bottom. Rim sliced off and polished.

Condition: Surface iridescent in places.

Literature: OAK for 1880, c. XX—XXI (without ill.); Художественное стекло, с. 6 (without ill.)

Analogies: Recent Important Acquisitions // JGS, XI, 1969, p. 111, no. 11; Dusenbery 1967, p. 46, fig. 41; Sammlung Hentrich, Nr. 246; compare also SH, П.1861.2; П.1861.3 (straight walls); Hayes, no. 134; Matheson, no. 99

298.
BEAKER

Eastern Mediterranean (Syro-Palestinian region ?). 40s—70s AD

H 9; D: rim 6.7; base 6.5; pad-base 3.9
Received in 1872; found in 1872 in Pantikapaion necropolis (grave III, together with cat. 63, 163, 213)
П.1872.97

Cone-shaped body; walls widening upwards and downwards, projecting over narrowing rounded lower section of body; with protruding rim, on thin, flat, ring-shaped base; concave bottom. Clear light-aquamarine glass. One polished groove at top, one at bottom and doubled one in middle. Rim sliced off and polished.

Condition: Good.

Literature: OAK for 1880, 1882, с. XXII

Analogies: SH, П.1872.107 (Кунина, Сорокина, с. 149, ил. 2, *4*); П.1896.31 (АДЖ, табл. LXI, 3); Сорокина 1978, с. 270, ил. 2, *10* (from Pantikapaion); Dusenbery 1967, p. 47, fig. 42; Dusenbery 1971, p. 21, fig. 30; Vanderhoeven, no. 30, pl. VI, 30; Auth, no. 376; Hayes, no. 137; Matheson, no. 112, 113

299.
BEAKER

Eastern Mediterranean (Syria ?). Second half of 1st century — early 2nd century AD

H 8.7; D: rim 5.7; pad-base 4.3

295 □

296 □

297 □

298

299

300 □

301

302 □

303

304

305–307 □

308

309

310 □

311

Received in 1850; found in 1850 in Pantikapaion necropolis (kurgan III, grave 3)
П.1850.7

Body with rounded walls narrowing sharply downwards; with slightly flanged rim, on massive, flat pad-base; semi-spherical, concave bottom. Clear aquamarine glass; with various-sized bubbles. Wide polished groove between two thin engraved girdles on upper section of body, one engraved groove on lower section. Rim sliced off and polished.

Condition: Iridescent film on surface.

First ever publication

Analogies: SH, П.1905.39; Сорокина 1962, с. 220, ил. 7, *3* (с. 224, ил. 9, *1*); Filarska, Nr. 77, tabl. XVI, 3; Hayes, no. 136; Sammlung Hentrich, Nr. 248, 249; Benko, tabl. XXXIII, 6 (12.f/9); compare with cat. 295, 296

300.
BEAKER

Eastern Mediterranean. Mid — second half of 1st century AD

H 9.4; D: rim 7.2; pad-base 4.5
Received in 1872; found in 1872 in Pantikapaion necropolis (grave I; together with cat. 230, 240)
П.1872.84   ill.144

Ovoid body with walls narrowing downwards; with bolster-like rim, on flat pad-base; slightly concave bottom. Clear light-aquamarine glass. Rim melted (?). Pontil-mark (D 2.2) on bottom.

Condition: Good.

Literature: OAK for 1872, с. XXI—XXII

Analogies: Vessberg 1952, pl. IV, 3; Vessberg 1963, pl. 58, *64*; Hayes, no. 192, Antik Kunst, nr. 353

301.
BEAKER

Eastern Mediterranean. Second half of 1st century AD

H 9.4; D: rim 6.5; bottom 4.9
Received in 1912; found in 1910 in ruined grave of Pantikapaion necropolis
П.1910.116

Body with concave walls widening upwards and downwards; with smooth rim; flat bottom. Clear greenish glass. One polished girdle under rim, one in middle and one at bottom of body; two thin engraved girdles between them. Rim sliced off and polished.

Condition: Glued together from pieces; surface iridescent.

Literature: ИАК, 1913, вып. 47, с. 72

Analogies: Compare with mould-blown glasses with relief ornamental design: Dusenbery 1971, p. 13, fig. 6; Fogolari e Scarfi, tav. 66, *3*

302.
BEAKER

Northern Italy (?). 1st century AD

H 7.5; D: rim 8; pad-base 5
Received in 1900 from A.Novikov collection; found on the territory of Nymphaion, probably in necropolis
E663   ill.168

Body widening upwards; with rounded walls and thirteen ribs on outside; smooth rim, on massive flat protruding pad-base; semi-spherical, concave bottom. Clear aquamarine glass. Rim sliced off.

Condition: Surface slightly iridescent.

First ever publication

Analogies: Compare: Benko, tabl. XXIX, II (12c/3, 10), tabl. XXX, I (12c/3, 11); Berger, Taf. 16, *6*

303.
BEAKER

Cyprus. Second half of 1st century AD

H 14; D: rim 7.1; pad-base 3.9
Received in 1976; found in 1976 in Nymphaion necropolis (grave B-2)
ННФ.76.206

High, cone-shaped body with small flat pad-base formed by lower part of walls with twelve vertical cavities; with protruding rim; semi-spherical, concave bottom. Clear slightly greenish glass. Rim sliced off.

Condition: Glued together from pieces; part of base lost; surface iridescent.

First ever publication

Analogies: Compare: cat. 304; Vessberg 1952, pl. IV, 14; Myres, p. 511, no. 5686; Fremersdorf IX, Nr. 62; Bucovala 1984, p. 62, fig. 7

304.
BEAKER

Cyprus. Second half of 1st century AD

H 13.6; D: rim 7.5; pad-base 4.3
Received in 1893 from J.Lemme' collection
E 414

Analogous in shape and decoration to cat. 303. Clear greenish glass.

Condition: Glued together from pieces; parts of walls and rim lost; surface iridescent.

First ever publication

Analogies: See cat. 303

305.
BEAKER

Cyprus. Second half of 1st century AD

H 6.5; D: rim 6.8; bottom 4
Received in 1904; found in 1903 in Pantikapaion necropolis (grave 100; together with cat. 215)
П.1903.68

Ovoid body, with four oval cavities; with protuberant rim on the outside; slightly concave bottom. Clear bluish glass. Rim sliced off.

Condition: Surface iridescent.

Literature: ИАК, 1905, вып. 17, с. 25

Analogies: Cat. 307; SH, П.1873.139; П.1902.182; Сорокина 1978, с. 270, ил. 2, *22*, А.К.Коровина. Тирамба (городище и некрополь). Итог археологических работ экспедиции Государственного музея изобразительных искусств им. А.С.Пушкина за 1959, 1961—1963 и 1968 годы // Сообщения ГМИИ им. А.С.Пушкина, 1968, вып. IV, с. 79 (склеп 54); Vessberg 1963, p. 116, fig. 1b; Harden, 1936, pl. XV, 391; Bucovala 1968, p. 48, no. 48; Simonett, S. 115, Abb. 94, *8* (Taf. 12, *1*); Berger, Taf. 7, *107* (Taf. 19, *54*, *107*); Isings, Form 32; Sammlung Niessen, Band II, Taf. XVIII, 257; Nr. 109, 373; compare with Hayes, no. 187

306.
BEAKER

Eastern Mediterranean (Cyprus ?). Second half of 1st century AD

H 8.8; D: rim 6.8; bottom 5
Found in 1946 in Pantikapaion necropolis (kurgan X, grave 8)
П.1846.47   ill.170

Almost pear-like body; with four rounded cavities on walls, with flanged rim; concave bottom. Clear aquamarine glass.

Condition: Surface iridescent.

First ever publication

Analogies: See cat. 309; compare: Vessberg 1952, no. 34, 35; Hayes, no. 191; Antik kunst, Nr. 344; Petru 1972, tabl. CIV, 13, 15

307.
BEAKER

Cyprus. Second half of 1st century AD

H 8.1; D: rim 7.2; bottom 3.7
Received in 1906; found in 1900 in Pantikapaion necropolis (grave 52)
П.1900.25   ill.170

Analogical in form and decoration to cat. 305. Clear bluish glass.

Condition: Surface iridescent.

Literature: ИАК, 1902, вып. 2, с. 49

Analogies: See cat. 305

308.
BEAKER

Eastern Mediterranean (Cyprus ?) Second half of 1st century AD

H 8.8; D: rim 6.8; bottom: 4.5x4.5
Received in 1904; found in 1903 in Pantikapaion necropolis (grave 278/155/; together with cat. 293)
П.1903.168

312—314   □   315   □   316, 317

318   319   320

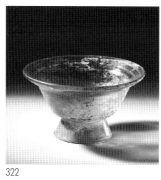

321   322   323

High, almost ovoid body; with four deep, oval cavities, slightly outsplayed rim; square, slightly concave bottom. Clear light-aquamarine glass. Thirteen and a half coils of applied thread on body (on one of protuberances is a piece of glass, the starting point for the first coil); cavities made after application of thread.

Condition: Glued together from pieces; surface iridescent.

Literature: ИАК, 1905, вып. 17, с. 57; Кунина, Сорокина, с. 151, ил. 3, *12*

Analogies: All without thread; see Vessberg 1952, pl. III, 28, 29; Vessberg 1963, p. 166, fig. 1b, pl. 56d; Benko, tabl. XXXIII, 1 (12e/41); Bucovala 1968, p. 46, nr. 43; Sammlung Hentrich, Nr. 120

309.
BEAKER

Cyprus. Second half of 1st century AD (?)

H 6.2; D: rim 7.1; bottom 4.2
Received in 1875; found in 1875 in Pantikapaion necropolis (grave 11)
П.1875.445

Rounded body with walls narrowing upwards; with four rounded cavities near base, curved, bolster-shaped rim; slightly concave bottom. Clear bluish glass.

Condition: Surface iridescent.

Literature: OAK for 1875, c. XXIX

Analogies: Compare: cat. 306, also Vessberg 1952, pl. III, 31; Hayes, no. 190; Petru 1972, tabl. CIV, 14

310.
BEAKER

Eastern Mediterranean (Cyprus ?)
Mid — third quarter of 1st century AD

H 14.8; D: rim 4.4; foot 3.7; bottom: 4x4.6
Received in 1905; found in 1902 in Pantikapaion necropolis (grave 225/37/; together with cat. 337)
П.1902.69   ill.171

High, pear-shaped body with conical base and four cavities; flanged rim; low cone-shaped foot; almost square bottom. Clear colourless glass. Thin engraved girdle at top of body; rim polished.

Condition: Glued together from two pieces; part of foot lost; surface iridescent, dull in places.

Literature: ИАК, 1904, вып. 9, с. 113, ил. 29

Analogies: A.P. di Cesnola. Salaminia (Cyprus). London, 1882, pl. XVIII, 23; H.Dragendorff. Theraische Graeber. Thera. Zweiter Band. Berlin, 1903, S. 286, Abb. 481; compare with Benko, tabl. XXXIII, 2 (12e/42)

311.
JAR

Gaul or Germany. 2nd—3rd centuries AD

H 7.4; D: rim 6.1; GD 7.7; pad-base 4.3
Received in 1913; bought from A.Elterman in Kertch
E 908

Spherical body; with four rounded cavities in walls; with funnel-shaped orifice; on ring-shaped base. Clear colourless glass. Pontil-mark (D 2) on bottom.

Condition: Brown film on surface in places.

First ever publication

Analogies: Vanderhoeven, pl. VI, no. 29; Fremersdorf IX, Nr. 128; compare: Fremersdorf IV, Taf. 20; Morin-Jean, p. 145, fig. 199

312.
ONE-HANDLED JAR

Eastern Mediterranean. 1st century AD

H 5.8; D: rim 5.8; GD 6.4; bottom 1.5
Received in 1900 from A.Novikov collection; found on the territory of Nymphaion, probably in necropolis
E694   ill.166

Spherical body; with slightly outsplayed rim; flat bottom. Loop-shaped handle. Clear blue glass; handle of dull glass. Coils of spiral thread of white dull glass on body, girdle of same glass along rim.

Condition: Only traces of thread on body; part of coil on bottom; silvery-white crust of iridescence on surface.

First ever publication

Analogies: SH, E 667; П.1874.95; cat. 313, 314; compare: cat. 315; Sammlung Oppenländer, Nr. 641; Antik Kunst, pl. 339, 340; Fortuna 1969, p. 24, fig. 23

313.
ONE-HANDLED JAR

Eastern Mediterranean. 1st century AD

H 5.2; D: rim 6.1; GD 7.3; bottom 2.5
Received in 1931 from the RAS collection; found in 1854 in Pantikapaion necropolis
П.1854.79   ill.166

Squat spherical body; with slightly flanged rim; flat bottom. Thin, loop-shaped handle. Clear yellow glass; handle of dull white glass. Coils of spiral applied thread of white dull glass on body.

Condition: Crack on bottom; surface iridescent.

First ever publication

Analogies: See cat. 312

314.
ONE-HANDLED JAR

Eastern Mediterranean. 1st century AD

H 6.5; D: rim 6; GD 8; bottom 4.1

Received in 1924 from SAHMC; found in 1913 in Pantikapaion necropolis
П.1913.20   ill.166

Spherical body; with flanged rim; flat bottom. Loop-shaped handle, slightly elevated above rim. Clear greenish-blue glass. On body, coils of spiral applied thread of white dull glass ending in spiral at bottom.

Condition: Crack near handle; surface iridescent.

First ever publication

Analogies: See cat. 312

315.
ONE-HANDLED JAR

Eastern Mediterranean. 1st century AD

H 6; D: rim 5.5; GD 7.5; bottom 2.8
Received in 1900 from A.Novikov collection; found on the territory of Nymphaion, probably in necropolis
E 689   ill.167

Spherical body; with protruding rim; flat bottom. Thin, loop-shaped handle, slightly elevated above rim. Clear dark-blue glass with dimmed white patterns.

Condition: Surface iridescent in places.

First ever publication

Analogies: See cat. 312; Fortuna 1969, p. 24, fig. 23; compare Sammlung Oppenländer, Nr. 383a (Farbtaf. 124)

316.
BEAKER

Eastern Mediterranean. Second half of 1st century AD

H 6.2; D: rim 6; GD 7.7; pad-base 4.3
Received in 1924; found in Pantikapaion necropolis (grave 5)
П.1914.18

Spherical body with flat, ring-shaped pad-base; with flanged rim; slightly concave bottom. Clear aquamarine glass. Horizontal girdles under rim and near bottom; wide polished groove between two engraved lines in middle section. Rim sliced off and polished.

Condition: Cracks on walls; surface iridescent.

First ever publication

Analogies: See cat. 317; compare with Sammlung Hentrich, Nr. 149; compare shape: mould-blown cups; Sammlung Löffler, Taf. 6, *3*, Nr. 60; Sammlung Oppenländer, Nr. 447

317.
BEAKER

Eastern Mediterranean
Second half of 1st century AD

H 7.7; D: rim 6.5; GD 7; pad-base 4.3

Received in 1925; found in 1901 in Pantikapaion necropolis (grave 58/55/)
П.1901.34

Spherical body with flat base formed by lower part of walls; with high neck; flanged rim. Clear aquamarine glass. Engraved girdle under rim and near bottom; three close girdles in middle section. Rim sliced off.

Condition: Surface iridescent.

Literature: ИАК, 1903, вып. 7, с. 91

Analogies: See cat. 316; compare: Hayes, no. 135; Benko, tabl. XXXVII, 8 (14b/2)

318.
BEAKER

Eastern Mediterranean. 3rd century AD

H 7; D: rim 5.8; GD 6.2; bottom 4.2
Received in 1904; found in 1903 in Pantikapaion necropolis (grave 159/36/; together with cat. 279)
П.1903.92

Almost spherical body on small thick base formed by lower part of walls; with flanged rim; flat bottom. Clear greenish glass, with many bubbles. Two girdles of close thin engraved lines under rim; one below. Rim sliced off.

Condition: Cracks; surface iridescent in places.

Literature: ИАК, 1905, вып. 17, с. 35

Analogies: Bucovalia 1968, nr. 55; reproduces the form of earthenware jugs from various parts of the ancient world popular in the 3rd century AD

319.
BEAKER

Eastern Mediterranean. Second half of 1st century — early 2nd century AD

H 8.4; D: rim 5.3; GD 7; pad-base 3.6
Received in 1904; found in 1903 in Pantikapaion necropolis (grave 157/34/)
П.1903.90

Cone-shaped body, with walls narrowing towards bottom; with bolster-shaped rim, on low, ring-shaped base; flat bottom. Clear aquamarine glass. Base made separately; Pontil-mark (D 1) on bottom.

Condition: Surface iridescent.

Literature: ИАК, 1905, вып. 17, с. 35, grave 157 (34)

Analogies: Liepmann, Nr. 74; Sammlung Hentrich, Nr. 137

320.
BEAKER

*Eastern Mediterranean (Cyprus ?)
2nd — 3rd centuries AD*

H 7.4; D: rim 4.5; GD 7.5; pad-base 3.2

Received in 1927 from SAHMC; bought in Parutino, Nikolaev Region, as having been found on the territory of Olbia
Ол. 3575

Biconical body; with bolster-shaped rim, on low ring-shaped base; flat bottom. Clear colourless glass. Two girdles of applied thread at top and foot of body. Pontil-mark (D 0.8—1) on bottom.

Condition: Glued back together from pieces; hole; surface iridescent.

First ever publication

Analogies: Vessberg 1952, pl. IV, no. 33—35; Matheson, no. 264; compare with La Baume, Nr. D36 (Taf. 23, *3*)

321.
ONE-HANDLED JAR

Egypt. Second half of 2nd century AD

H 8.4; D: rim 6; GD 8; foot 4.5
Received in 1874; found in Pantikapaion necropolis (grave 5; together with cat. 272, 323, 374)
П.1874.118

Ovoid body with flattened, cone-shaped foot; with wide neck, flanged bolster-shaped rim; strongly concave bottom. Loop-shaped handle, with flat oval protuberance over rim. Clear olive-greenish glass. Pontil-mark (D 2) on bottom.

Condition: Glued together again from pieces; losses; holes in walls; surface iridescent in places.

Literature: OAK for 1874, с. XI; Кунина, Сорокина, с. 185, ил. 9, *53*

Analogies: Compare with two-handled cups: Сорокина 1978, с. 270, ил. 2, *7*; Hayes, no. 597; Harden 1936, pl. XVI, 488, pl. XVII, 511

322.
BOWL

Syria. Second half of 2nd century AD

H 6; D: rim 11; foot 5.4
Received in 1874; found in 1874 in Pantikapaion necropolis (grave 5; together with cat. 272, 321, 374)
П.1874.117

With thick rounded, walls; flanged elevated rim; on high, conical foot. Clear almost colourless glass, with tint of light-green. Two polished grooves under rim; polished circle (D 1.6) on inside bottom, possibly traces of polishing by buffing.

Condition: Yellowy-silver film of iridescence on surface in places.

Literature: OAK for 1874, с. XI; Кунина, Сорокина, с. 165, ил. 9, *54*

Analogies: Vessberg 1952, pl. II, 16; Fitzwilliam Mus., no. 99; Edgar, pl. II, 32.452

323.
BOWL

Eastern Mediterranean. 3rd century AD

H 5.2; D: rim 12.5; pad-base 6.1
Received in 1904; found in 1903 in Pantikapaion necropolis (grave 203/80/)
П.1903.100

Cone-shaped body with small ring-shaped base formed by lower part of walls; with bolster-shaped rim curved inwards; bottom flat on outside and slightly convex inside. Clear almost colourless glass, with tint of light yellow-green. Small disc-shaped lump (D 1.1; H 0.4) for attaching the pontil on outer bottom.

Condition: Two small cracks; surface iridescent.

Literature: ИАК, 1905, вып. 17, с. 43

Analogies: Edgar, pl. II, 32.462; compare: Isings, Form 80; Benko, tabl. XXV, 2 (8b/7)

324.
BEAKER

*Eastern Mediterranean (Cyprus ?)
First half of 2nd century AD*

H 6.6; D: rim 7.2; bottom 3.5
Found in 1846 in Pantikapaion necropolis (kurgan X, grave 6; together with cat. 370)
П.1846.44

Body narrowing downwards, with rounded walls, with slightly flanged rim; slightly concave bottom. Clear almost colourless glass, with tint of light-green, with many bubbles. Embossed girdle of applied thread under rim. Pontil-mark (D 0.9) on bottom.

Condition: Good.

First ever publication

Analogies: Compare with Vessberg 1952, pl. IV, 24

325.
BEAKER

*Eastern Mediterranean
2nd—3rd centuries AD (?)*

H 8.4; D: rim 6; bottom 2.8
Date and circumstances of acquisition unknown
E 43   ill.160

High body narrowing upwards; with slightly flanged rim; small, slightly concave bottom. Clear bright-green glass. Four thin engraved girdles in centre of body; rim sliced off and polished.

Condition: Glued together again from pieces; surface corroded; pearly crust or iridescent film in places.

First ever publication

Analogies: Vessberg 1952, pl. III, 40; compare with La Baume, Nr. D37 (Taf. 23, *4*)

326.
BEAKER

Bosporan Kingdom (?). Late 2nd — early 3rd century AD

H 6.8; D: rim 7.1; bottom 6.1
Received in 1925; found in 1900 in Pantikapaion necropolis (grave 17; together with cat. 265, 375)
П.1900.6

Cylindrical shape; with flanged bolster-shaped rim; flat bottom. Clear colourless glass.

Condition: Surface covered in golden-iridescent film.

Literature: ИАК, 1902, вып. 2, с. 43; Кунина, Сорокина, с. 165, ил. 9, *47*

Analogies: Cat. 328; SH, П.1903.30 (two coils of applied thread under rim); Сорокина 1962, с. 220, ил. 7, *2*; с. 224, ил. 9, *8*; Кобылина, с. 80, ил. 117; Spartz, Nr. 29, Taf. 7, *29* (from Olbia); with engraved girdles see Сорокина 1965 (2), с. 206, ил. 1, *2–8*

327.
BEAKER

Bosporan Kingdom (?). Second half of 2nd century — first half of 3rd century AD

H 5.3; D: rim 7.2; bottom 5.3
Received in 1905; found in 1902 in Pantikapaion necropolis (grave 285/97/)
П.1902.75

Cylindrical shape; with flanged rim; flat bottom. Clear colourless glass. Three horizontal engraved girdles of several close lines on walls.

Condition: Cracks on bottom; surface heavily iridescent and shine almost completely lost.

Literature: ИАК, 1904, вып. 9, с. 123, 124

Analogies: Compare with Сорокина 1965 (2), с. 206, ил. 1, *2–8*

328.
BEAKER

Bosporan Kingdom (?) Late 2nd century — early 3rd century AD

H 7; D: rim 7.1; bottom 5.5
Received in 1905; found in 1902 in Pantikapaion necropolis (grave 243/55/)
П.1902.73

Analogous in form and decoration to cat. 326. Clear colourless glass. Pontil-mark (D 1) on bottom.

Condition: Cracks in walls and bottom; golden-iridescent film on surface.

Literature: ИАК, 1904, вып. 9, с. 116

Analogies: See cat. 326

329.
BEAKER

Eastern Mediterranean or Bosporan Kingdom. 2nd — 3rd centuries AD

H 7; D: rim 5.1; bottom 4.7
Received in 1912; found in 1910 in Pantikapaion necropolis (grave 14)
П.1910.15

Almost cylindrical form, narrowing slightly upwards; with slightly flanged, bolster-shaped rim; flat bottom. Clear olive-greenish glass. Embossed girdle of applied thread on upper section of body. Pontil-mark (D 1.1) on bottom.

Condition: Surface iridescent.

Literature: ИАК, 1913, вып. 47, с. 48

Analogies: Compare: Edgar, pl. III, 32.464; compare with cat. 326, 328

330.
BEAKER

Eastern Mediterranean. 2nd — early 3rd centuries AD

H 6; D: rim 8.1; bottom 3.2
Received in 1914; found in 1912 in Pantikapaion necropolis
П.1912.45

Almost cylindrical body, slightly convex in middle section, with flanged rim; bottom concave in centre. Clear light-aquamarine glass. Two circuits of thin, applied thread under rim. Rim melted; pontil-mark (D 2) on bottom.

Condition: Surface iridescent.

First ever publication

Analogies: Compare with Fremersdorf IX, Nr. 30; Алексеева 1982 (2), с. 62, ил. 35, *7*

331.
KANTHAROS

Gaul or Rhineland. 2nd century AD

H 10; D: rim 10.1; foot 5.5
Received in 1924; found in 1914 in Pantikapaion necropolis (grave 1)
П.1914.32   ill.165

Semi-spherical body; with slightly flanged rim, on hollow conical foot. Thin vertical handles with flat horizontal shoulders; fastened low down. Clear slightly yellowy glass. Thin engraved girdles at top and foot of body; rim sliced off and polished.

Condition: Part of rim and wall glued back on again; cracks; foot glued back together from pieces; surface destroyed; film of silvery-pearl iridescence in places.

Literature: Сорокина 1965 (2), с. 206, ил. 1, *9*

Analogies: Fremersdorf IX, Nr. 86; compare: Sorokina 1965 (2), с. 213, ил. 7, *7*, с. 216, ил. 8, *8*; La Baume, Nr. L5 (Taf. 50, *1*); Doppelfeld, Taf. 153

332.
BOWL

Rhineland (Cologne ?). Second half of 2nd century — early 3rd century AD

H 5; D rim 7.7
Received in 1904; found in 1903 in Pantikapaion necropolis (grave 49; together with cat. 222, 371)
П.1903.46

Semi-spherical shape; with thin walls, protruding outer rim; flat bottom. Clear almost colourless glass. Five equidistant thin engraved girdles under rim and on body; rim unwrought at top.

Condition: Cracks; part of rim lost; golden-iridescent crust on surface in places.

Literature: ИАК, 1905, вып. 17, с. 15

Analogies: Сорокина 1965(2), с. 213, ил. 7, *1*; с. 212, ил. 6, *7* (with polished ornamental design); compare: Fr.Fremersdorf. Figurlich geschliffene Gläser eine Kölner Werkstatt des 3. Jahrhunderts. Berlin, 1951, Taf. 2, *2*; Morin-Jean, p. 236, fig. 319

333.
BOWL (WITH POLISHED ORNAMENTAL DESIGN)

Rhineland (Cologne ?). 3rd century — early 4th century AD

H 7.7; D rim 12.1; thickness of walls 0.2
Received in 1900 from A.Novikov collection, bought in Kertch probably in Pantikapaion necropolis
E 668   ill.183, 184

Semi-spherical body; with flanged rim; small, flat bottom. Clear colourless glass. Continuous polished four-tier ornamental design: two girdles of horizontal ovals alternating with friezes of vertical double ovals. Smooth rim; rosette of circles on bottom. Rim sliced off and polished.

Condition: Cracks; milky-white and rainbow-coloured film of iridescence on surface in places.

Literature: Художественное ремесло, кат. 300; Кунина 1984, с. 158, № 21, табл. III, 21

Analogies: Fremersdorf VIII, Taf. 75, 78, 80, 81; compare: Сорокина 1965 (2), с. 208—215; с. 207, ил. 2, *9, 10*; с. 210, ил. 4, *1*; с. 211, ил. 5, *1–5*; compare also: E.М.Алексеева, Т.М.Арсеньева. Стеклоделие Танаиса // CA, 1966, № 2, с. 180, ил. 3, *4, 7, 11*; the authors (p. 176—178) consider vessels of this type to be mould-blown, with ornamental design subsequently finished by cutting.

334.
BOWL

Eastern Mediterranean. 3rd century AD

H 6.4; D: rim 8.8; GD 9.3; bottom 2.9
Received in 1909; bought in 1904 in Pantikapaion necropolis (grave 61)
П.1904.24

Semi-spherical body; with slightly protuberant small rim outside; flat bottom. Clear colourless glass. Rim sliced off.

324

325

326

327—329

330

331

332

333 а

333 б

334

335

336

337

338

339

Condition: Silvery-iridescent film on surface.

Literature: ИАК, 1907, вып. 25, с. 16

Analogies: Vessberg 1952, pl. I, 21, 22; Harden, 1936, pl. XV, 343; Hayes, no. 173; Auth, no. 372; Sammlung Hentrich, Nr. 151; Сорокина 1963, с. 137, ил. 1, *10*, SH, П.1902.154

335.
BOWL

Eastern Mediterranean. 4th century AD

H 7.8; D: rim 17.5; GD 14; foot 4.5
Received in 1954 from MAE; previously in the
D. & I.Tolstoy collection
E 3136

Semi-spherical body; with wide flanged profiled rim, on low conical foot. Clear yellow glass. Festoons at edge of rim; bolster protecting over walls under rim. Foot crudely wrought: rim uneven, traces of the tool can be seen.

Condition: Good.

First ever publication

Analogies: OAK for 1905, с. 63, ил. 74 (found in Kertch); Sammlung Löffler, Nr. 183, Taf. 25, *4*; Sammlung Cohn, Nr. 107; Sammlung Hentrich, Nr. 163; compare silver cup: Искусство Византии, с. 61, № 48

336.
AMPHORA

Syria or Northern Italy
Mid — second half of 1st century AD

H 25; GD 7
Received in 1852; found in 1852 in the environs of Kertch
П.1852.55   ill.172

Conical body with sharp bottom; with rounded shoulders, high conical neck. Thin vertical handles bent at sharp angle. Clear bluish glass. Embossed bolster on neck between handles.

Condition: One of handles glued together from two pieces; cracks under handle; upper and lower ends of vessel lost; surface iridescent.

Literature: ДБК, табл. LXXVIII, 7, 8; ABC, pl. LXXVIII, 7, 8; Художественное ремесло, кат. 252 (without ill.)

Analogies: Cat. 337; SH, П.1901.22; Sammlung von Kirchner-Schwarz, Taf. 3, Nr. 90 (from Syria); Bucovala 1968, nr. 272; Kisa, III, Formentafel B, 112

337.
AMPHORA

Syria or Northern Italy. Mid — third quarter of 1st century AD

H of remnant 20.6; GD 6.2
Received in 1905; found in 1902 in Pantikapaion necropolis (grave 225/37; together with cat. 310)
П.1902.68   ill.171

Analogous in shape to cat. 336; handles slightly asymmetric, with smooth curve. Clear light-aquamarine glass.

Condition: Top of neck and lower end of vessel lost; surface iridescent.

Literature: ИАК, 1904, вып. 9, с. 113, ил. 28

Analogies: See cat. 336

338.
AMPHORISKOS

Eastern Mediterranean or Northern Italy. Second — third quarter of 1st century AD

H 12.4; D: rim 2.8; GD 5.9; bottom 3.6
Received in 1909; found in 1905 in Pantikapaion necropolis (grave 147/39/; together with cat. 210)
П.1905.153   ill.177

Ovoid body with narrow flat base formed by lower part of walls; with high neck widening downwards, muff-shaped rim; concave bottom. Narrow, vertical handles, with rib in centre, curved near rim. Clear honey-yellow glass; handles of clear dark-blue glass.

Condition: Silvery-lilac crust of iridescence on surface in many places.

Literature: ИАК, 1909, вып. 30, с. 42, 43

Analogies: Isings, Form 15; Smith Collection, no. 63; La Baume, Nr. N11, Taf. 55, *3*; Vessberg 1952, pl. VI, 24; Simonett, Taf. 10, *5* (right); Notizie degli scavi di Antichita, Anno 1922. Roma, 1922, Fasc. 1, p. 18, fig. 19 (tomba 39); compare shape with Sammlung Cohn, Nr. 34

339.
AMPHORISKOS

Eastern Mediterranean. Second half of 1st century AD

H 15.2; D: rim 4.7; GD 8.2; pad-base 4
Received in 1904; found in 1903 in Pantikapaion necropolis (grave 237/114/)
П.1903.112

Ovoid body, with flattened base formed by lower part of walls; with cylindrical neck, outsplayed rim; slightly concave bottom. Clear greenish glass. Engraved girdles of thin close lines on body: two on shoulders; three in middle and one at the bottom.

Condition: Surface iridescent.

Literature: ИАК, 1905, вып. 17, с. 50

Analogies: La Baume, Nr. D52, Taf. 27, *4*; SH, П.1875.392

340.
AMPHORISKOS

Eastern Mediterranean. Mid — third quarter of 1st century AD

H 10.2; D: rim 3.7; GD 7.3; bottom 3.7

Found in 1842 in Pantikapaion necropolis (kurgan III, grave 1; together with cat. 230, 287, 296, 361, 362)
П.1842.70

Spherical body; with short cylindrical neck, outsplayed rim; slightly concave bottom. Narrow vertical handles, smoothly bent. Clear bluish glass. Neck deformed during production, handles asymmetric; one of them has extension at top. Pontil-mark (D 2) on bottom.

Condition: Crack on neck; surface iridescent in places.

Literature: ЗООИД, 1844, т. I, с. 616 сл.; Спасский, с. 144; Кунина, Сорокина, с. 152, ил. 4, *11*

Analogies: Кунина, Сорокина, с. 155, ил. 5, *19*; compare with Hayes, no. 120, 122

341.
AMPHORISKOS

Eastern Mediterranean. 1st century AD

H 6.9; D: rim 2.5; GD 4.9; bottom 1.3
Received in 1932 from SAM; previously in the Rayevskaya collection
E 2790   ill.176

Spherical body; with short neck widening slightly downwards, outsplayed bolster-shaped rim; small, slightly concave bottom. High vertical handles. Clear honey-yellow glass; handles of semi-clear yellow-grey glass.

Condition: Surface iridescent in places.

Literature: Художественное ремесло, кат. 264 (without ill.)

Analogies: Sammlung Oppenländer, Nr. 541, 542; Hayes, no. 119, 120; compare form: cat. 342, 343; Hayes, no. 122; La Baume, Nr. N11, *2*, Taf. 55, *4*; Fremersdorf III, Taf. 31

342.
AMPHORISKOS

Eastern Mediterranean. 1st century AD

H 7; D: rim 2.4; GD 5; bottom 1.8
Received in 1900 from A.Novikov collection; found in Kertch, probably in the Pantikapaion necropolis
E 688   ill.176

Spherical body; with short, cylindrical, slightly protuberant neck, with constriction at body, with slightly outsployed rim; small, slightly concave bottom. Vertical handles fastened to middle of neck. Clear cobalt-blue glass. Carelessly made: rim is bent, handles slightly asymmetric.

Condition: Surface iridescent.

Literature: Художественное ремесло, кат. 263 (without ill.)

Analogies: See cat. 341

340

341, 342

343—345   □   □

346—348

349

350—352   □

353—355

356—358

359

360

343.

AMPHORISKOS

Eastern Mediterranean. 1st century AD

H 7.5; D: rim 3.5; GD 6.2; bottom 1.9
Received in 1926 from S.Stroganov collection
E 1200   ill.175

Spherical body; with short cylindrical neck; wide bolster-shaped rim; small, flat bottom. Narrow vertical handles; with groove in centre. Clear emerald-green glass.

Condition: Body glued back together from pieces.

First ever publication

Analogies: See cat. 341

344.

SMALL JUG

Eastern Mediterranean. 1st century AD

H 9.3; D: rim 2.6; GD 6.2; bottom 4.6
Received in 1931 from SAHMC; previously in A.Bobrinsky collection
E 2217   ill.175

Intricately shaped body: sphere flattened at the upper end, with constriction near high cylindrical base formed by lower part of walls; with high cylindrical neck, narrow curved rim; slightly concave bottom. Wide tape-shaped handle, with three ribs, loop-shaped protuberance above rim. Clear cobalt-blue glass; handle of clear, dark-aquamarine glass. Note its clear proportions and beautiful silhouette.

Condition: Thin silvery-iridescent film on surface in places.

First ever publication

Analogies: Vessberg 1952, pl. VI, 11, 12, 15; compare: Berger, Taf. 6, *89,* 20, *76* (*89*); Matheson, no. 93; compare with large jug (cat. 250)

345.

SMALL JUG

Eastern Mediterranean or Italy. 1st century AD

H 7.5; D: rim 2.8; GD 6.5; bottom 3
Received in 1926 from S.Stroganov collection
E 1237   ill.175

Squat biconical body on low cylindrical base formed by lower part of walls; with wide neck, collar-shaped rim; concave bottom. Tape-shaped handle with three pointed ribs, bent almost at right angle. Clear violet-pink glass; colour intensity increases downwards; handle of semi-clear green glass. Form dates back to earthenware lagenoi.

Condition: Silvery-iridescent film on surface.

First ever publication

Analogies: Vessberg 1952, pl. VI, 14; Berger, Taf. 16, *4;* Simonett, S. 80, Abb. 62, *32,* Taf. 11, *3;* 12, *6;* compare with Matheson, no. 93

346.

ARYBALLOS

Eastern Mediterranean. Second half of 1st century AD

H 7.2; D: rim 3; GD 6.8; bottom 3.2
Received in 1909; found in 1906 in Pantikapaion necropolis (grave 65/11/; together with cat. 166)
П.1906.82

Spherical-shaped body; with short neck, muff-shaped rim; slightly concave bottom. Small handles bent under rim. Clear light-blue glass.

Condition: Surface iridescent in places.

Literature: ИАК, 1909, вып. 30, с. 73; Кунина, Сорокина, с. 162, ил. 7, *24*

Analogies: Cat. 347; 348; SH, П.1847.43; П.1900.12; П.1906.75; П.1910.78; П.1884.44 (see Кунина, Сорокина, с. 152, ил. 4, *43;* с. 155, ил. 5, *25, 33;* с. 167, ил. 10, *14*); Vessberg 1952, pl. IX, 33—36; Fortuna 1967, p. 48, fig. 48; Bucovala 1968, p. 82, nr. 131; p. 83, nr. 135; Isings, Form 61

347.

ARYBALLOS

Eastern Mediterranean. Second half of 1st century AD

H 8.4; D: rim 3.6; GD 7.8; bottom 2.6
Found in 1846 in Kertch
П.1846.58

Analogous in form to cat. 346; rim carelessly made; flat bottom. Clear light-aquamarine glass.

Condition: Surface iridescent in places.

First ever publication

Analogies: See cat. 346

348.

ARYBALLOS

Eastern Mediterranean. Second half of 1st century AD

H 5.2; D: rim 2.8; GD 6.1; bottom 2.5
Received in 1874; found in 1874 in Pantikapaion necropolis (grave 2; together with cat. 232)
П.1874.88

Analogous in form to cat. 346, 347; rim flattened on surface. Clear light-aquamarine glass.

Condition: Surface iridescent in places.

First ever publication

Analogies: See cat. 346

349.

ARYBALLOS

Western provinces of the Roman Empire Second half of 1st century — early 2nd century AD

H 6.9; D: rim 3.1; GD 6.5; bottom 2.9

Received in 1875; found in 1875 in Pantikapaion necropolis (grave 9)
П.1875.444

Spherical body, with thick walls; with short neck, massive horizontally curved rim; slightly concave bottom. Thick, dolphin-shaped handles. Clear greenish-bluish glass. Pontil-mark (D 1.5) on bottom.

Condition: Film of silvery iridescence on surface.

Literature: OAK for 1875, с. XVIII; Кунина 1984, с. 155, № 15, табл. III, 15

Analogies: Morin-Jean, p. 82, fig. 84; p. 84, fig. 87; Fremersdorf IV, Taf. 36, 37; Spartz, Taf. 37, Nr. 65; Sammlung Oppenländer, Nr. 565; compare with Fremersdorf IX, Nr. 223, 224

350.

SMALL FLASK

Eastern Mediterranean. First half of 1st century AD

H 5.5; D: rim 1.5; GD 3.7; bottom 2.2
Received in 1929 from N.Romanchenko collection
E 1738   ill.179

Almost spherical body; with high neck widening downwards, outsplayed rim; flat bottom. Clear glass, from pink to dark-violet in colour. Two close thin grooves in middle section of body.

Condition: Part of rim lost; iridiscent film on surface.

First ever publication

Analogies: Compare: Hayes, no. 111; Matheson, no. 56

351.

SMALL FLASK

Eastern Mediterranean. First half of 1st century AD

H 5.7; D: rim 1.8; GD 3.2; bottom 1
Received in 1929 from N.Romanchenko collection
E 1735   ill.179

Spherical body; with high neck widening upwards, outsplayed rim; small flat bottom. Clear dark-blue glass.

Condition: Iridescent film on surface in places.

First ever publication

Analogies: Auth, no. 505; Hayes, no. 96

352.

SMALL FLASK

Eastern Mediterranean or Italy. First half of 1st century AD

H 5.9; D: rim 2; GD 3.5; bottom 1
Received in 1900 from A.Novikov collection; found in Kertch, probably in Pantikapaion necropolis
E 699   ill.179

Pear-shaped body; with short, almost cylindrical, neck, horizontal profiled rim; small flat bottom. Clear dark-aquamarine glass.

Condition: Surface iridescent in places.

First ever publication

Analogies: Fitzwilliam Mus., no. 64a; compare with Liepmann, Nr. 37

353.
SMALL FLASK

Eastern Mediterranean. Early 1st century AD

H 5.8; D: rim 1.8; GD 3.9; bottom 0.9
Received in 1909; found in 1905 in Pantikapaion necropolis (grave 24; together with cat. 37, 354, 355, 359)
П.1905.28

Spherical body; with slightly protuberant cylindrical neck, outsployed rim; small flat bottom. Clear dark-blue glass.

Condition: Glued together from pieces; parts of walls lost; surface iridescent.

Literature: ИАК, 1909, вып. 30, с. 8; Кунина, Сорокина, с. 170, ил. 11, *15*

Analogies: Кунина, Сорокина, с. 170, ил. 11, *29*; Simonett, S. 80, Abb. 62, *27*; S. 135, Abb. 116, *19*; Sorokina 1978, p. 270, ill. 2, *16*; Hayes, no. 98; Liepmann, Nr. 38; compare: Dusenbery 1967, p. 42, fig. 24; Auth, Nr. 505

354.
SMALL FLASK

Eastern Mediterranean (Syria ?). First half of 1st century AD

H 9.4; D: rim 1.5; GD 2.7
Receved in 1909; found in 1905 in Pantikapaion necropolis (grave 24; together with cat. 37, 353, 355, 359)
П.1905.25

Almost ovoid body with pointed bottom; with high cylindrical neck, outsployed rim. Clear light-bluish glass.

Condition: Surface has almost totally lost its shine.

Literature: ИАК, 1909, вып. 30, с. 8; Кунина, Сорокина, с. 170, ил. 11, *17*

Analogies: SH, П.1902.146; П.1843.40; Vessberg 1952, pl. VII, 44, 45; Simonett, S. 80; Abb. 62, *16a*; Hayes, no. 102, 103; Sammlung Oppenländer, Nr. 638, 639; Smith Collection, no. 157, 356; compare: Calvi 1968, cat. 13, tav. 1, *6*

355.
SMALL FLASK

Eastern Mediterranean or Italy. Early 1st century AD

H 7.4; D: rim 1.7; GD 4.2; bottom 1.6
Received in 1909; found in 1905 in Pantikapaion necropolis (grave 24; together with cat. 37, 353, 354, 359)
П.1905.26

Spherical body; with high neck narrowing sharply upwards, outsployed rim; small flat bottom. Clear pink-violent glass.

Condition: Film of milky-white iridescence on neck and part of body.

Literature: ИАК, 1909, вып. 30, с. 8; Кунина, Сорокина, с. 170, ил. 11, *14*

Analogies: SH, П.1908.46; П.1908.47; П.1905.136; Кунина, Сорокина, с. 170, ил. 11, *4*; Smith Collection, no. 155; G.Eisen, Glass, vol. I, New York, 1927, pl. 44; Sammlung Hentrich, Nr. 167; compare: Hayes, no. 111; Sammlung Oppenländer, Nr. 340

356.
SMALL SPHERE-FLASK

Western part of Roman Empire or Italy · 1st century AD

H 4.2; D: orifice 1; GD 4.6; bottom 1.8
Received in 1875; found in 1875 in Pantikapaion necropolis (grave 5)
П.1875.406

Spherical form; with short rim around small aperture in centre; flat bottom. Clear colourless glass.

Condition: Surface iridescent.

Literature: OAK for 1875, с. XXI—XXII; Кунина 1984, с. 154, № 11, табл. II, 11

Analogies: Sometimes found with soldered orifice; on one occasion containing pink powder: Isings, p. 25, 26, Form 10; compare also: Simonett, S. 65, Abb. 44, *9*; S. 76, Abb. 59, *2, 3, 4*; S. 97, Abb. 80, *8*; S. 116, Abb. 95, *7*; S. 153, Abb. 130, Nr. 18

357.
SMALL FLASK

Eastern Mediterranean. First half of 1st century AD

H 11; D rim 2.1; GW 3.4
Received in 1871; found in 1871 in Pantikapaion necropolis
П.1871.54

Flat body; with rounded shoulders, low almost cylindrical neck, outsployed rim; sharp bottom. Clear bluish glass. Asymmetric: one shoulder is steep, the other sloping.

Condition: Good.

First ever publication

Analogies: Compare shape with cat. 354

358.
MINIATURE AMPHORISKOS

Eastern Mediterranean. Second half of 1st century AD

H 5.6; D: rim 1.9; GD 3.2; foot 1.8
Received in 1904; found in 1901 in Pantikapaion necropolis (submound grave 30/28/)
П.1901.2

Ovoid body with flattened ring-shaped foot formed by lower part of walls; with short, almost cylindrical, neck, outsployed rim. Clear greenish glass. Handles of clear dark-green glass.

Condition: Good.

Literature: ИАК, 1903, вып. 7, с. 81

Analogies: Сагинашвили, кат. 15

359.
MINIATURE UNGUENTARIUM

Eastern Mediterranean (Syria ?) Early 1st century AD

H 3.7; D: rim 1.5; bottom 1.2
Received in 1909; found in 1905 in Pantikapaion necropolis (grave 24; together with cat. 37, 353—355)
П.1905.27

Pear-shaped body; with high cylindrical neck, clear-cut intake below; with flanged rim; flat bottom. Clear greenish glass.

Condition: Pieces of rim and parts of body lost; surface iridescent.

Literature: ИАК, 1909, вып. 30, с. 8; Кунина, Сорокина, с. 170, ил. 11, *16*

Analogies: Сагинашвили, кат. 27, 29, 38; Simonett, S. 97, Abb. 79, *11e*; Vessberg 1952, pl. VII, 47; compare with Matheson, no. 170

360.
UNGUENTARIUM

Egypt. Circa mid—1st century AD

H 15.7; D: rim 3.4; GD 6.1; bottom 3.9
Received in 1872; found in 1872 in Pantikapaion necropolis (grave 4; together with cat. 162)
П.1872.110

Pear-shaped body; with high, wide, cylindrical neck with clear-cut constriction near base, horizontally curved rim; flat bottom. Clear bottle-green glass with many oblong (on neck) and spherical (on body) bubbles.

Condition: Good.

Literature: OAK for 1872, с. XXII—XXIII; Кунина, Сорокина, с. 149, ил. 2, *1*

Analogies: Edgar, pl. VIII, no. 32.647; Dusenbery 1967, p. 43, fig. 26; Стекло девней Армении, кат. 53; Кунина, Сорокина, с. 149, ил. 2, *2, 9*; compare also Сагинашвили, кат. 140

361.
UNGUENTARIUM

Egypt. Mid — third quarter of 1st century AD

H 11.5; D: rim 3.5; bottom 3.5
Found in 1842 in Pantikapaion necropolis (kurgan III, grave 1; together with cat. 230, 287, 296, 340, 362)
П.1842.76   ill.178

Pear-shaped body; with high, wide, cy-lindrical neck; with protuberance and constriction near base, curved horizon-tal rim; flat bottom. Clear bottle-green glass.

Condition: Surface iridescent in places.

Literature: ЗООИД, 1844, т. I, с. 616 сл.; Спасский, с. 144; Кунина, Сорокина, с. 152, ил. 4, *4*

Analogies: A multitude of similar unguentaria were found in the necropoleis of the Bosporan Kingdom: see, for example,Кунина, Сорокина, с. 151, ил. 3, *1–5, 13, 14, 35, 36*; с. 152, ил. 4, *1–3, 5–8, 16–20, 29, 35, 38–41, 45*; also Сагинашвили, кат. 74—78, 80, 83—85; Стекло древней Армении, кат. 2, 20; Bucovala 1968, p. 148, fig. VIII; Edgar, pl. VIII, 36.243; Harden 1936, pl. XX, 797; Toll, pl. XLIV, 12; Fortuna 1965, p. 19, fig. 4; Isings, Form 28b

362.
UNGUENTARIUM

Egypt. Mid — third quarter of 1st century AD

H 14.7; D: rim 3.3; bottom 4.2
Found in 1842 in Pantikapaion necropolis (kurgan III, grave 1; together with cat. 230, 287, 296, 340, 361)
П.1842.78   ill.178

Pear-shaped body; with very high, wide, cylindrical neck; with clear-cut constric-tion near base; wide, sliced rim; flat bottom. Clear bottle-green glass.

Condition: Surface heavily iridescent.

Literature: ЗООИД, 1844, т. I, с. 616 сл.; Спасский, с. 144; Кунина, Сорокина, с. 152, ил. 4, *10*

Analogies: A multitude of similar unguentaria were found in the necropoleis of the Bosporan Kingdom: see, for example,Кунина, Сорокина, с. 151, ил. 3, *15, 37*; с. 152, ил. 4, *9*; с. 155, ил. 5, *1–4, 13, 23, 31, 36–39, 47*; also Harden 1936, pl. XX, 797; Edgar, pl. VIII, 32.640; Toll, pl. VII; Fortuna 1965, p. 19, fig. 4; p. 21, fig. 12; p. 23, fig. 15; Bucovala 1968, p. 106, fig. 203; p. 107, fig. 205; p. 148, fig. VII; Сагинашвили, кат. 62—68, 71

363.
UNGUERENTARIUM

Egypt. Second half of 1st century AD

H 12.3; D: rim 3.3; bottom 3.1
Received in 1906; found in 1900 in Pantikapaion necropolis (grave 69; together with cat. 258)
П.1900.47

Analogous in form to cat. 361. Clear bottle-green glass.

Condition: Silvery-iridescent film on surface in places; shine totally lost.

Literature: ИАК, 1902, вып. 2, с. 53; Кунина, Сорокина, с. 152, ил. 4, *22*

Analogies: See cat. 361

364.
UNGUENTARIUM

Syria. Mid — second half of 1st century AD

H 7.3; D: rim 3.5; bottom 3.8
Received in 1904; found in 1903 in Pantikapaion necropolis (grave 251/128/)
П.1903.116

Squat, conical body; with very high, wide, almost cylindrical neck; funnel-shaped orifice; flat, thick bottom. Clear greenish glass; bright-green in thicker places.

Condition: Crack on neck; carved spiral grooves on body (traces of buffing ?); silvery-iridescent film on surface in places.

Literature: ИАК, 1905, вып. 17, с. 53

Analogies: Сагинашвили, кат. 110, 111, 125, 128; Toll, pl. LVI (tomb 46); Hayes, no. 165; Auth, no. 426; Matheson, no. 171; compare with Harden 1936, pl. XX, 803

365.
UNGUENTARIUM

Bosporan Kingdom. Second half of 1st century AD

H 10.7; D: rim 2.2; bottom 3.5
Received in 1935; found in 1906 in Myrmekion necropolis (grave 116/38/; together with cat. 366)
П.1906.145

Conical body; with high, almost cylindri-cal neck widening upwards; with wide outsployed rim; slightly concave bottom. Clear greenish glass; with multitude of small bubbles. Rim carelessly made.

Condition: Surface iridescent.

Literature: ИАК, 1909, вып. 30, с. 87, 88

Analogies: A multitude of similar unguentaria were found in the necropoleis of the Bosporan Kingdom: see Кунина, Сорокина, с. 162, ил. 7, *17, 18, 22, 26, 28, 31, 36–38, 43–46*; с. 163, ил. 8, *1, 5, 8, 10, 13, 17, 22, 23, 27, 28, 30, 32–34, 37, 38, 40, 44*; с. 165, ил. 9, *1, 2, 17, 19, 32*; compare with Auth, no. 422

366.
UNGUENTARIUM

Syro-Palestinian region. Second half of 1st century AD

H 10.8; D: rim 1.8; bottom 2
Received in 1935; found in 1906 in Myrmekion necropolis (grave 116/381/); together with cat. 365)
П.1906.146

Body with waist (in shape of two spheres); with high, almost cylindrical, neck widening downwards; horizonal rim; slightly concave bottom. Clear co-lourless glass.

Condition: Surface iridescent.

Literature: ИАК, 1909, вып. 30, с. 87, 88

Analogies: Cat. 367; SH, E 445; E 3242 (Кунина 1975, с. 103, ил. 2); E 2103; П.1845.22

(Кунина, Сорокина, с. 162, ил. 7, *39*); Vessberg 1952, pl. IX, 26; Fortuna 1965, p. 21, fig. 12; Basserman-Jordan, Taf. VIII, 129 (from Syria); Edgar, pl. VII, 32.623, 32.624; Filarska, nr. 210, tabl. XLIV, 1; Auth, no. 416; Matheson, no. 169; Сорокина 1978, с. 270, ил. 2, *29*

367.
UNGUENTARIUM

Syro-Palestinian region. Second half of 1st century AD

H 10.9; D: rim 2; bottom 2.8
Received in 1912; found in 1909 in a looted grave of the Pantikapaion necropolis
П.1909.7

Shape analogical to cat. 366 (bottom sphere flattened out; neck is shorter and slightly protuberant near the base). Clear colourless glass.

Condition: Surface iridescent.

Literature: ИАК, 1913, вып. 47, с. 40, раздел V

Analogies: See cat. 366

368.
UNGUENTARIUM

Syro-Palestinian region. Late 1st century — early 2nd century AD

H 12.4; D: rim 3; bottom 4.4
Received in 1912; found in 1909 in the environs of Kertch (grave 98/9/; together with cat. 254)
П.1909.119

Bell-shaped body; with high, cylindrical, protuberant neck; with constriction near base, with curved horizontal rim; con-cave bottom. Clear colourless glass, with many bubbles. Pontil-mark (D 1.3) on bottom.

Condition: Film of milky-white and golden iridescence on surface in places.

Literature: ИАК, 1913, вып. 47, с. 33; Кунина, Сорокина, с. 167, ил. 10, *24*

Analogies: Cat. 369; SH, П.1841/42.28; Vessberg 1952, pl. IX, 6; Fortuna 1965, p. 21, fig. 11; Fortuna 1969, p. 22, fig. 10

369.
UNGUENTARIUM

Syro-Palestinian region. First half of 2nd century AD

H 11; D: rim 2.7; bottom 5.1
Received in 1912; found in the environs of Kertch (grave 106/17/; together with cat. 263)
П.1909.135

Bell-shaped body; with high, almost cylindrical, neck; bolster-shaped rim; slightly concave bottom. Clear green-ish glass; with many bubbles.

Condition: Film of silvery iridescence on surface in places.

361, 362 ▫

363

364

365, 366

367

368

369

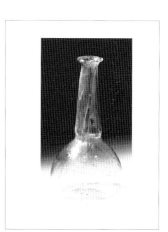

370

371

372–374

375

Literature: ИАК, 1913, вып. 47, с. 35, 36; Кунина, Сорокина, с. 167, ил. 10, *33*

Analogies: See cat. 368

370.
UNGUENTARIUM

Eastern Mediterranean (Cyprus ?). First half of 2nd century AD

H 12.5; D: rim 2.3; bottom 5.6
Found in 1846 in Pantikapaion necropolis (kurgan X, grave 6; together with cat. 324)
П.1846.45

Pear-shaped body; with high conical neck; with clear-cut intake near base, outsplayed rim; flat bottom. Clear bluish glass, many bubbles. Accidental stain of yellow glass on neck and body. Pontil-mark (D 1.6) on bottom.

Condition: Crack on neck.

First ever publication

Analogies: Vessberg 1952, pl. VIII, 13; Myres, p. 511, no. 54240; compare with Hayes, no. 487–490

371.
UNGUENTARIUM

Bosporan Kingdom. Second half of 2nd century — early 3rd century AD

H 14.2; D: rim 2; bottom 5
Received in 1904; found in 1903 in Pantikapaion necropolis (grave 49; together with cat. 222, 332)
П.1903.44

Low conical body; with very high, almost cylindrical, neck; with wide outsplayed rim; concave bottom. Clear greenish glass.

Condition: Surface iridescent.

Literature: ИАК, 1905, вып. 17, с. 15

Analogies: Кунина, Сорокина, с. 165, ил. 9, *9, 18, 33, 37*; Bucovala 1968, p. 147, fig. VI

372.
UNGUENTARIUM

Syro-Palestinian region. Second half of 2nd century AD

H 18.6; D: rim 2.4; bottom 8.1
Received in 1875; found in 1875 in Pantikapaion necropolis (grave 6; together with cat. 241, 373)
П.1875.440

Low conical body; with very high, almost cylindrical neck widening upwards; with bolster-shaped rim; concave bottom. Clear colourless glass. Rim carelessly made. Pontil-mark on bottom.

Condition: Good.

Literature: OAK for 1875, c. XXVIII; Кунина, Сорокина, с. 165, ил. 9, *42*

Analogies: Cat. 373—375; SH, П.1908.21; ПАН.601; Vessberg 1952, pl. IX, 1; Harden 1936, pl. XX, 799; Edgar, pl. VII, 32.628; Abdul-Hak, p. 30, fig. 9; Hayes, no. 259;

E.M.Stern. Ancient Glass at the Fondation Custodia (Collection Frits Lugt). Paris; Groningen, 1977, pl. 12, no. 20

373.
UNGUENTARIUM

Syro-Palestinian region. Second half of 2nd century AD

H 19.5; D: rim 2.8; bottom 8.5
Received in 1875; found in 1875 in Pantikapaion necropolis (grave 6; together with cat. 241, 372)
П.1875.439

Analogous in form to cat. 371, 372; painstakingly made. Clear colourless glass. Pontil-mark.

Condition: Good.

Literature: OAK for 1875; c. XXVIII; Кунина, Сорокина, с. 165, ил. 9, *41*

Analogies: See cat. 372

374.
UNGUENTARIUM

Syro-Palestinian region. Second half of 2nd century AD

H 16.1; D: rim 1.7—2.2; bottom 7.4
Received in 1874; found in 1874 in Pantikapaion necropolis (grave 5; together with cat. 272, 321, 322)
П.1874.119

Low conical body; high, narrow, almost cylindrical neck widening upwards, sunk into shoulders; bolster-shaped rim; concave bottom. Clear light-aquamarine glass. Upper part of neck and rim bent. Pontil-mark (D 1) on bottom.

Condition: Surface iridescent.

First ever publication

Analogies: Hayes, no. 264; Vessberg 1952, pl. VIII; compare with cat. 372

375.
UNGUENTARIUM

Syro-Palestinian region. Second half of 2nd century AD

H 18.9; D: rim 2.2; bottom 7.2
Received in 1925; found in 1900 in Pantikapaion necropolis (grave 17; together with cat. 266, 326)
П.1900.5

Analogous in form to cat. 372, 373; with sloping shoulders; bent neck. Clear bluish-green glass, with many bubbles. Pontil-mark (D 1.2) on bottom.

Condition: Surface iridescent.

Literature: ИАК, 1902, вып. 2, с. 43; Кунина, Сорокина, с. 165, ил. 9, *45*

Analogies: See cat. 372

376.
BIRD ASKOS

Eastern Mediterranean. 1st century AD

H 20.8; L 22.4; GD 12; D pad-base 7.5
Received in 1915; bought from A.Elterman; found in Olbia
E957   ill.182

Vessel in shape of stylized figure of bird; ovoid, horizontal body with dent on back, extended, pointed bottom (tail) and sloping, cylindrical neck (neck). With bolster-shaped rim, nose-spout; on foot in shape of upturned saucer. Flat handle with three ribs bent twice at an angle, with flat protuberance at top. Clear bluish glass.

Manufacturing technique: End of pointed part of body is broken off, a glass sphere is fastened to the aperture and cemented by plaster. The foot is produced separately; protuberance on handle is compressed by tongs.

Condition: Cracks on body; surface iridescent in places.

First ever publication

Analogies: Compare Sammlung Löffler, Nr. 96; Taf. 11, *4*; Sammlung Oppenländer, Nr. 574; Vessberg 1952, pl. X, 1; Fogolari e Scarfi, tav. 64, *2*

377.
BIRD GUTTUS

Eastern Mediterranean. Second half of 1st century AD

GH 12.1; L body 9; D: body 7.2; orifice 4.5; bottom 5x4.5
Received in 1894; found in 1894 in Pantikapaion necropolis (crypt with four bays (northern); together with cat. 214)
П.1894.23   ill.181

Vessel in form of stylized figure of bird (duck ?); oval-shaped horizontal body with high curved neck and thick cylindrical tail-extension with rounded end. With wide funnel-shaped orifice; concave bottom. Clear light-blue glass of very high quality. "Tail" completely made of bright-aquamarine glass. Rim sliced off, "tail" attached to body through aperture.

Condition: Surface slightly iridescent in places.

Literature: OAK for 1894, c. 45

Analogies: Cat. 378; compare: Berger, Taf. 15, 224; Taf. 22, *101 (224)*; Morin-Jean, p. 161, fig. 214; p. 182, fig. 240; Sammlung Hentrich, Nr. 237

378.
BIRD GUTTUS

Eastern Mediterranean (?). Second half of 1st century AD

GH: 10; body: 6.8; L body 10.3; D orifice 3.8; bottom: 4.4x4.3
Received in 1854; found in 1852 (1853 ?) in a grave in the environs of Kertch
П.1852/53.26   ill.180

376 □

377 □

378 □

379

380

381 □

382, 383 □

384, 385 □

386 □

387 □

Analogous in form to cat. 377; neck and tail shorter. Clear colourless glass; tail of yellowish glass.

Condition: Surface iridescent.

Literature: Извлечение, с. 182, ил. 75

Analogies: See cat. 377

379.
BIRD GUTTUS

Eastern Mediterranean. 1st century AD

H 8.6; L body 8.5; D rim 1.8
Received in 1874; found in 1874 in
Pantikapaion necropolis (grave 4)
П.1874.54

Horizontally extended, arc-shaped, curved body with protuberant shoulders in shape of bird's chest; long, almost cylindrical, sloping neck with funnel-shaped orifice; outsplayed rim and slightly raised spout in shape of tail. Clear colourless glass. End of spout sliced off, melted; aperture of spout D 0.1. Carelessly made: fold outside under rim encompasses half of circumference of orifice.

Condition: Part of rim lost; surface iridescent.

Literature: OAK for 1874, с. VII

Analogies: Compare: Hayes, no. 118; Doppelfeld, Taf. 23; SH, П.1877.37 — vessel is close in dimensions, shape, quality, colour of glass and details of workmanship ("fold" on funnel-shaped orifice, the same small aperture of the spout), suggesting that both sprang from the hand of the one master; compare with Vessberg 1952, pl. X, 1

380.
BIRD GUTTUS

Eastern Mediterranean. 1st century AD

H 8.9; L body 6.7; D rim 1.5
Received in 1854; found in 1852 in
Pantikapaion necropolis (grave 29)
П.1852.10

Spherical body of irregular shape; with high vertical neck widening downwards, bolster-shaped rim, extended "tail" spout formed by lower part of the body; oval, flat bottom. Clear bluish glass. Rim sliced off and melted; D spout 0.3.

Condition: Surface iridescent.

Literature: ДБК, табл. LXXVII, 2; ABC, pl. LXXVII, 2

Analogies: Compare with cat. 379; compare also: Benko, tabl. XLIII, 9, 10; Hayes, no. 118; Bucovala 1968, p. 143, fig. IV; A Decade of Glass Collecting. Selections from the Melvin Billups Collection. The Corning Museum of Glass. Corning, New York, 1962, no. 14; Сорокина 1990, с. 72, ил. 1, 2; с. 74, кат. 2

381.
GUTTUS

Eastern Mediterranean. 1st century AD

H 7.7; rim: 3.9x4.2; GD 6.3; D bottom 4.3
Received in 1875; found in 1875 in
Pantikapaion necropolis (grave 5)
П.1875.390 ill.185

Intricately shaped body: spherical, on a narrowing conical base formed by lower part of walls, with protruding base and conical nose-spout in middle of body. With short, wide neck and wide orifice; rim curved inwards; slightly concave bottom. Narrow, rounded handle. Nose with aperture cut through; rim sliced off and melted; orifice of spout D 0.3.

Condition: Cracks on neck and orifice; surface iridescent.

Literature: OAK for 1875, с. XXIV

Analogies: Hayes, no. 279 (compare with no. 299); Benko, tabl. XLIII, 9—11; compare: Doppelfeld, Taf. 80 (bottom); SH, П.1903.63; П.1914.79 (nose extends from the lower part of the body); compare with Сорокина 1990, с. 72, ил. 1, 10

382.
INK-WELL OR PYXIS

Eastern Mediterranean. 1st century AD

H 3.5; D: rim 5.7; bottom 4.2
Received in 1851; found in 1850 in Kertch
П.1850.32

Semi-spherical body with profiled "lid" top, aperture in centre (D 1.3) and bolster-shaped rim; on base formed by lower part of walls; concave bottom. Three small, loop-shaped handles. Clear colourless glass.

Condition: Lower part of one handle, upper part of other lost; surface slightly iridescent.

First ever publication

Analogies: Sammlung Oppenländer, Nr. 572

383.
INK-WELL (PYXIS FOR COSMETICS ?)

Eastern Mediterranean. 1st century AD

H 5.8; D: rim 4.8; bottom 4; thickness of walls 0.5; thickness of bottom 1
Found in 1841 (1842 ?) in Pantikapaion necropolis
П.1841/42.24 ill.174

Cylindrical body; with distinctly modelled protecting rim; slightly protruding horizontal "lid" top; with aperture in centre on top (D 1.5); flat bottom. Clear aquamarine glass.

Condition: Much cracked; parts of walls and bottom lost; surface iridescent.

First ever publication

Analogies: Hayes, no. 129; Dusenbery 1971, p. 18, fig. 21; Auth, no. 145, 146; Sammlung Oppenländer, Nr. 298, 299; La Baume, Nr. D13, Taf. 18, 1; Smith Collection, no. 64

384.
FUNNEL

Western regions of the Roman Empire Second half of 1st century — early 2nd century AD

H remnant 10.7; D: orifice 6.4; neck 1.1
Received in 1911; found in 1908 in
Pantikapaion necropolis (grave 52/15/)
П.1908.123

With rounded walls; narrow neck, narrowish smoothly flanged rim. Clear colourless glass.

Condition: Lower section of foot lost; surface almost completely covered in yellowy film of iridescence.

Literature: ИАК, 1911, вып. 40, с. 90, 91; Кунина 1984, с. 154, № 12, табл. II, 12

Analogies: Cat. 385; SH, E 723; E 2295; ПАН.839 (Кунина 1984, с. 154, № 14, табл. II, 14); Fremersdorf IV, Taf. 132; Vanderhoeven, pl. XXV, 108; Morin-Jean, p. 147, fig. 202; Isings, Form 74

385.
FUNNEL

Western regions of the Roman Empire Second half of 1st century — 2nd century AD

H 12.7; D: orifice 7.2; neck 0.8
Found in Kertch
ПАН.602

With rounded walls; horizontally curved rim, narrow neck. Clear bluish glass.

Condition: Surface iridescent.

Literature: ДБК, табл. LXXVII, 4; ABC, pl. LXXVII, 4; Кунина 1984, с. 154, № 13, табл. II, 13

Analogies: See cat. 384

386.
URN WITH LID (WITH ASHES INSIDE)

Rhineland or Gaul. 1st — 2nd centuries AD

Urn: H 20.2; D: rim 14.7; GD 17.8; bottom 12.2. Lid: H 3.2; D 11; upper handle 3
Received in 1928 from E.Shuvalova collection (bought in Italy ?)
E 1493 ill.186

Body almost spherical; with base formed by lower sections of walls; with short, wide neck, massive protruding bolster-shaped rim; flat bottom. Round lid with handle in shape of conical projection ending in irregular, carelessly made disc. Clear aquamarine glass; bluish glass on lid.

Condition: Surface iridescent. Cremation ashes inside urn.

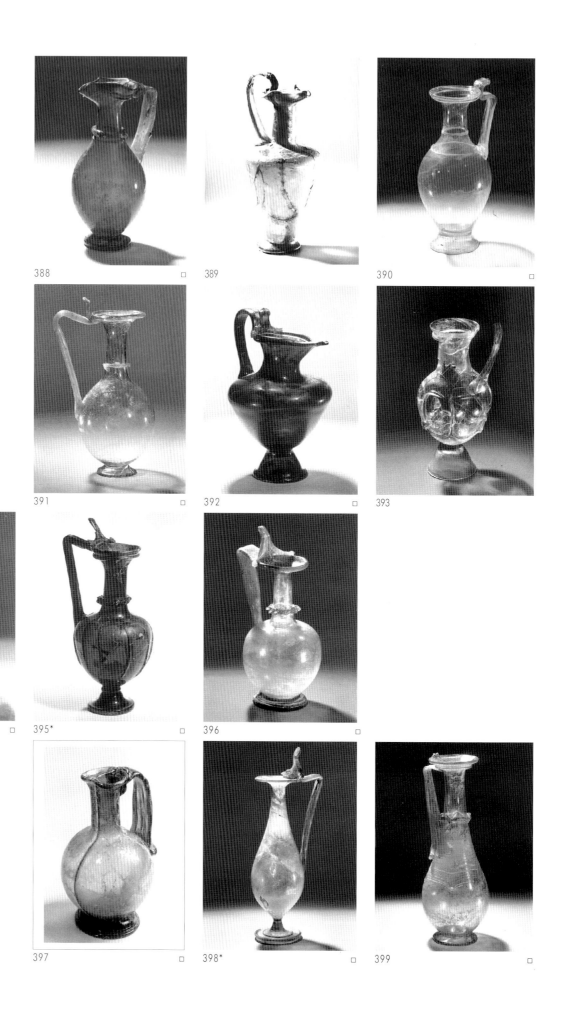

388 ☐   389   390 ☐

391 ☐   392 ☐   393

394* ☐   395* ☐   396 ☐

397 ☐   398* ☐   399 ☐

First ever publication

Analogies: *Urn:* Sammlung Hentrich, Nr. 145; Fortuna 1969, p. 21, fig. 3; compare: Hayes, no. 615, 616; Liepmann, Nr. 50; Morin-Jean, p. 46, fig. 17; Isings, Form 65. *Lid* Isings, Form 66b; Doppelfeld, Taf. 35; Sammlung Niessen, Band II, Taf. XLIX, 966

387.
URN

Rhineland or Gaul. 2nd—3rd centuries AD

H 26.1; D: rim 21.3; GD 25.4; bottom 10.5
Received by Department of Antiquities from Department of the Middle Ages, Hermitage, in 1912
E 881   ill.187

Ovoid body; with massive, flanged rim; slightly concave bottom. Clear bright-aquamarine glass.

Condition: Surface iridescent.

First ever publication

Analogies: Morin-Jean, p. 44, fig. 13; Vanderhoeven, pl. XXIII, no. 99, 101; Fremersdorf, IX, Nr. 79, 82, 83; Sammlung Löffler, Nr. 236; Petru, tabl. CV, 2; Isings, Form 67; Fortuna 1969, p. 21, fig. 2; Hayes, no. 618

388.
OENOCHOE

Eastern Mediterranean (Syro-Palestinian region ?). 3rd century — first half of 4th century AD

H 16.6; rim: 6x6.1; GD 7.9; D foot 5.2
Received in 1914 from Ya.Buksil collection
E 930   ill.195

Ovoid body, with almost cylindrical short neck, on short foot. Wide, flat, curved handle. Applied braided noop under rim and on neck. Clear bluish glass; handle, foot and decoration of dirty-green glass, with small dark lumps inside. Foot carelessly made, small lump of blue glass from bottom.

Condition: Surface completely iridescent on one side.

Literature: Художественное ремесло, кат. 262 (without ill.)

Analogies: La Baume, Nr. D66, Taf. 31, *3;* Sammlung Hentrich, Nr. 213; Hayes, no. 336; compare with Dusenbery 1971, p. 26, fig. 47

389.
OENOCHOE

Syria. 2nd—3rd centuries AD (?)

H (without handle) 21; rim: 7x6.4; D: shoulders 10; bottom 5.5
Received in 1909; found in 1906 in Pantikapaion necropolis (grave 21)
П.1906.17

Cone-shaped body on flat base formed by lower section of walls; with horizontal shoulders, high, slightly cylindrical, protruding neck with constriction near body; flat bottom. Narrow handle, with groove in middle, rounded curve above rim. Clear violet glass; rim outlined with dulled white glass.

Condition: Glued together from many parts; losses; some losses supplemented by film.

Literature: ИАК, 1909, вып. 30, с. 58, ил. 1; B.Pharmakowsky. Archaeologische Funde im Jahre 1906 // AA, 1907, 2, S. 139, Abb. 10

Analogies: Compare: Auth, no. 115; Sammlung Löffler, Nr. 174, Taf. 24; Sammlung Oppenländer, Nr. 599; Sammlung Cohn, Nr. 104; Sammlung Niessen, Band II, Taf. XXXIV, 1006

390.
JUG

Syria (?). Second half of 3rd century — early 4th century AD

H 21.3; D: rim 7.1; GD 10.6; foot 6.7
Received in 1880; found in 1880 in Pantikapaion necropolis (stone sarcophagus 2)
П.1880.27   ill.189

Ovoid body with conical leg formed by lower section of walls; with short, almost cylindrical neck, funnel-shaped orifice, profiled protruding rim. Wide tape-shaped handle, with protuberance in shape of pressed loop above rim. Clear bright-bluish glass. Two coils of applied thread on neck, one on shoulders. Foot carelessly made, rim uneven. Pontil-mark (D 2.5) on bottom.

Condition: Surface iridescent.

Literature: OAK for 1880, с. XVIII

Analogies: Compare: Kisa I, S. 75, Abb. 38 (right); S. 79, Abb. 40 (left)

391.
JUG

Eastern Mediterranean (Syria ?) Second half of 3rd century AD

H 19.3; D: rim 6.8; GD 9.6; foot 5.2
Received in 1904; found in 1903 in Pantikapaion necropolis (grave 111)
П.1903.85

Spherical body on conical foot formed by lower section of walls; with narrow, almost cylindrical, neck, funnel-shaped orifice, rim curving inwards. Handle bent at an angle, with flat finger-shaped protuberance at top. Clear olive-yellow glass. Embossed applied braid round neck. Foot carelessly made. Pontil-mark (D 2.2) on bottom.

Condition: Cracks; parts of braid on neck lost; surface iridescent in places

Literature: ИАК, 1905, вып. 17, с. 27, ил. 24

Analogies: Compare: cat. 396; Hayes, no. 276, 397; Sammlung Cohn, Nr. 123; Auth, no. 382, 389

392.
JUG (WITH SPOUT)

Eastern Mediterranean. 3rd—4th centuries AD

H 19.8; D: rim 6.6; shoulders 13.6; foot 7.5
Received in 1900 from A.Novikov collection; found in Nymphaion, probably in necropolis
E 683

Wide cone-shaped body; with horizontal shoulders, short wide neck, funnel-shaped orifice with narrow extended spout and rim slanting inward. On high, hollow, bell-shaped foot with protruding base. Tape-shaped handle, round curve above rim, with three vertical protuberances at top (one large and two small). Clear dark-cherry glass.

Condition: Small side protection lost; surface iridescent in places.

Literature: Художественное стекло, ил. 16

Analogies: Compare foot with cat. 393; compare protuberance above rim with cat. 395, 396, 398

393.
JUG

Syria. Second half of 3rd century — early 4th century AD

H: 15.3; foot 3.4; D: rim 5.2; GD 8.2; foot 5.2
Received in 1854; found in 1842 in Pantikapaion necropolis
П.1841/42.27   ill on p.25

Almost spherical body; with low wide neck, profiled rim; on high, bell-shaped foot. Flat, curved handle. Clear greenish glass. Embossed ornamental design of seven oval bordered cells on body.

Condition: Glued together from many small pieces; upper part of handle and parts of walls and rim lost; surface dulled in places.

Literature: ДБК, табл. LXXVII, 1; AVS, pl. LXXVII, 1

Analogies: Compare ornamental design with Smith Collection, no. 296

394.
JUG

Syria. Late 3rd century — early 4th century AD

H 30.3; D: rim 7.9; neck 3.5—6.1; body 16.9; foot 10
Received in 1900 from A.Novikov collection; found in Kertch, probably in the Pantikapaion necropolis
E 596   ill.198

Spherical-shaped body; with neck widening downwards; almost horizontally outsplayed bolster-shaped rim; on wide, flat, profiled foot. Tape-shaped handle with ribs, bent at an angle, with high vertical protuberance over rim. Clear greenish glass. Modelled applied braid on neck; embossed ornament in imitation of wicker-work on body.

Condition: Surface slightly iridescent in places.

Literature: Художественное стекло, ил. 22

Analogies: Antik Kunst, Nr. 357; compare with Sammlung Cohn, no. 85, 86; compare details with cat. 395, 396, 398

395.
JUG

Syria. 4th century AD

H (without handle) 29.5; foot 3.5; D: rim 9.4; neck 4.5—5.5; shoulders 14.4; foot 9
Received in 1900 from A.Novikov collection; found in Nymphaion, probably in necropolis
E 682

Almost ovoid body with eleven thin ribs; with wide shoulders, high bell-shaped cylindrical neck, profiled horizontal rim; bell-shaped, profiled foot; flat bottom. Narrow handle bent at an angle, with vertical protuberance and two horizontal extensions above rim; with ribs. Clear dark-violet glass. Modelled applied braid on neck; bolster between body and foot.

Manufacturing technique: Outer side of bottom extended down and individually made foot affixed, after which the end of the extended bottom is broken off — a trace of which can be clearly seen.

Condition: Glued together from pieces; chip on handle; surface iridescent in places.

First ever publication

Analogies: Compare: cat. 394, 396, 398

396.
JUG

Syria. Late 3rd century — early 4th century AD

H 25.2; D: rim 8.4; body 14; foot 10.2
Receved in 1931 from SAHMC; previously in A.Bobrinsky collection
E 2196

Spherical body; with high, narrow, cylindrical neck, funnel-shaped orifice, wide bolster-shaped rim, on massive leg. Flat, wide handle bent at an angle; with high triangular protection (rounded at ends) above rim. Clear light-green glass; handle and decoration of dark olive-green glass. Modelled braid with festoons applied on neck. Foot carelessly made; closes off bottom in wide ring, except for central section (D 3.8). Pontil-mark (D 2) on bottom.

Condition: Surface iridescent.

Literature: Шелковников, ил. 2 (слева); Художественное ремесло, кат. 258

Analogies: SH, E 1902; Bronzegefässe und Bronzegeräte der Antike. Römishen Tonlampen. Antike Gläser. Bücher über Archäeologie, Basel, März 1968, Nr. 152; Sammlung Cohn, Nr. 127; Sammlung Löffler, Nr. 152, Taf. 20, 3; Sammlung Hentrich, Nr. 55; compare with cat. 394, 395

397.
JUG (WITH TWO SECTIONS)

Eastern Mediterranean (Syria ?). 3rd — 4th centuries AD

H 20.3; rim: 5x6.8; GD 13.5; D foot 9.7
Received in 1953 from I.Tolstoy collection
E 3089   ill.200

Spherical body with vertical partition inside; with high, cylindrical neck, thick bolster-shaped rim, on wide, profiled foot (base in form of irregular oval). Massive tape-shaped handle, smoothly curved at rim; with four blurred ribs. Clear honey-yellow glass. Foot bent and asymmetrically affixed to bottom. Pontil-mark (D 1.7) on bottom.

Condition: Part of partition lost; surface iridescent.

First ever publication

Analogies: Compare form (without foot): Morin-Jean, p. 101, fig. 120; Auth, no. 116. Compare foot: cat. 394, 396; Smith Collection, no. 274; Spartz, Nr. 98, Taf. 29; Sammlung Hentrich, Nr. 55 (a jug of yellow glass and similar proportions)

398.
JUG

Syria. 4th century AD

H (without protuberance of handle) 34.3; D: rim 9.6; GD 11.6; base of foot 10.2
Received in 1931 from SAHMC; previously in A.Bobrinsky collection
E 2232   ill.193

Ovoid body smoothly turning into conical neck; wide, almost horizontal, lip with thickened rim; small cone-shaped foot with massive profiled base. Tape-shaped handle bent at an angle, with high triangular protuberance above rim. Clear light-green glass; handle and foot of clear dark-green glass. Mark of tool (D 2, depth 0.6) employed when affixing leg to base. Note its beautiful silhouette and elegant proportions. Shape repeats the silver jugs of the day.

Condition: Glued back together from pieces; "extension" of handle protuberance lost; surface iridescent in places.

First ever publication

Analogies: Masterpieces, no. 117 (amazingly similar in colour, shape, layout of all details; made in the same workshop ?). Compare with silver ones: Искусство Византии, с. 60, № 44

399.
JUG

Syria. Mid — 5th century AD

H 27.8; D: rim 7.5; GD 10.8; foot 7
Received in 1869; found in 1869 in Kertch (grave 3 of Bosporos' necropolis)
1820/34   ill.191

Pear-shaped body; without shoulders, with short neck widening downwards, funnel-shaped rim, on short conical foot; concave bottom. Flat, ribbed handle bent at an angle; with protuberance above rim. Clear bright-aquamarine glass. Four rows of applied thread and thick bolster on outside of rim; thick applied braid with zigzags on neck. Nine rows of applied thread forming five festoons (tops downwards) on body. Foot carelessly made. Pontil-mark (D 2.5) on bottom.

Condition: Handle protuberance lost; surface iridescent.

Literature: Скалон 1974, с. 44—48, ил. 2 (с. 45)

Analogies: Скалон, op. cit, с. 44, ил. 1; с. 46, ил. 3; Sammlung von Kirchner-Schwarz, Taf. 5, 291; Basserman-Jordan, Taf. VI, 1; Liepmann, Nr. 114; Auth, no. 121; compare with Recent Important Acquisitions // JGS, 1969, vol. XI, p. 110, no. 7

400.
AMPHORA

Rhineland (Cologne ?). 4th century AD

H 33.5; D: rim 9.6; bottom 11.4
Received in 1932; found in 1914 in Kertch (earthen crypt; together with cat. 175)
1820/1041   ill.190

Cylindrical body; with horizontal shoulders, narrow short neck widening downwards; funnel-shaped orifice, massive profiled rim. Vertical, wide, flat handles with thin dense ribs. Clear greenish-yellow glass. Carved geometrical ornamental design of horizontal tiers between double lines on body in following order (from the top downwards): slanting parallel lines; narrow vertical polished ovals; diamonds from interlacing double lines; narrow vertical polished ovals; slanting parallel lines. Ornamental design carelessly made.

Condition: Good.

Literature: OAK for 1913—1915, с. 101, ил. 167; Художественное стекло, ил. 21

Analogies: Doppelfeld, Taf. 150, 151; F.Fulep. Roman Cemeteries on the Territory of Pecs (Sopiane). Budapest, 1977, pl. 24, 1, Grave K/191, p. 36; Sammlung Hentrich, Nr. 259 (Abb. auf S. 167 und Farbtaf. auf Titel); Benko, tabl. XXIII, 1 (6c/6); compare: Fr.Fremersdorf,

Figürlich geschliffene Gläser eine Kölner Werkstatt des 3. Jahrhunderts. Berlin, 1951, S. 9, Abb. 4, *3*; Taf. 21, *2*; Smith Collection, no. 378; Засецкая 1993, с. 92, кат. 367, табл. 63, № 367

401.
AMPHORA
Syria. 4th century AD

H 22.1; D: rim 4.2; shoulders 9.7; bottom 5.6
Received in 1928 from Gaman-Gamon collection; previously in M.Botkin collection
E 1609   ill.202

Body with ribs narrowing sharply downwards; with wide shoulders; high neck widening downwards; bolster-shaped rim; slightly concave bottom. Clear green glass. On body two applied ribbons with curls forming two small ornamental looped handles above shoulders and two under rim. Pontil-mark in form of small glass protuberance on bottom.

Condition: Surface iridescent, film of silver iridescence in some places.

First ever publication

Analogies: Sammlung Niessen, Band II, Taf. LII, Nr. 1006; compare: Sammlung Hentrich, Nr. 206; Auth, no. 171, 452; Hayes, no. 333, 389, 436

402.
FLASK
Syria. 4th century AD

H 19; D: rim 2.6; body 8.1; bottom 3.8
Received in 1908; found in 1905 in looted grave of the Pantikapaion necropolis
П.1905.8

Spherical body; with high narrow neck, widening upwards and downwards; concave bottom. Clear light-aquamarine glass. Blue applied braid along rim; rows of super-imposed spiral threads, light-bluish above and navy-blue below, on neck. Circle of several close blue strands in middle of neck. Tier of vertical thin oval cavities in middle of body.

Condition: Parts of walls lost, surface dimmed in places.

Literature: ИАК, 1909, вып. 30, с. 32, ил. 21

Analogies: SH, E 3137; E 1338; Neuburg pl. 61; Vessberg 1952, pl. VII, 21; Hayes, no. 403

403.
FLASK
Syria. 3rd—4th centuries AD

H 23.4; D rim 3.9; GD 6; foot 4.6
Received in 1898 from M.Sivadjan collection; bought in Syria
E 1352   ill.192

Spindle-shaped body with linear oval cavities and conical constricted foot

formed by lower part of walls. Funnel-shaped wide neck, flat rim. Clear honey-yellow glass. Rim sliced off and melted. Pontil-mark (D 1.5) on bottom.

Condition: Crack on foot; pattern of golden iridescence on surface.

First ever publication

Analogies: Compare: Liepmann, Nr. 102; Sammlung Löffer, Nr. 128, Taf. 16, *2*

404.
FLASK
Syria. 3rd — 4th centuries AD

H 19; D: rim 3.3; GD 5.7; foot 4.3
Received in 1898 from M.Sivadjan collection; bought in Syria
E 1332   ill.209

Pear-shaped body, with cone-shaped foot formed by lower part of walls; with cylindrical neck, flat rim; concave bottom. Clear bluish glass. Girdles of applied thread under rim and at lower part of neck. Blue applied braids on neck form three loop-shaped ornamental handles, turning into comb-shaped ribbons on walls along body. Pontil-mark (D 1.2) on bottom.

Condition: Surface iridescent.

Literature: Художественное стекло, ил. 20; Художественное ремесло, кат. 286

Analogies: Cat. 405; Auth, no. 165, 453; La Baume, Nr. D78, Taf. 34, *3*; Sammlung Cohn, Nr. 98; Basserman-Jordan, Taf. IV, 32

405.
FLASK
Syria. 3rd — 4th centuries AD

H 21.5; D: rim 3.6; GD 7; foot 6.5
Received in 1898 from M.Sivadjan collection; bought in Syria
E 1358   ill.203

Pear-shaped body; without shoulders, with high, slightly swollen and almost cylindrical neck; funnel-shaped orifice; on wide profiled cone-shaped foot. Clear honey-yellow glass. On the lower part of neck two round loops with protuberance above, turning into comb-shaped ribbons on walls along body.

Condition: Glued back together from pieces; parts of walls lost; surface iridescent.

Literature: Художественное ремесло, кат. 285 (without ill.)

Analogies: Cat. 404; SH, E 1610; La Baume, Nr. D78, Taf. 34, *3*

406.
JAR
Syria. 4th century AD

H 8.6; D: rim 6.8; body 8.7; bottom 4.6
Received in 1898 from M.Sivadjan collection; bought in Syria
E 1342   ill.208

Spherical body; with massive profiled rim; slightly concave bottom. Loop-shaped handles. Clear bluish glass. Handles and applied decorations of dull blue glass. Ornamental design of three and a half coils of thread and row of zigzags near base on body. Pontil-mark (D 1.1) on bottom.

Condition: Cracks on foot; golden iridescent patterns on surface.

Literature: Художественное ремесло, кат. 293 (without ill.); Glass, p. 255, no. 233

Analogies: Neuburg, pl. 59; Auth, no. 176, 180, 476—479; Liepmann, Nr. 123; La Baume, Nr. D102, 1, Taf. 41, *1*; Sammlung Hentrich, Nr. 98—100; Filarska, nr. 60, tabl. XIII, 1; SH, E 1327

407.
JAR
Syria. 4th century AD

H 10.2; D: rim 7; body 9.8; bottom 5
Received in 1898 from M.Sivadjan collection; bought in Syria
E 1326   ill.206

Spherical body; with short neck, thick bolster-shaped rim; flat bottom. Thick, rounded handles in shape of braids. Clear aquamarine glass. Applied ornamental design of rows of zigzags on body; applied six-sided rosette of loops with intricate contours meeting ends of zigzags to form a network pattern on bottom.

Condition: Surface iridescent; with silvery-lilac or pearl crust in places.

First ever publication

Analogies: Compare: Matheson, no. 311; Sammlung Oppenländer, Nr. 675, 677

408.
JAR
Syria. 4th century AD

H 10; D: rim 7.4; shoulders 10; bottom 2.2
Received in 1914; bought from Ya.Buksil
E 934   ill.207

Squat body narrowing downwards; with wide shoulders, funnel-shaped orifice slightly sunk into shoulders; small, slightly concave bottom. Four ribbon-shaped vertical handles, with three ribs, with small curve near rim. Clear violet glass; handles and thin embossed band under rim of semi-clear greenish glass. Edge sliced off and melted.

Condition: Thin silver coating of iridescence in places on surface.

400

401

402

403*

404, 405

406

407

408

409, 410

411, 412

413

414

Literature: Художественное ремесло, кат. 294 (without ill.)

Analogies: Bronzegefässe und Bronzegeräte der Antike. Römische Tonlampen. Antike Gläser. Bücher über Archäologie. Basel, März 1968, Nr. 151; Basserman-Jordan, Taf. V, 196; Sammlung von Kirchner-Schwarz, Taf. 1, *106*; compare Sammlung Cohn, Nr. 106; La Baume, Nr. D62, Taf. 30, *3*; Sammlung Hentrich, Nr. 224

409.
FLASK

Syria. 4th century AD

H 13; D: rim 4.2; foot 3.8
Received in 1928 from M.Botkin collection
E 1601   ill.201

Pear-shaped body; on conical foot. Clear aquamarine glass. Applied lace zigzag ornamental design of braids under rim. Pontil-mark (D 1.2) on bottom.

Condition: Surface iridescent.

Literature: Художественное ремесло, кат. 283 (without ill.)

Analogies: Hayes, no. 452, 455; La Baume, Nr. D81, Taf. 35; Collection de M.Louis Courtin. Antiquités et monnaies requeillies en Syrie. Paris, 1896, pl. II, 2

410.
FLASK

Syria. 4th century AD

H 11; D: rim 3.7; foot 3.2
Received in 1928 from E.Shuvalova collection (bought in Italy ?)
E 1492   ill.201

Pear-shaped body; on wide flattened foot. Handles smoothly curved. Clear aquamarine glass. Spiral flutes on body. Pontil-mark (D 0.8) on body.

Condition: Silvery film of iridescence on surface.

Literature: Художественное ремесло, кат. 284 (without ill.)

Analogies: Hayes, no. 450 (compare: no. 447, 448, 451, 393—395); Filarska, nr. 181, tabl. XXXIX, 6; La Baume, Nr. D72, Taf. 33, *1*; Fitzwilliam Mus., no. 107; Neuburg, pl. 58; Sammlung Hentrich, Nr. 68; Smith Collection, no. 321; compare: Liepmann, Nr. 129; Matheson, no. 317—320; Basserman-Jordan, Taf. VI, Nr. 149, 150, Taf. VIII, 146, 148

411.
FLASK

Syria. 4th century AD

H 11.6; D: rim 4.4; GD 6; foot 3.8
Received in 1928 from Gaman-Gamon collection
E 1620   ill.205

Squat body narrowing sharply downwards; with wide shoulders, narrow neck, funnel-shaped orifice, on short conical foot; concave bottom. Clear bluish glass. Triple loop-shaped ornamental handles and ornamental design of spiral applied thread of semi-clear blue-green glass. Pontil-mark in form of lump of glass on bottom.

Condition: Good.

First ever publication

Analogies: Compare: Hayes, no. 350, handles: no. 392; Auth, no. 450; Sammlung Oppenländer, Nr. 676; Sammlung Hentrich, Nr. 133

412.
FLASK

Syria. 4th century AD

H 12.7; D: rim 4.6; GD 5.3; foot 3.5
Received in 1909; presented by Partriarch Grigory IV of Antioch
E 1407   ill.205

Body in shape of two spheres with narrow waist between them; with funnel-shaped orifice, on short conical foot; concave bottom. Handles bent at an angle. Clear bluish glass. Spiral of three and a half coils of thick applied thread on orifice. Braid-girdle on neck under handles. Pontil-mark in form of lump of glass on bottom.

Condition: Surface iridescent.

First ever publication

Analogies: Compare with Hayes, no. 392

413.
DOUBLE   TUBE

Syria. 4th century AD

H: without handle 11.1; with handle 16; rim: one section 2.5x3; other section 2x3
Received in 1898 from M.Sivadjan collection; found in Syria
E 1297   ill.199

Body in shape of two tubes connected by common wall, slightly widening upwards and rounded below; with bolster-shaped rims. Handles in shape of braid, upper one crescent-shaped, side ones with curve near rim. Clear bluish glass. Handles and spiral ornamental design of six coils of applied thread on body of dark-blue glass.

Condition: Spiral ornamental design (with exception of section of bottom coil) lost (though a trace has survived); upper part glued back on; surface very iridescent; covered by golden-lilac film and corroded.

First ever publication

Analogies: La Baume, Nr. D84, Taf. 36, *1*; Auth, no. 183; Matheson, no. 323—325; Hayes, no. 360, 361, 456, 458; Sammlung Hentrich, Nr. 104; Sammlung Oppenländer, Nr. 680a; Neuburg, pl. 28, 59; Filarska, nr. 178, tabl. XXXIX, 3; Basserman-Jordan, Taf. VII, Nr. 168, 169; Collection de M.Louis Courtin. Antiquitiés et monnaies requeillies en Syrie. Paris, 1896, pl. III, 3; SH, E 1300; E 1367; compare handle with cat. 414

414.
VASE-UNGUENTARIUM

Syria. 4th — 5th centuries AD

H: without handle 12.9; with handle 19.2;
D: rim 4.3; foot 6.2
Received in 1922 from Gaman-Gamon collection
E 1622   ill.204

Cone-shaped body on wide, massive (two-layered) foot formed by lower part of walls; with bolster-shaped rim. Thick, crescent-shaped handle. Clear light-blue glass. Thirteen and a half coils of thin spiral applied thread on body. Open-work applied decoration on sides in shape of loops: six loops on one side and five on the other. Pontil-mark (D 1.5) on foot; compare handle with cat. 413.

Condition: Good.

First ever publication

Analogies: Sammlung Hentrich, Nr. 103

415.
JAR (WITH EMBOSSED ORNAMENTAL DESIGN)

Eastern Mediterranean (Syria ?)
Late 4th century — early 5th century AD

H 13.3; D rim 7.4; GD 10.4; bottom 6.7
Received in 1873; found in 1873 in Kertch in Bosporos' necropolis (grave 21)
П.1873.199   ill.210

Virtually spherical body; with short, wide, funnel-shaped neck; bolster-shaped rim; concave bottom. Clear light-green glass. One and a half coils of applied thread on neck. Embossed ornamental design of diamond-shaped facets on body. Pontil-mark (D 2.5) on bottom.

Condition: Surface highly iridescent and corroded.

First ever publication

Analogies: Cat. 416; SH, E 393; E 640; 1820/1052 (Искусство Византии, с. 77, № 100); Сорокина 1962, с. 220, ил. 7, *4*; Сорокина 1978, с. 272, ил. 3, *14*; Сорокина 1971, с. 96, ил. 5, *1*; compare: Harden 1936, pl. XVIII, 593; Doppelfeld, Taf. 130, 131; Sammlung Cohn, Nr. 108; Sammlung Hentrich, Nr. 227; without ornamental design — SH, E 2219

416.
JAR (WITH EMBOSSED ORNAMENTAL DESIGN)

Eastern Mediterranean (Syria ?). Late 4th century — early 5th century AD

415 □   416 □   417* □

418 □   419—421   422, 423 □

424 □   425* □

426   427*

H 12.5; D: rim 7.7; GD 9.1; bottom 5.6
Received in 1912; found in 1909 in Kertch in
Bosporos' necropolis (grave 75/22/)
П.1909.101   ill.211

Spherical-shaped body; with short, wide,
funnel-shaped neck; thick bolster-shaped
rim; concave bottom. Clear olive-green
glass. Two and a half coils of applied
thread on neck, embossed ornamental
design of diamond-shaped facets on
body. Pontil-mark (D 2.5) on bottom.

Condition: Surface iridescent.

Literature: ИАК, 1913, вып. 47, с. 29

Analogies: See cat. 415

417.
SMALL JUG (WITH PAINTED DECORATION)

*Eastern Mediterranean. 4th — 5th
centuries AD*

H 12.4; D: rim 7.6; body 9.5; bottom 4.6
Received in 1916; bought from L.Gauhman;
probably originates from Southern Russia
E 959   ill.209

Spherical body; with short, wide, funnel-
shaped neck; concave bottom. Wide,
flat handle bent at an angle. Clear olive-
green glass. White enamel painting:
continuous scaly ornamental design on
neck; stylized branch on shoulders; network pattern of loops and thin diagonal
lines on body and along handle. Rim
melted. Pontil-mark (D 2.8) on bottom.
Vessels with similar enamel paintings are
unknown.

Condition: Good.

First ever publication

Analogies: Compare (without handle and
design): Doppelfeld, Taf. 131; Hayes, no. 154;
Auth, no. 460; with white thread ornamental
design, without handle and with narrow neck
see Smith Collection, no. 424 (scallops ornamental
design); compare form with cat. 415, 416

418.
BEAKER

Syria. 4th century AD

H 11.1; D: rim 6.2; foot 4.1; thickness (top) 0.3
Received in 1854; found in 1853 in
Pantikapaion necropolis (grave 2; together with
cat. 429)
П.1853.59   ill.214

Almost cylindrical body with massive
rounded foot formed by lower part of
walls; with rim protuding outwards;
concave bottom. Clear olive-green
glass. Rim sliced off at top; engraved
girdle of close thin lines under rim, two
similar girdles on body.

Condition: Surface iridescent.

Literature: Извлечение, с. 182, ил. 75

Analogies: Compare: Auth, no. 112, 494;
Sammlung Cohn, Nr. 119; Hayes, no. 379;
Recent Important Acquisitions // JGS, 1963,
vol. V, p. 145, no. 16

419.
BEAKER

*Bosporan Kingdom (?). Mid — third quarter
of 4th century AD*

H 8.5; D: rim 6.6; bottom 3.9
Received in 1931 from SAHMC; previously in
A.Bobrinsky collection
E 2169

Almost cylindrical body; with rim protruding outwards; slightly concave bottom. Clear olive-green glass. On body,
between two engraved girdles of double thin lines, embossed ornamental
design of large blue separate drops
twice in alternation with groups of six
small drops of blue glass. Embossed
ornamental design was applied after
engraving, as lower small drops cover
girdle. Rim sliced off.

*Condition: Piece glued on at upper end,
surface slightly iridescent.*

First ever publication

Analogies: Сорокина 1971, с. 86, ил. 1, *3a*,
с. 88, ил. 2, *9*; compare: Сорокина 1979,
с. 58, ил. 1, *1*; Сорокина 1978, с. 272,
ил. 3, *10*

420.
BEAKER

*Chersonesos (?). Late 4th century — early
5th century AD*

H 7; D: rim 7.1; bottom 3.4
Received in 1931 from SAHMC; previously in
A.Bobrinsky collection
E 2174

Ovoid body; with rim protruding outwards; flat bottom. Clear olive-yellow
glass. Embossed ornamental design of
large separate drops twice in alternation
with groups of five small drops of blue-
green glass on body; engraved girdle
over ornamental design. Rim sliced off.

*Condition: Glued together from pieces;
losses to rim; surface iridescent.*

First ever publication

Analogies: Сорокина 1971, с. 86, ил. 1, *5*,
с. 98, ил. 6, *3*; compare: с. 95, ил. 4, *6*;
Сорокина 1978, с. 272, ил. 3, *5*

421.
BEAKER

*Eastern Mediteranean or Black Sea coast
4th century — early 5th century AD*

H 10.1; D: rim 7.5; bottom 3
Received in 1900 from A.Novikov collection; found
in Kertch, probably in Pantikapaion necropolis
E 658

Body in shape of truncated cone; with
slightly curved rim protruding outwards; slightly concave bottom. Clear
greeny-yellow glass. On body, between two slight polished girdles, embossed ornamental design of large
blue separate drops thrice in alternation with groups of three small drops.

*Condition: Surface iridescent, shine lost
almost everywhere.*

First ever publication

Analogies: Сорокина 1971, с. 86, 87, ил. 1, *86*;
с. 95, ил. 4, *3*; compare: Сорокина 1979,
с. 58, ил. 1, *2*, cat. 423

422.
BEAKER

Eastern Mediterranean. 4th century AD

H 7.1; D: rim 6.6; bottom 2.3
Received in 1893 from J.Lemme' collection
E 503   ill.217

Ovoid body; with outsplayed rim protruding outwards; slightly concave bottom. Clear olive-yellow glass. Embossed ornamental design of several
separate drops of blue glass under
barely visible engraved girdle on body.

Condition: Cracks on walls, surface iridescent.

First ever publication

Analogies: Сорокина 1971, с. 86, ил. 1, *26*;
с. 98, ил. 6, *1, 2*; Сорокина 1963, с. 139,
ил. 2, *2*; Сорокина 1979, с. 58, ил. 1, *20*;
Сорокина 1978, с. 272, ил. 3, *10*;
Morin-Jean, pl. 10, (right); Auth, no. 501

423.
BEAKER

*Eastern Mediterranean or Black Sea coast
4th century — early 5th century AD*

H 10; D: rim 7; bottom 3.8
Received in 1931 from SAHMC; previously in
A.Bobrinsky collection
E 2171   ill.217

Analogous in shape to cat. 421. Clear
olive-green glass. Embossed ornamental design from large relief drops of
various sizes and configurations on
body.

*Condition: Surface iridescent, shine lost in
many places.*

First ever publication

Analogies: Сорокина 1971, с. 86, 87,
ил. 1, *8*; с. 91, ил. 3, *3* (compare with
ил. 3, *2*), с. 97; ил. 5, *5* (compare with
ил. 5, *2*); Сорокина 1973, с. 184, ил. 1, *1*;
Liepmann, Nr. 140; Auth, no. 196; compare:
Сорокина 1963, с. 144, ил. 4, *28*; Сорокина
1978, с. 272, ил. 3, *4*; Сорокина 1979,
с. 58, ил. 1, *21*; compare shape with
Скалон 1973, с. 52, ил. 5

428 a ☐   428 б ☐

429

430

431 ☐

432

433

434 ☐

424.
LAMPADA

Egypt or Syria. 4th century AD

H 13.9; D: rim 6.1; bottom 0.9
Received in 1859; found in 1857 in
Pantikapaion necropolis (grave I)
П.1857.54   ill.216

Conical form; with rim protruding outwards; small flat bottom. Clear olive-
yellow glass. Girdle of eight relief ovals of
blue glass on upper part of body.

Condition: Surface iridescent.

First ever publication

Analogies: Сорокина 1971, с. 91, ил. 3, *5*;
Morin-Jean, pl. 10, Hayes, no. 380;
Sammlung Löffler, Nr. 197; Taf. 28, *2*; Smith
Collection, no. 426; Masterpieces, no. 87;
compare: Harden 1936, pl. XVI, no. 460;
Sammlung Hentrich, Nr. 112. For the use of
such vessels as lamps in suspended
candelabra see Recent Important Acquisitions
// JGS, 1974, vol. XVI, p. 126, no. 9

425.
LAMPADA

Egypt or Syria. 4th century AD

H 20.3; D rim 6.7
Received in 1908; found in 1904 in Kertch
(crypt 154/10/)
1820/314   ill.215

Conical body; with curved rim protruding
outwards; small rounded bottom. Clear
dark-blue glass. Embossed ornamental
design from drops of dulled glass, in
imitation of grains, on body. Ornamental
design consists of three tiers: two rows of
triangles in each between horizontal girdles. Girdles, in their turn, consist of three
rows of grains — red between yellow. In
each tier triangles are in upper and lower
tiers; formed from grain points alternate in
colour in chess-board fashion: red and
yellow; yellow and light-blue in central tier.

Condition: Glued from pieces.

Literature: OAK for 1904, с. 77, ил. 122;
ИАК 1907, вып. 25, с. 42, ил. 17; AA, 1905, 2,
S. 60 (without ill.); Художественное стекло,
ил. 24; Сорокина 1971, с. 91, ил. 3, *1*; Засецкая
1993, с. 73, кат. 213, табл. 47, № 213

Analogies: Compare shape with cat. 424;
compare, for example: Harden 1936,
pl. XVI, 436; Edgar, pl. III, 32.491

426.
LAMP

Syria. 4th—5th centuries AD

H 14.8; D: rim 10; base 2.7
Received 1932—1935 from LILI Museum of
Antiquities collection; found in 1904 in
Pantikapaion necropolis (crypt 162/18/)
П.1904.77

Bell-shaped body; with base in shape of
sphere. Clear olive-green glass. Several
coils of applied thread on upper body,
embossed ornamental design of ovals
joined by bridges in middle. Round trace
With embossed circumference and chip
(Pontil-mark or broken foot ?) on base.

*Condition: Glued together again from
pieces; parts of walls lost; fastened
together by film in places; surface
iridescent.*

Literature: ИАК, 1907, вып. 25, с. 45, ил. 18

Analogies: Compare: Masterpieces, no. 131;
G.Ekholm, Scandinavian Glass Vessels of
Oriental Origin from the First to the Sixth
Century // JGS, 1963, vol. V, p. 37, fig. 35;
G.D.Weinberg 1963, p. 28, fig. 7; Harden 1936,
pl. XVI, 464, 465; Edgar, pl. III, 32.483

427.
FLASK (ON FOOT)

Syria. 4th — 5th centuries AD

H 28.7; D: rim 5.2; GD 6.8; foot 9
Received in 1924 from SAHMC; bought in 1914
in Kertch; found on the territory of the
Pantikapaion necropolis
П. 1914.89

Elegant spindle-shaped body on high
conical foot formed by lower part of
walls. Wide funnel-shaped neck, with
curved rim protruding outwards. Clear
colourless glass. Rim sliced off and
unwrought.

*Condition: Surface almost completely
covered with film of iridescence.*

Literature: OAK for 1913—1915, с. 100, ил. 165

Analogies: Compare: G.D.Weinberg 1963,
p. 24, fig. 1; p. 27, fig. 5 (foot of vessel has a
more intricate profile)

428.
SMALL PLATE

*Eastern Mediterranean or Egypt
3rd — 4th centuries AD*

H 2.5; D: rim 11.6; foot 4.9
Received in 1894; found in 1893 in
embankment on the territory of the Chersonesos
necropolis
X.1893.53   ill.212, 213

Wide-open conical body on short foot
formed by lower part of walls. Irregular
circle in section; no rim-band; concave
bottom. Clear blue glass. Cavity in circumference of irregular contours (D 1 —
pontil-mark ?) in centre of base.

*Condition: Surface corroded, very
iridescent, silver crust from within.*

Literature: OAK for 1893, с. 74

Analogies: Compare with Harden 1936,
pl. I, *8, 17*; Hayes, no. 592; Edgar, pl. I,
32.408; Sammlung Cohn, Nr. 139

429.
DISH

Egypt. 4th century AD

H 6.5; D: 37.5; foot 12.7
Received in 1854; found in 1853 in
Pantikapaion necropolis (grave 2; together with
cat. 418)
П.1853.58

Almost flat form, rim slightly raised and
curved; on conical foot. Clear grass-
green glass, bright-green on the foot. Foot
carelessly made, traces of toolwork can
be seen; pontil-mark (D 2.7) on bottom.

Condition: Surface iridescent in places.

Literature: Извлечение, с. 182, ил. 75

Analogies: Compare with Hayes, no. 592

430.
DISH

Eastern Mediterranean. 3rd—4th centuries AD

H: 2.9; foot 1.4; D: 29.1; foot 12; thickness of
foot 0.4—0.5; thickness of rim 0.5
Received in 1909; presented by Partriarch
Grigory IV of Antioch
E 1408

Flat, on circular tape-shaped foot. Clear
aquamarine glass, emerald-green in
protuberances. Bolster (W, H 0.6) parallel to rim on outside.

Condition: Surface slightly iridized.

First ever publication

Analogies: Compare with Hayes, no. 592

431.
DISH (WITH PAINTED DESIGN)

Egypt or Syria. 4th century AD

H: 7.6; foot 2.5; D: rim 24.2; bottom 14
Received in 1913 from Kertch
E 898   ill.218

Curved walls, sloping towards bottom;
with flanged rim, on high, almost vertical, tape-shaped foot; slightly concave
bottom. Clear olive-green glass; with
many horizontal bubbles. Paintings on
both sides: bird in profile (stork ?) encir-
cled by three ovals on inner side of
bottom; pointed zigzags on outer side of
walls. Foot carelessly modelled, bent,
rim unevenly cut.

*Condition: Surface iridescent, colour of
painting indistinct.*

First ever publication

Analogies: Сорокина 1978, с. 272, ил. 3, *15*
(this dish is identical to the Hermitage one in
form and is painted with the same motif of bird
amongst ovals. It originates from Kertch.
N.Sorokina believes that it is a peacock that is
depicted on the bottom and links this
representation to early Christian symbolism);
compare with cat. 432

432.

DISH (WITH PAINTED DESIGN)

Egypt or Syria. 5th century AD

H: 8.2; foot 2.5; D: rim 26.5; foot 14.3
Received in 1859 from S.Stroganov collection, found in 1857 in Kertch, in a crypt
1820/6

Rounded walls; with thick bolster-shaped rim; on high, almost vertical, thick foot. Clear olive-green glass; many horizontal bubbles. On outer side of walls zigzag ornamental design, probably painted. On inside of bottom ground ornamental design of two intersecting crosses and four circumferences; possible colouring over grinding. Foot crudely made.

Condition: Colour lost, surface iridescent.

Literature: Художественное стекло, ил. 25; Искусство Византии, с. 76, No. 93; V.F.Gaidukevic. Das Bosporanische Reich. Berlin; Amsterdam, 1971, Abb. 150, S. 502, Anm. 22; Засецкая 1993, с. 39, кат. 2, табл. № 2

Analogies: Compare with Hayes, no. 591, 593; compare shape: cat. 431; Smith Collection, no. 324

433.

BOWL

Syria or Palestine. Second half of 4th century AD

H 4; D rim 13
Received in 1900 from A.Novikov collection;

found on the territory of Nymphaion, probably in necropolis
E 676

Segment-shaped body; with rim protruding outwards and sliced off at top. Clear greenish glass. On lower part of outer walls is ground inscription in Greek ΠΙΕΖΗCΗC ("Drink to your health") intended to be read from above (retrograde). Inscription runs along circumference between engraved girdles of close lines. In centre, drawing of stylized tree in shape of palmetto between two ovals.

Condition: Insignificant chips along rim, glass in very good condition.

Literature: Кунина 1995, с. 46—48, ил. 1 и 2 на с. 47

Analogies: All analogous bowls have the same shape: a bowl with the same inscription from the Ashmolean Museum (A.M.1949.168): D.B.Harden, Tomb-groups of Glass of Roman Date from Syria and Palestina // Iraq, 1949, vol. XI, part 2, p. 157, fig. 3; compare also with the bowl in the Louvre with a similar inscription around a central palmetto (MHD1182), acquired in Kertch: Harden, op. cit., p. 157; bowl with the same inscription depicting a male figure amongst foliage — see Smith Collection, no. 380; bowl with representation of peacock and similar inscription found in Georgia at the Mtskheta-Samtavro burial ground: Н.Н.Угрелидзе. К истории производства стекла в раннесредневековой Картли (Иберии), Тбилиси, 1967, с. 27, ил. V

434.

BOTTOM OF VESSEL (WITH INTERGLASS GILDING)

Rome. 4th century AD

D 8.1; H pad-base 0.2; thickness of pad-base 0.3
Received in 1895; previously in A.Bazilevsky collection in Paris; found in catacombs in Rome
E 2039

Bottom of vessel on low circular base. Clear colourless, two-layered glass. Between layers half-length family portrait of woman, man and girl, cut from sheet of thin gold foil. Drawing in silhouette, engraved details. Portrait placed in two concentric circumferences of golden girdles with circular inscription between them: BALERI BALENTINA PERGAMIA ZESES ("Valeria, Valentina, Pergamia, good health"). Judging by the inscription, the bottom made part of a drinking vessel (bowl ?). The representation is intended to be seen from above.

Condition: Chips on edge.

First ever publication

Analogies: Vessels with portraits and toasts or religious pictures have been found in various necropoleis, particularly in the Roman catacombs. They may have been part of the burial ritual. See SH, E 2038 (with representation of St Peter); E 2037 (with scene of Abraham offering Isaac in sacrifice) (Искусство Византии, № 90, 91); see also SH, E 2040—42; Smith Collection, no. 443; Masterpieces, no. 90

GLOSSARY

ALABASTRON

Cat. 2—18, 94

Flask for holding perfume. Oblong in shape, with wide rim and circular bottom, often with ears for the purpose of hanging. Its name is derived from *alabaster* (Gr. *alebastr*), from which alabastra were first made, in ancient Egypt. Alabastra were also made from clay, glass and metal and were intended for everyday use, sporting activities and burial rites.

AMPHORA

Cat. 109, 178, 179, 229, 336, 337, 400, 401

Two-handled vessel. The Greek name for it is *amphoreus*, though a more ancient word is *amphiphoreus* — *amphi* (from two sides) and *phoreus* (carrying). Large clay amphoroi were used to hold and transport wine and olive oil. When full, an amphora was extremely heavy and required two men to lift it, one taking each handle. Clay amphoroi were also used for serving wine at the table. Amphoroi were made from gold and silver, though rarely from glass. They were of various shapes and were used for serving water and wine and in burial rites.

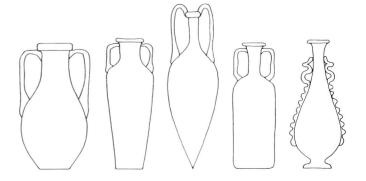

AMPHORISKOS

Cat. 27—38, 129, 137, 138, 140, 142, 143, 187—192, 338—343, 358

The Greek diminutive form of *amphora*. A small flask for holding perfumes, similar in shape to the amphora — two handles, pointed bottom, small foot or pad-base — only smaller.

ARYBALLOS

Cat. 22—26, 228, 346—349

Small perfume flask, spherical in shape, with a wide disc-like rim and short throat. Clay aryballoe could have one or two handles, though glass aryballoe always had two. Young men carried arybolloi suspended from their waists. They rubbed their bodies with oils prior to sporting events, afterwards using the perfumes to scrape off mud and dirt, prior to taking a bath. Aryballoe were also used by women.

ASKOS

Cat. 376

Vessel with a low body and upward protruding short neck and orifice. A handle joins the neck to the lower end of the body. The word *askos* in Greek means wine- or water-skin. Clay askoe were used for holding and pouring oil in the 6th and 5th centuries BC. The askos was first blown from glass in the first centuries AD. It could also be used as a wine receptacle.

BEAD, BEADS. *Cat. 45, 103, 104, 106—108*

BEAKER

Cat. 113—119, 291—293, 295—310, 316—320, 324—330, 418—423

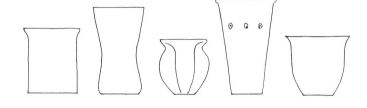

BOTTLE

Cat. 152, 213, 214, 217, 218

BOWL

Cat. 47—53, 86—90, 93, 120—122, 180, 284—290, 322, 323, 332—335, 433

RIBBED BOWL. *Cat. 54—56, 204—211*

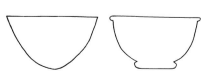

CAMEO. *Cat. 72*

CUP. *Cat. 294*

DISH
Cat. 203, 429—432

DOUBLE TUBE *Cat. 413*

FLASK

*Cat. 95, 96, 98—102, 126—128, 132—136, 139, 141,
145—151, 153—156, 158, 159, 170, 171, 173, 174, 177,
193—199, 212, 215, 216, 219, 222—227, 350—357,
402—405, 409—412, 427*

FUNNEL

Cat. 384, 385

GEM. *Cat. 68*

GUTTUS

Cat. 377—381

A ewer with a body and short narrow spout for holding liquids.
They were made from clay or glass, the latter with a throat. The
guttus was used for pouring oil into lamps, feeding children
(clay vessels), anointing hands with perfume, applying drops of
medicine, and for serving spices and dressings.

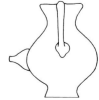

INK-WELL. *Cat. 382, 383*

IRIDIZATION

The process of the flaking away of the surface of glass. The result is an iridescent film, formed as a result of the refraction of light through the glass layers. The process derives its name from Iris, Greek goddess of the rainbow.

JAR

Cat. 311—315, 321, 406—408, 415, 416

JUG

Cat. 124, 130, 131, 144, 157, 162—169, 172, 175, 176, 230—248, 250—268, 274—281, 344, 345, 390—399, 417

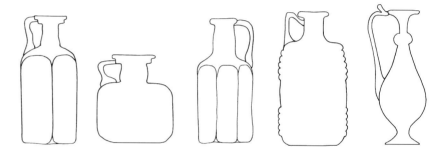

KANTHAROS

Cat. 59—62, 283, 331

Drinking vessel in the form of a two-handled cup with a deep receptacle, often on a foot. The word *kantharos* in Greek means "beetle" and the protuberances on the handles are what gives it its beetle-like shape. The kantharos was made from various materials — clay, silver, bronze or glass.

KRATERISKOS

Cat. 1, 183, 184

Greek diminutive of the word *krater* or crater. In ancient Greece the krater was a large two-handled clay vessel with a foot and wide orifice, used for mixing water and wine. The krateriskos resembles the form of the krater in miniature. The Greeks later used the word *krateros* to describe the crater of a volcano.

LAMPADA

Cat. 424—426

MEDALLION. *Cat. 65—67*

MODIOLUS

Cat. 185, 186

Tankard similar in shape to a *modius* (the Latin word for a basket used for measuring grain).

NEEDLE. *Cat. 84*

OENOCHOE

Cat. 19—21, 110—112, 123, 125, 249, 269—273, 388, 389

Greek diminutive of the word *krater* or crater. In ancient Greece the krater was a large two-handled clay vessel with a foot and wide orifice, used for mixing water and wine. The krateriskos resembles the form of the krater in miniature. The Greeks later used the word *krateros* to describe the crater of a volcano.

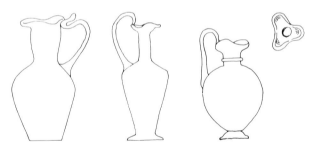

PATERA

Cat. 160, 161

Ritualistic vessel in the form of a bowl with a straight handle (Latin: cup for libations). Paterae were manufactured at the start of the present millenium from bronze, clay and (rarely) glass.

PENDANT. *Cat. 39—44*

PHALERA

Cat. 73—77

Military decoration, worn on armour, in the form of a medallion with an ornamental design in relief.

PLAQUE. *Cat. 105*

PLATE. *Cat. 63, 64, 428*

PONTIL

A special instrument in the form of an iron rod used for finishing off the decoration of a glass vessel. The end of the pontil was used to attach a glob of heated glass to the base of the vessel. Holding the vessel on the pontil, the master formed its upper section (neck, rim) and attached a handle. Detaching the foot of the glass from the pontil often resulted in the formation of a chip or mark. The pontil was also employed as a glass-blowing pipe; in such cases the pontil-mark would be in the shape of a circumference.

PORTRAIT. *Cat. 78*

PYXIS

Cat. 46 (with lid), 97, 181 (with lid), 182 (with lid), 291, 292, 382, 383

Cosmetics box with a lid used for holding foundation and rouge. They were made from wood, bone, metal and glass. Derived from the Greek word for beech wood (*pyxos*).

RING. *Cat. 69, 70*

ROD. *Cat. 79—83*

SEAL. *Cat. 71*

SKYPHOS

Cat. 57, 58, 282

Deep, two-handled drinking vessel on a foot or a pad-base.

SPOON. *Cat. 85*

TRULLA. *Cat. 202*

UNGUENTARIUM

Cat. 220, 221, 359—375, 414

Scent-bottle with a high, narrow throat and a low body. They were of various size and shape and were commonly used in burial rites.

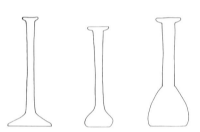

URN

Cat. 386, 387

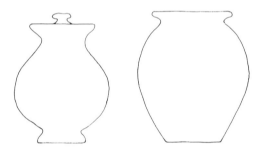

VASE. *Cat. 414*

VESSEL (INCLUDING FIGURED)

Cat. 91, 92, 200, 201, 434

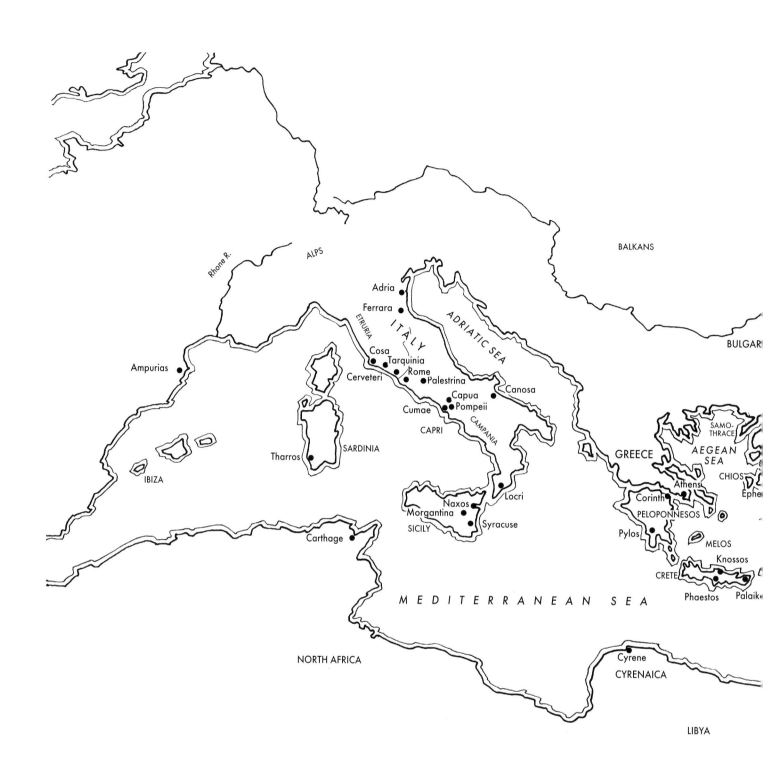

Rhone R. ALPS BALKANS

Adria
Ferrara
ETRURIA ITALY ADRIATIC SEA BULGAR
Cosa
Ampurias Tarquinia
Cerveteri Rome
Palestrina Canosa
Capua
Cumae Pompeii
CAPRI CAMPANIA
SARDINIA GREECE AEGEAN
Tharros SEA CHIOS
Athens Ephe
IBIZA Corinth
PELOPONNESOS
Naxos Locri Pylos MELOS
Morgantina
Carthage SICILY Syracuse Knossos
CRETE
MEDITERRANEAN SEA Phaestos Palaik

NORTH AFRICA Cyrene
CYRENAICA

LIBYA

The Mediterranean and the Middle East
15th — 4th centuries BC

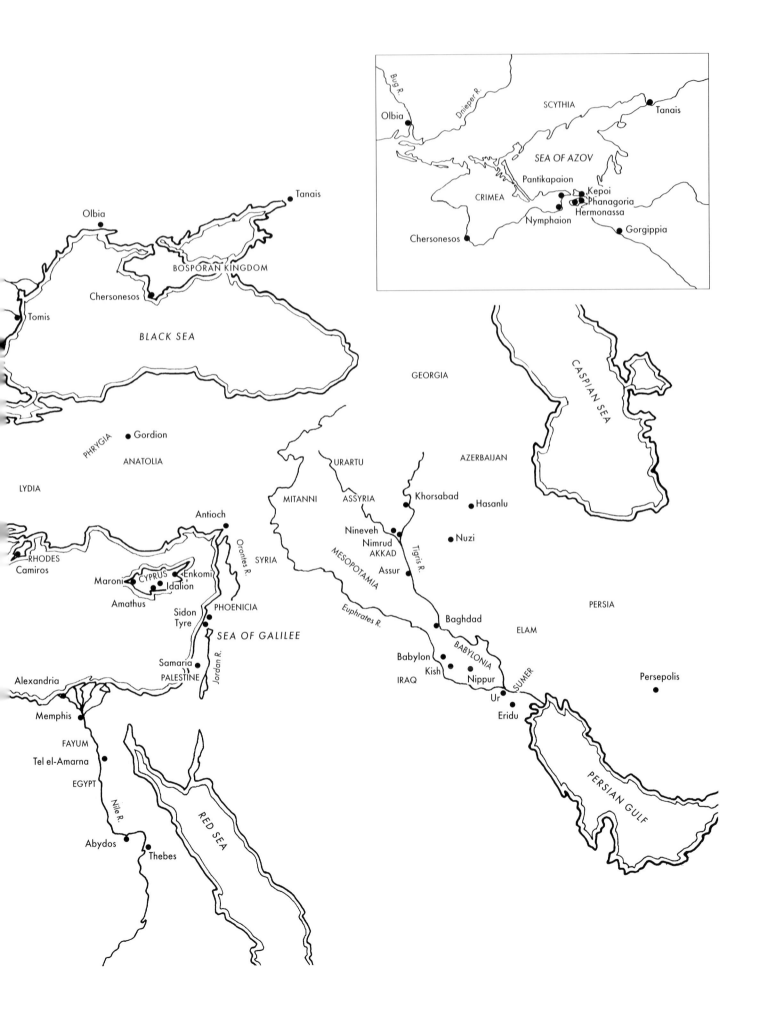

Inset map (top right):

Bug R.
Dnieper R.
Olbia
SCYTHIA
Tanais
SEA OF AZOV
Pantikapaion
CRIMEA
Kepoi
Phanagoria
Hermonassa
Nymphaion
Chersonesos
Gorgippia

Main map:

Olbia
Tanais
BOSPORAN KINGDOM
Chersonesos
Tomis
BLACK SEA
GEORGIA
CASPIAN SEA
PHRYGIA
Gordion
ANATOLIA
URARTU
AZERBAIJAN
LYDIA
MITANNI
ASSYRIA
Khorsabad
Hasanlu
Antioch
Nineveh
Nuzi
Nimrud
AKKAD
RHODES
Camiros
SYRIA
Orontes R.
Assur
Maroni
CYPRUS
Enkomi
Idalion
Amathus
PHOENICIA
MESOPOTAMIA
Tigris R.
PERSIA
Sidon
Tyre
SEA OF GALILEE
Baghdad
ELAM
Samaria
Jordan R.
Euphrates R.
BABYLONIA
Persepolis
Alexandria
PALESTINE
Babylon
Kish
SUMER
Memphis
Nippur
IRAQ
Ur
FAYUM
Eridu
Tel el-Amarna
EGYPT
Nile R.
RED SEA
PERSIAN GULF
Abydos
Thebes

GEOGRAPHICAL INDEX
Sites of Production, Sites of Excavation, Sites of Acquisition

ALPHABETICAL INDEX
Collections, Donations, Acquisitions

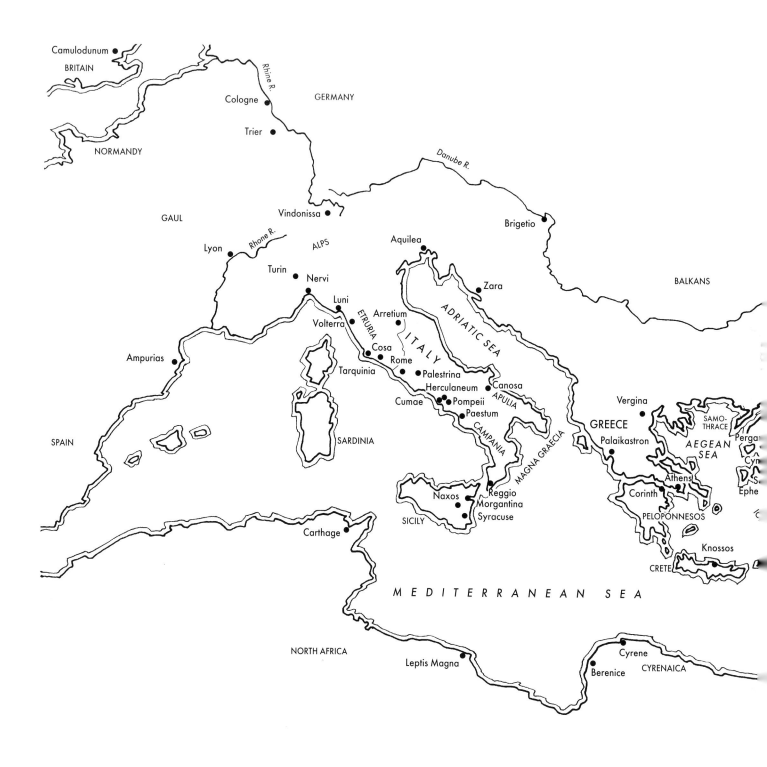

Camulodunum •

BRITAIN

NORMANDY

Rhine R.

Cologne •

Trier •

GERMANY

Danube R.

GAUL

Vindonissa •

Brigetio •

Lyon •

Rhone R.

ALPS

Aquilea •

BALKANS

Turin •

Nervi •

Zara •

Luni •

Volterra •

ETRURIA

Arretium •

ITALY

ADRIATIC SEA

Ampurias •

Cosa •

Rome •

Tarquinia •

Palestrina •

Herculaneum •

Canosa •

APULIA

SPAIN

SARDINIA

Cumae •

Pompeii •

Paestum •

CAMPANIA

MAGNA GRAECIA

GREECE

Vergina •

SAMO-
THRACE

AEGEAN
SEA

Perga

Palaikastron •

Athens

Naxos •

Reggio •

Morgantina •

Syracuse •

SICILY

Corinth •

Ephe

PELOPONNESOS

Carthage •

Knossos •

CRETE

MEDITERRANEAN SEA

NORTH AFRICA

Leptis Magna •

Cyrene •

Berenice •

CYRENAICA

The Mediterranean and the Middle East
4th century BC — 5th century AD

Olbia

Bug R.

Dnieper R.

SCYTHIA

Tanais

SEA OF AZOV

Pantikapaion

CRIMEA

Kepoi

Phanagoria

Hermonassa

Alma-Kermen

Nymphaion

Gorgippia

Chersonesos

Olbia

BOSPORAN KINGDOM

Chersonesos

BLACK SEA

Constantinople

CASPIAN SEA

ASIA MINOR

Antioch

Oronfes R.

Nimrud

Tigris R.

RHODES

SYRIA

Dura Europos

CYPRUS

Hama

MESOPOTAMIA

PARTHIA

Palmyra

Kourion

Amathus

Damascus

Sidon

Tyre

Tel Anafa

Euphrates R.

Baghdad

GALILEE

Alexandria

JUDAEA

Jerusalem

Jordan R.

FAYUM

Karanis

Oxyrhynchos

Nile R.

Cusae

EGYPT

Coptos

RED SEA

PERSIAN GULF

Thebes

SETS OF VESSELS
from the burial vaults of the Pantikapaion necropolis

Grave 24. 1905. *Cat. 353, 354, 359, 355*

Kurgan III, grave 1. 1842. *Cat. 361, 362, 230, 287, 296*

Grave 1. 1872. *Cat. 300, 240*

Grave 225/37. 1902. *Cat. 337, 310*

Grave 69. 1900. *Cat. 258, 363*

Kurgan X, grave 6. 1846. *Cat. 370, 324*

Grave 98/9. 1909. *Cat. 254, 368*

Grave 106/17/. 1909. *Cat. 263, 369*

Grave 116/38/. 1906. *Cat. 365, 366*

Grave 49. 1903. *Cat. 222, 371, 332*

Grave 17. 1900. *Cat. 326, 266, 375*

CHRONOLOGICAL INDEX
Period of Production, Year of Excavation, Year of Acquisition

BIBLIOGRAPHY

Алексеева Е.М.
Античные бусы
Северного
Причерноморья // САИ,
1982, вып. Г 1—12

*Алексеева Е.М.,
Арсеньева Т.М.*
Стеклоделие Танаиса
// СА, 1966, № 2,
с. 176—188

*Аракелян Б.Н.,
Тирацян Г.А.,
Хачатрян Ж.Д.*
Стекло древней
Армении (I—IV вв.)
// Археологические
памятники Армении. 3.
Памятники древней
эпохи. Вып. I. Ереван,
1969

Безбородов М.А.
Химия и технология
древних и средневеко-
вых стекол. Минск, 1969

*Безбородов М.А.,
Островерхов А.С.*
Стеклоделательная
мастерская в
Северном Причерно-
морье в VI в. до н. э.
// Стекло и керамика,
1978, № 2, с. 32—33

Белов Г.Д.
Стеклоделие в
Херсонесе // СА, 1965,
№ 3, с. 237—239

Белов Г.Д.
Стеклоделательная
мастерская в
Херсонесе // КСИА,
1969, вып. 116, с. 80—84

Висотська Т.М.
Про виробництво скла

в Пізньоантичному
Криму. Археологія. 1964.
Київ, т. XVI, с. 7—20

Галанина Л.К.
Стеклянные сосуды из
Курджипского кургана
// АСГЭ, 1970, вып. 12,
с. 35—44

Галибин В.А.
Состав стекла как
археологический
источник. Л., 1989

*Засецкая И.П.,
Марченко И.И.*
Классификация
стеклянных канфаров
позднеэллинистического
и раннеримского
времени // АСГЭ, 1995,
№ 32, с. 90—104

Качалов Н.
Стекло. М., 1959,
с. 40—96

Кунина Н.З.
Сирийские выдутые
в форме стеклянные
сосуды из некрополя
Пантикапея
// Памятники
античного прикладного
искусства. Л., 1973,
с. 101—150

Кунина Н.З.
К вопросу о западном
импорте стекла на
Боспор (по материалам
некрополя Пантикапея
из собрания Отдела
античного мира
Эрмитажа) // ТГЭ, 1984,
Т. XXIV, с. 147—164

Кунина Н.З.
О боспорском стекло-
делии в I и III вв. н. э.
// Боспор и античный
мир // Сборник
научных трудов.
Нижний Новгород, 1997,
с. 39—82

*Кунина Н.З.,
Сорокина Н.П.*
Стеклянные бальзама-
рии Боспора // ТГЭ,
1972, Т. XIII, с. 146—177

Лукас А.
Материалы и ремес-
ленные производства
Древнего Египта. М.,
1958

Николаева Э.Я.
Стеклоделие Боспора
// КСИА, вып. 204,
1991, с. 50—55

Островерхов С.А.
Древнейшее античное
производство стеклян-
ных бус в Северном
Причерноморье // СА,
1981, № 4, с. 214—228

Сагинашвили М.Н.
Стеклянные сосуды
Урбнисского могиль-
ника. Каталог. Тбилиси,
1970 (на рус. и груз. яз.)

Смішко М.Ю.
Поселення III—IV ст. н.
е. із слідами скляного
виробництва біля
с.Комарів, Чернівецької
області // Матеріали
із археології
Прикарпаття і Волині.
Вип. 5. Київ, 1964

Сорокина Н.П.
Стекло из раскопок
Пантикапея 1949—
1959 гг. // МИА.
Пантикапей. № 103,
1962, с. 210—236

Сорокина Н.П.
Стеклянные сосуды
из Танаиса // МИА.
Древности Нижнего
Дона. № 127, М. 1965,
с. 202—248

Сорокина Н.П.
Античные стеклянные
сосуды из раскопок
некрополя боспор-
ского города Кепы на
Таманском полуост-
рове // Античный мир
и археология. Вып. 3.
Саратов, 1977,
с. 115—144

Сорокина Н.П.
Стеклянная посуда как
источник по истории
экономических связей
Причерноморья и
локального стекло-
делия первых веков н. э.
// Труды ГИМ.
Археологические
исследования на юге
Восточной Европы.
Часть вторая. 1982,
вып. 54, с. 40—42,
99—106

Сорокина Н.П.
Основные направления
изучения стекла первых
веков н. э. Северного
Причерноморья
(по материалам отечест-
венной литературы).
// Труды ГИМ.

Археологические
исследования на юге
Восточной Европы.
1989, вып. 70, с. 142—149

Угрелидзе Н.Н.
К истории
производства стекла
в раннесредневековой
Картли (Иберии)
(на груз. яз., резюме на
рус. яз.). Тбилиси, 1967

Фармаковский М.В.
Римские стеклова-
ренные печи //
Известия Института
археологической
технологии. Т. I. Пг.,
1922, с. 126—176

Флитнер Н.
Стекольно-керамичес-
кие мастерские Тель-
Амарны // Ежегодник
Российского института
истории искусства. Т. I.
Вып. 2. Пг., 1922,
с. 137—164

Шелковников Б.А.
Художественное
стекло. Л., 1962

Щапова Ю.Л.
О химическом составе
древнего стекла // СА,
1977, № 3, с. 95—106

Щапова Ю.Л.
Очерки истории
древнего стеклоделия.
М., 1983. Эллинистичес-
кая техника. М.; Л.,
1948, с. 232—244

Энтелис Ф.С.
Формование и горячее

декорирование стекла. СПб., 1992

Auth S.H.
Ancient Glass at the Newark Museum from the Eugene Schaefer Collection of Antiquities. Newark, New Jersey, 1976

Brill R.H.
Ancient Glass // Scientific American, 1963, vol. 209, no. 5, p. 120—131

Calvi M.C.
I vetri romani del Museo di Aquileia. Aquileia, 1968

Carleston R.J.
Glass Furnaces throughout the Ages // JGS, 1978, vol. 20, p. 9—23

Doppelfeld O.
Römisches und Fränkisches Glas in Köln. Köln, 1966

Dusenbery E.B.
Ancient Glass from the Cemeteries of Samothrace // JGS, 1967, vol. IX, p. 34—49

Dusenbery E.B.
Ancient Glass in the Collections of Wheaton College // JGS, 1971, vol. XIII, p. 9—33

Flinders Petrie W.M.
Arts und Crafts of Ancient Egypt. London, 1910

Flinders Petrie W.M.
Glass in the Early Ages // Journal of Society of Glass Technology, 1926, vol. X, no. 39, p. 229—234

Forbes R.J.
Studies in Ancient Technology. Leiden, 1966, vol. V, p. 112—241

Fossing P.
Glass Vessels before Glass-Blowing. Copenhagen, 1940

Fremersdorf Fr.
Die Anfänge der römischen Glashütten Kölns // Kölner Jahrbuch fur Vor-und Frühgeschichte. Bd. 8. 1965/66. S. 24—43

Glass from the Ancient World.
The Ray Winfield Smith Collection. The Corning Museum of Glass. Corning, New York, 1957

Grose D.F.
The Toledo Museum of Art. Early Ancient Glass. Core-Formed, Rod-formed, and Cast Vessels and Objects from the Late Bronze Age to the Early Roman Empire, 1600 B.C. to A.D. 50. New York, 1989

Harden D.B.
Roman Glass from Karanis. Ann Arbor, 1936

Harden D.B.
Glass and Glasses // A History of Technology, vol. II. Oxford, 1957, p. 311—346

Harden D.B.
Glass-making Centres and the Spread of Glass-making from the First to the Fourth Century A.D. // Annales du Ier Congrés des "Journées internationales du verre". Liège, 1958, p. 47—62

Harden D.B.
The Canosa group of Hellenistic Glases in the British Museum // JGS, 1968, vol. 10, p. 21—47

Harden D.B., Hellenkemper H., Painter K. and Whitehouse D.
Glass of Caesars. Exhibition Catalogue. Milan, 1989

Harden D.B., Painter K.S., Pinder-Wilson, Hugh Tait.

Masterpieces of Glass. London, 1968

Hayes J.W.
Roman and Pre-Roman Glass in the Royal Ontario Museum. A Catalogue. Toronto, 1975

Isings C.
Roman Glass from Dated Finds. Groningen; Djakarta, 1957

Kisa A.
Das Glas im Altertume. T. I—III. Leipzig,1908

La Baume P.
Glas der antiken Welt. Bd. 1. Römisch-Germanisches Museums Köln. Köln, 1973

La Baume P., Salomonson J.W.
Römische Kleinkunst. Sammlung Karl Löffler. Wissenschaftliche Kataloge des Römisch-Germanischen Museums Köln. Bd. 3. Köln (sans date)

Labino D.
The Egyptian Sand-core Technique: a New Interpretation // JGS, 1966, vol. VIII, p. 124—127

Lucas A.
Ancient Egyptian Materials and Industries. 4th ed., revised by J.R. Harris. London,1962, p. 179—194

Matheson S.B.
Ancient Glass in the Yale University Art Gallery. Yale, 1980

Morin-Jean.
La verrerie en Gaule sous L'Empire Romain. Paris,1913

Nolte B.
und Haevernick T.E.
Ägyptische und griechische früche Glasgefässe // Wissenschaftliche Zeitschrift der Universität

Rostock, 16. Jahrgang, 1967. Gesellschafts und sprach-wissenschaftliche Reihe. Rostock, 1967, Heft 7/8, S. 491—493, 611

Oliver A.Jr.
Late Hellenistic Glass in the Metropolitan Museum // JGS, 1967, vol. IX, p. 13—33

Oliver A.Jr.
Millefiori Glass in Classical Antiquity // JGS, 1968, vol. X, p. 48—70

Oliver A.Jr.
Persian Export Glass // JGS, 1970, vol. XII, p. 9—16

Saldern A. von.
Glass Finds at Gordion // JGS, 1959, vol. I, p. 23—49

Saldern A. von.
Ancient Glass in Split // JGS, 1964, vol. VI, p. 42—46

Saldern A. von.
Two Achaemenid Glass Bowls and a Hoard of Hellenic Glass Vessels // JGS, 1975, vol. XVII, p. 38—46

Saldern A. von, Nolte B., La Baume P., Haevernick T.E.
Gläser der Antike. Sammlung Erwin Oppenländer. Hamburg, 1974

Schuler Fr.
Ancient Glassmaking Techniques: The Molding Process // Archaeology, 1959, vol. 12, no. 1, p. 47—52

Schuler Fr.
Ancient Glassmaking Techniques: The Blowing Process // Archaeology, 1959, vol. 12, no. 2, p. 116—122

Schuler Fr.
Ancient Glassmaking Techniques: The Egyptian

Core Vessel Process // Archaeology, 1962, vol. 15, no. 1, p. 32—37

Seefried M.
Glass Core Pendants Found in the Mediterranean Area // JGS, 1979, vol. 21, p. 17—26

Stern E.M., Schlick-Nolte B.
Frühes Glas der alten Welt 1600 v. Chr — 50 n. Chr. Sammlung Ernesto Wolf. Stuttgart, 1994

Trowbridge M.L.
Philological Studies in Ancient Glass. University of Illinois Studies in Language and Literature. XIII, № 3—4, Urbana, Illinois, 1930

Vanderhoeven M.
Verres Romains (Ier — IIIme siécle) des Musées Curtius et du Verre à Liége. Liége, 1961

Vessberg O.
Roman Glass in Cyprus // Opuscula Archaeologica. VII. Lund, 1952, p. 109—165, pl. I—XXIV

Voščinina A.I.
Frühantike Glasgefässe in der Ermitage (Gruppe der Salbgefässe in der Sandkern-Technik) // Wissenschaftliche Zeitschrift der Universität Rostock, 16. Jahrgang 1967. Gesellschafts und sprachwissenschaftliche Reihe. Rostock, 1967, Heft 7/8. S. 555—560

Weinberg G.D.
Glass Manufacture in Ancient Crete // JGS, 1959, vol. I, p. 11—21

Weinberg G.D.
Hellenistic Glass from Tel Anafa in Upper Galilee // JGS, 1970, vol. XII, p. 17—27

Weinberg G.D.
Notes on Glass from Upper Galilee // JGS, 1973, vol. XV, p. 35—51